Grahame Lloyd is a freelance broadcaster and journalist based in Cardiff. As well as commentating and reporting on football for radio and television, he is the author of *Daffodil Days: Glamorgan's Glorious Summer* and Cardiff City's centenary book, *C'mon City! A Hundred Years of the Bluebirds*. He also runs his own independent television production company, Celluloid.

Jan the Man
From Anfield to Vetch Field

Jan Molby
with Grahame Lloyd

ORION

For Mandy, Kingsley and Karina

An Orion paperback
First published in Great Britain by Victor Gollancz in 1999
This paperback edition published in 2000 by Orion Books Ltd,
Orion House, 5 Upper St Martin's Lane, London WC2H 9EA

A CIP catalogue record for this book is available
from the British Library.

ISBN: 0 75282 779 0

Printed and bound in Great Britain by
The Guernsey Press Co. Ltd, Guernsey, C.I.

Contents

Part Four

Part Five

Part Six

Epilogue

Index   281

PROLOGUE

No Place for Losers

I looked up at Wembley's electronic scoreboard. Northampton 0 Swansea City 0. 90 mins. I knew we were into injury time and Northampton had just been awarded a free-kick just outside the box. The 1997 Nationwide Third Division promotion play-off final was just about to go into extra time. Fifteen minutes earlier, I'd been worried whether I would be able to last another thirty minutes, but now I felt fine. Like the 1986 FA Cup Final, I'd got second wind and the prospect of extra time, even penalties, appealed to me.

It seemed a harsh decision to penalize Keith Walker for his challenge on Christian Lee, but as we lined up I told the lads not to worry. 'No danger,' I assured them, 'he's not going to score.'

I was standing right in the middle of our seven-man wall. Carl Heggs to my left, Joao Moreira to my right, my hands in the usual place. My heart, if not in my mouth, then certainly working overtime.

Our keeper, Roger Freestone, was well positioned behind the wall. There didn't seem to be a problem. The referee, Terry Heilbron, pushed us back the required ten yards and blew his whistle. Jonathan Coates rushed forward from the wall seconds before John Frain's free-kick smashed into him. I didn't think there was anything wrong but when the referee ordered the kick to be retaken, the thought went through my mind: This is going to be the last kick of the game!

We put two men on the posts and prepared ourselves for Frain's second attempt. The original kick had been taken from a spot just outside the semicircle, right in the middle of the pitch. Almost dead

7

centre. Just as Frain was about to try again, Terry Heilbron made a crucial intervention. He decided the kick should be retaken from three yards further to the right. Frain later admitted that this gave him a much better chance of scoring because it improved the angle for a left-foot shot. We saw the ball being moved and tried to shuffle across to counter it, but we didn't have time.

I think Roger realized what was happening a little too late. As Frain hit the ball, Roger was moving to his left and couldn't get back to his right in time to keep it out. The ball flew into the net as clean as a whistle. We had been caught cold.

All around me the lads had their heads in their hands. The North-ampton players and supporters had gone bananas. I just wanted to get hold of the ball and restart the game. 'Let's go and get the equalizer!' I shouted. I didn't realize we were already in the 94th minute. Fifteen seconds later, the ball had just been passed back to me from the restart when the referee's final whistle confirmed my worst fears. The goal was the last meaningful kick of the final. After forty-nine games over a gruelling eight months, our season was over.

I couldn't believe it. I felt most aggrieved that we hadn't had a chance to equalize. I had a quick word with the referee about the free-kick being taken twice and then looked around me. Sheer despair had swallowed up our players. They were lying down, face down, some of them crying, all of them distraught. I knew they would be looking to me for a lead. The worst place to be when you've lost at Wembley is out on the pitch watching the winners celebrating.

I quickly shook hands with the officials and led the lads on a lap of honour to say thank you to the Swansea supporters. They had been magnificent. There were so many of them at the other end of the ground that it took a couple of minutes to reach the tunnel. On my way past the Northampton supporters, I applauded them and they returned the compliment. As the lads filed past me, I did a radio and television interview and then headed down the tunnel.

As soon as I arrived in the dressing room, I realized what was needed. All the players were sitting there waiting for me. They didn't know what to do. When you've never had a major disappointment like that, you don't know how to handle it. I knew I had to gee them up. I told them to take off their kit, have a bath and try to forget about it.

'You can walk out of this dressing room with your heads held high,' I said. 'You've got nothing to be ashamed of. You can be proud of yourselves because you've come a long way this season. Go and see your wives and girlfriends as a group of men because you've all come of age. I think on the day we've proved we were the better team, but we didn't get our reward. Don't let anyone see us feeling sorry for ourselves.'

They didn't say anything. I think they were just pleased that I had come in and broken the ice. For me, this was the biggest disappointment of my whole career. Worse than losing to Wimbledon in the 1988 FA Cup Final or being pipped to the title a year later by that last-minute Michael Thomas goal at Anfield. If you lose a Cup Final, you still go up and collect your medal and do a lap of honour. It's a day out for everyone. But this game was entirely different: it was solely about winning. The losers could always turn around and say it was a day out, but when the stakes are as high as that, it's not really the case.

We were grateful for the play-offs because of our dreadful start. It was the only way we were going to go up. We knew the rules when we went into the semi-finals – there'd only be one team celebrating and the other three would be gutted – but if you had written a novel, you could hardly have come up with a worse ending – a dubious, twice-taken, injury-time free-kick.

Luckily, as a manager, I didn't have time to sit around moping. I had people to see (from Liverpool and Denmark), things to do (talk to some of our younger players), and places to go (like the post-match press conference). I think defeat would have been easier to accept had we lost, say, 2–0 in normal time with a goal in each half, or to a better team on the day. But we'd been beaten by a team whom we'd outplayed until those final moments. There was some compensation at the press conference, which the Northampton manager Ian Atkins was leaving just as I arrived.

'It's very quiet in here,' he said. 'What's wrong with you lot? Are you all Swansea fans?'

'I don't think they're all Swansea fans, Ian,' I replied. 'I think they're all football fans.'

He knew what I meant but didn't say anything and just walked out. He didn't have to say anything. We may have been the better footballing side but he was on his way to the Second Division – somewhere I desperately wanted my players to be. I resolved there and then that our Wembley disappointment would be a salutary experience. There must be no play-offs for us next season.

Before we left the Twin Towers to head home to Swansea, I stressed the importance of winning automatic promotion to the players.

'Remember this day,' I told them. 'Remember it next season when we spend seven hours travelling to places like Hartlepool, Darlington and Scarborough, and just make sure we don't make the same mistakes again. We mustn't give other teams a fifteen-to-twenty-point start.'

Losing at Wembley had been a huge blow – as I say, the biggest disappointment of my career. Fewer than five months later, worse was to come. We made another poor start to the season, history repeated itself, and this time I was sacked as player-manager of Swansea City. For the first time since arriving in Britain, more than thirteen years earlier, I was out of work.

PART ONE

An Independent Spirit

Jan Molby was born on 4 July 1963 – the American Day of Independence, on which, nearly two hundred years earlier, it had been declared that all people have the right to 'life, liberty and the pursuit of happiness'. How appropriate that those three words should figure so prominently in the career of one of the most gifted foreign footballers to have ever graced the English game.

In his 36 years, Jan Molby has lived a full and rewarding life. He was deprived of his liberty for a spell during his heyday, but he has provided a huge amount of happiness for thousands of fans, both in Liverpool and beyond. From the moment he first kicked a ball, as a young boy on his own outside the family home in Denmark, Jan has displayed a rare independence of spirit. By blazing a trail through three countries, he has demonstrated that not all imports are inclined to take the money and run.

As a 15-year-old, Jan was the youngest player to represent Denmark at any level; he became the first footballer from his home-town club Kolding to win a cap in the full Danish national side; and he was the first Dane to play in three English FA Cup Finals. When he was sold to Ajax as an 18-year-old, the £75,000 transfer fee was the biggest ever paid for a Danish player to leave Denmark and, after nearly twelve years with Liverpool, Jan became the first foreigner to be awarded a testimonial by one of the most successful clubs in English football history.

Yet fascinating facts tell only half the story. At his peak, in the hurly-burly of the old First Division, Jan Molby stood out in the crowd, an artist among artisans. Two-footed and beautifully balanced, he could turn a match with a devastating pass or shot. A sharpshooter with a licence to thrill, Jan was deadly with a dead ball, mesmeric with a moving one. His talent gave him the time to step outside the hustle and bustle of a congested workplace and perform at his own elegant pace.

But unlike some crowd-pleasing free spirits, Jan Molby has almost always been a winner: with Kolding, Ajax, Liverpool, and so nearly with Swansea City of the Nationwide League Third Division. Opposition supporters and critics may have poked fun at his size but the Great Dane usually had the last laugh as girth triumphed over mirth. Having helped Kolding into the Danish First Division for the first time, Jan left to complete the Dutch Double with Johan Cruyff and Ajax in 1983 before playing a pivotal role in Liverpool winning the English version three years later.

'I first came across Jan in 1981,' says Knud Engedahl, Kolding's coach during their first season in the Danish First Division in 1982. 'People had told me he was a great player, and I soon realized they were right when I saw him with my own eyes. He was a good dribbler and he had an excellent shot from distance. I was struck by his maturity – he played like a 25-year-old even though he was only 18. His long passing was very clever, but unfortunately he was a little bit lazy.

'We went to a pre-season training camp near Kolding and I sent the players on a long run. I checked their times and most of the squad returned after about thirty-five minutes. Jan turned up ten minutes after them – even though he could have run it in twenty-five minutes!

'I talked to him about his performance and he explained to me that he was a footballer not a runner. Jan didn't like training without the ball. If he had a ball with him he could run the whole day. I told him that if he wanted to be a great player, he had to be fit.'

Knud Engedahl, now 57, is a technical director with a steel manufacturing firm at Herneng, about seventy miles from Kolding. He maintains his link with football by coaching promising young Danish goalkeepers.

'When Jan's last season with Kolding started, he began in defence but later I allowed him to go into the attack, where he scored several goals for us. He could play anywhere and as the season progressed, the better he became. Jan's only weakness was his heading – even so, he was a defender I could trust. I played in goal in the Kolding first team behind Jan, and although he was not a good header of the ball then, I can see that he worked on that part of his game at Ajax and Liverpool.'

Knud Engedahl wasn't surprised when Ajax moved in on his young star with only a quarter of his second season gone. 'Jan had a great overview of the game. He could read it so well, he was fast and he was strong.'

The young Molby turned to his coach for advice when the offer from Amsterdam arrived, but then displayed his independent streak. 'I told him he should stay and be discovered in Denmark rather than move abroad,' says Knud. 'I said he would soon be playing for the national team and be worth more as a result. But he was offered a lot of money for an 18-year-old, and he was worried about getting injured and losing such a lucrative contract.

'I understood Jan's position but I wish he had listened to my advice and stayed here. I think he made the wrong decision. Every club in Denmark would have bought Jan; he was that good. He was young and he went to Amsterdam and made a lot of money, but I'm sure he missed out on something. He was a little wild in Denmark, and then again a little later in England – he hadn't grown up properly – and I think it would have been better for him to have stayed in Denmark for, say, another two years. If he had, I'm sure he would have been as big a name as Michael Laudrup. He only played First Division football here for a short time so people don't recognize him in the same way as Michael. I'm sure if he'd played a few games for Denmark, Ajax would have paid a lot more money for him.

'But looking at what he achieved with Liverpool – the Double in his second season – maybe he did make the right decision. Who knows? I couldn't understand why he didn't play more for his country. Brian and Michael Laudrup are very popular in Denmark because they appeared more times for the national team than Jan and played more of their football here – Jan would rank in most Danish people's top ten but, in my view, he's one of the top five best players ever produced by Denmark, if not the best. He was such a complete footballer.'

It was that quality of embryonic total footballer which persuaded Ajax to bring Jan Molby south to Holland. Aad de Mos, the Amsterdam club's coach from 1980–85, had just signed Jesper Olsen and was looking for a new *libero* to replace Ruud Krol. He had travelled to Denmark to check out another Kolding player when he saw the number 10 warming up.

'Jan was standing on the edge of the box shooting at the goalkeeper using both feet,' says de Mos. 'I said to my assistant, "If he shoots like this in the game, he must be the new Beckenbauer."

'I didn't know who he was, I only knew the number he was wearing. I was very surprised by his physical and technical possibilities. He turned out to be better in the game than in the warm-up. He had a big, direct personality, intelligence and good technique – his only fault was his speed.'

That view was shared by one of Jan's new team-mates, Frank Rijkaard, who later left for AC Milan before returning to Holland to end his career with Ajax.

'He was a very strong young man and he combined that strength with great skill. He made up for a lack of pace by

16

being in the right spot at the right time – he was a fast-thinking footballer.'

Jan's new coach Aad de Mos almost expected him to struggle initially at his new club. 'That's always been a problem with sides like Ajax, Liverpool or AC Milan, because they have a special tradition. With Kolding, Jan was the best player, but at Ajax he was just one of the squad which included a lot of experienced players, like Johan Cruyff, Wim Jansen and Soren Lerby. But he was at the same level as the club's outstanding youngsters like Ronald Koeman, Jesper Olsen and Frank Rijkaard.

'We were sure of Jan, but he had to learn the system with a new club in a new country,' says de Mos, who after leaving Ajax had spells with Anderlecht and Mechelen in Belgium, PSV Eindhoven and Werder Bremen, and Standard Liège. 'He settled in quite well – I think he was speaking perfect Dutch within two or three months – and he played an important part in our Double year. When Cruyff left for Feyenoord the next season, it was the year of the youngsters. They were alone, and we missed the experienced players like Johan.'

'Jan was a multi-functional player,' recalls Rijkaard. 'Because of his ability to read the game, he was perfect for the coach to work with. I was more or less the same as Jan – playing in midfield or defence – but the side was not that well balanced. There were too many youngsters and, at that time, we weren't ready for the big European games.

'It was a great experience for us to play alongside Johan Cruyff. Often during games we were winning easily, we would just stand and watch Johan doing his things – he was so skilful, it was wonderful to look at him.'

Jan's transfer from Ajax to Liverpool after two years in Amsterdam was the move which made his career. It was precipitated by a dressing-room row with Aad de Mos over a wet towel, which was witnessed by Frank Rijkaard.

'It was very tense but, fortunately, they didn't come to blows. This incident made it much more difficult for Jan at

Ajax. He had had a special relationship with Aad but, from that moment on, he didn't get the support he needed to become one of the most important players in the team. That was the reason for the separation between Ajax and Jan.'

As well as being out of favour, Jan was one of the latest crop of young players which Ajax had decided to sell. The club's prolific production line would, inevitably, continue to deliver the goods. For the moment, it was time to cash in, so Jan found himself in the shop window.

'Jan was sold to Liverpool because the board was not serious with the young players,' says Aad de Mos. 'Their contracts in this period were not very good. It was easy for the youngsters to get out of them. It was very easy for AC Milan to take Marco Van Basten and Frank Rijkaard because there was a financial problem at Ajax. The board were happy to sell Jesper Olsen to Manchester United, Ronald Koeman to Barcelona and Jan Molby to Liverpool for big fees, and the players could earn more money abroad. So everyone was happy apart from me!

'It was very frustrating, but the youth-education programme at Ajax always brings forward new stars. It is the Ajax philosophy. They give the young players a chance to gain some experience in the first team and then capitalize on the education they've received. It's always been a problem with Ajax and you could see history repeating itself with Patrick Kluivert and Edgar Davids going to AC Milan.'

History shows that all those Ajax teenagers of the early eighties went on to make their mark with their new clubs – none more so than Jan Molby.

'I wasn't surprised by Jan's success with Liverpool,' says Frank Rijkaard, now coaching the Dutch national side, 'because I knew what kind of footballer Jan was. I did wonder how he would get on because I remember that English football was very fast, it was kick-and-rush, and I thought a skilful player like Jan might have difficulties over there, but he coped fantastically.'

'He was made for the Liverpool system,' says Aad de Mos. 'Two in the middle of midfield, one-touch, two-touch – Jan was born to play their style of football.'

And so it proved. The good habits learned lovingly at Kolding were honed to near perfection in Amsterdam with Ajax before blossoming under the tutelage of the Anfield Boot Room and, in particular, Kenny Dalglish.

Training a Great Dane

In the beginning, I was Pelé. My second hero was Johan Cruyff and my third Liam Brady, but when I began playing the beautiful game at the age of five, I was Pelé – probably because it was an easy name to remember. (Edson Arantes do Nascimento was difficult enough for an adult to get his tongue around, let alone a young boy.) I would kick a ball around all day on my own pretending to be Pelé.

It's a mystery to me why I was so keen on football, because the only person in my family who was remotely interested in the game was one of my uncles. I used to play football in a lane between our house and next door which led down to a stream and a few other houses. Local people would drive about five miles an hour along the lane because they knew I'd be there. You don't start school until you're seven in Denmark, so I spent two years doing nothing but kicking a ball around. I played by myself because I had to. There was nobody else. My friend next-door-but-one wasn't interested and nearly everyone else in the neighbourhood was nowhere near my age group. They were either babies or older than me.

I'm not sure why I chose to play in the lane when we had a massive garden at the back of the house. We lived in a nice quiet area of Kolding, an industrial seaport in Jutland about fifty miles from the German border, with a population of about sixty thousand. Kolding's main claim to fame is that the town has the oldest stone church in Denmark, dating back to the thirteenth century. Our house was bought by my parents, Benno and Erna, when they married thirty-nine years ago and it's where their four children were born. My sister, Jytte, is a year older than me, and my brothers, twins Mikael and Torben, are five years younger. I had a very happy childhood, and the house I grew up in is still the family home.

As long as anyone can remember, the Molbys have always been involved in farming just outside Kolding. My father was the first to break with tradition and not work the land when he became a long-distance lorry driver with the Gulf Oil Company. He now works at their depot at nearby Fredricia, while my mother cleans in a private home and a school.

Although I had to play by myself, the man who lived next door was quite keen on football. He used to go and watch Kolding, and because Mum and Dad didn't know what to do with a football-mad son, he ended up taking me with him to games on the back of his pushbike. Bikes were – and still are – very big in Kolding. I would clutch him round the waist and we'd ride to the ground, me hanging on for dear life.

It wasn't long before I actually joined Kolding Football Club, where I was one of the youngest members. In Denmark, the first organized team for kids is at under-8 level, so I was two years younger than the boys in that group. After spending two years in the Under-8s, you moved on to the Under-10s and so on up until the Under-18s. We had five under-8 teams and I started in the fifth team. I'd only been there for a couple of weeks when I played my first competitive game of football, at right-back. I stood on the edge of the penalty area and didn't move for a full hour. We lost 17–0 – I'll never forget it. I just thought this was football. I didn't know anything else.

I played another game the following week – again at full-back – and we lost 4–0, but I was moving around a little more and I must have had four or five kicks of the ball. As a boy, I was very shy and I would come to the training and just stand there – nobody told me what to do. But then I started to get into it. I finished the season still in the fifth team, but when I was 6 I started making progress up into the fourth, third and second teams. I thought I was good enough to be in the first team but they felt I was a bit too young.

The following season, when I was 7, I started playing in midfield in the Under-8s first team. I was physically bigger than the others anyway, but it was more of my age group now and I just completely took over. We won everything and scored 119 goals – I got 97 of them. In those days, I used to take short corners from the edge of the penalty area and just bend them in.

It was about this time that Soren Peter Nielsen, the father figure of Kolding Football Club, started to sing my praises. He was 'Mr Kolding'; everybody knew him. Nobody had a bad word to say about Soren and, although he wasn't a former player, all the coaches respected his opinion. He started to say to my parents, to my grandparents, to anyone who would listen, that I was going to be a bit special. When I was 7, he said I would be the first footballer from Kolding ever to represent Denmark. It didn't bother me – I just wanted to play. I wanted to be the best and score lots of goals. I had no other interests at that time – it was nothing but football. I simply lived for the game.

Football wasn't officially on the curriculum at school. We had PE regularly but we'd probably play football only once a month – along with athletics, volleyball and basketball, all of which improved me as an athlete. I enjoyed school because it came very easy to me. I never used to work as hard as I should have done. I didn't think I had to put in that little bit of extra effort because I was almost top of the class anyway. My favourite subject was mathematics.

When I went into the Under-12 team, as a 10-year-old, I started to realize that I was a bit different. I was man- (or rather boy-) marked wherever I played. It didn't worry me, it just happened every time. The opposition didn't want to kick me, they weren't malicious, because everyone enjoyed seeing good players, but they just wanted to stop me playing in order to win.

It was really competitive in the Under-16 team. There were six regional groups throughout Denmark and the top four of each one qualified for the national Under-18 Championships. It was very unusual for Kolding to reach the final stages of this tournament. They had been there once or twice before but, all of a sudden, we had done it. We only just qualified in fourth position, but people still felt that if Kolding were ever going to do anything, then we were the boys who could pull it off.

Before the tournament began, we played a string of friendlies against senior sides. We even beat Kolding's first team who, at the time, were in the Danish Second Division. In fact, we beat everyone. The manager played me up front and I just kept on scoring . . . three, four, and even five in one match. But success brought with it one or two problems.

A week before the season started, one of the club's directors came up to me in the canteen after training. I was queueing for a bottle of pop. He said to me, 'You're Jan Molby, aren't you? I've heard bad things about you: that you don't want to play for the first team – you'd rather play with your mates in the Under-18s!' At the time, I didn't know what to make of it but, as I got to know him, I realized that that was his style. He'd obviously made the decision that I should play for the first team even though there was no pressure from the manager Ernst Netuka. This director was a big businessman in Kolding and I don't think he was too concerned about the rest of the club – he just wanted the first team to do well because he had an investment in there. He felt they had a better chance with me playing and he was probably fed up with people in the town telling him about my performances for the Under-18s.

I told him I did want to play in the first team but mentioned that I was only 17. He said the club wanted me to step up to the senior side and, in my naivety, I agreed. As I say, I was only 17 and completely ignorant about club politics. I had no idea of the kind of trouble I was going to cause.

You can imagine the reaction from the Under-18 team. All the players and the two managers wanted to walk out. When I agreed to play, I hadn't thought of the effect it would have on my team-mates. I had trained with the first team a couple of times and the manager Ernst Netuka had always taken a personal interest in me, but I think he felt I should stay in the Under-18s. In the end, the managers were persuaded to stay on and the players decided to get on with it – after all, Kolding's first team was the most important one in the club.

The following Sunday, I made my debut as sweeper in the first game of the season against Aalbourg. They had just been relegated from the First Division and we drew 0–0. In the meantime, the

Under-18 team managed to finish in the top half of their tournament.

I made my breakthrough into the first team at just the right moment. The previous season, Kolding had been on the brink of reaching the First Division of Danish football for the very first time. There were three divisions in Denmark and, at the time, the standard of football was on a par with that in other Scandinavian countries, but trailing behind the rest of Europe. Our First Division was equal to the then Third Division in England because in the late seventies and early eighties, there was a mass exodus of footballers from Denmark. Anyone who had any sort of talent left the country. I think at one stage there were over a hundred Danish footballers playing abroad. Although the game had gone professional, everything was still part-time – from the top to the bottom of the three divisions. Danish football was full of very promising youngsters who went abroad to seek fame and fortune ... like Jesper Olsen, John Sivebaek and Michael Laudrup. There were lesser-known players, like Jan Heinzte, who went to PSV Eindhoven for twelve years and is now in Germany, and Henrik Andersen, who picked up an horrific injury against Holland in the semi-finals of the European Championships in 1992. For a long time, Scandinavian players were cheap and the clubs in Denmark needed to sell just to keep afloat. The exodus benefited the national team too because, after making it with European clubs, they came back better players – there were Danes everywhere who returned to play for Denmark.

On top of that, there were another thirty or forty players who were good enough to become full-time professionals in other countries but didn't become part of the Danish national team. While in Denmark, they played for First Division teams like Vejle – just fifteen miles down the road from Kolding, and the most successful club in the history of Danish football. Until the early eighties, Kolding had played mainly in either the Second Division or the Danish equivalent of the Nationwide Conference – that is, one league away from the Danish Football League. After spending a couple of seasons in the Second Division in the seventies, they were relegated and dropped out of the league altogether. In 1977, they returned to the Third Division and, when the game went professional a year later, it was decided that Kolding ought to have a go. They were one of only four teams in that division to grasp the nettle.

As an industrial town, Kolding had a lot of businesses, and a five-year plan was drawn up to reach the big league. Many players on good money were brought in and everyone thought it was going to happen, but it didn't. In fact, it almost all went horribly wrong: they tried to run before they could walk and only avoided relegation by the skin of their teeth. The next season, though, they were promoted to Division Two and then narrowly missed out on reaching the First Division just before I made my debut. They actually achieved their target a year ahead of schedule but financial problems later caught up with the club. They pushed the boat out too far – they were too ambitious and slid down the divisions as players coming to the end of their careers left and no youngsters came through.

There was always a lot of rivalry between Kolding and our near neighbours Vejle – we had the bigger city, but they thought they had the better football team. They approached me to play for them when I was 16 but I didn't like the manager's attitude. He didn't seem to really want me to move to Vejle. Signing me would have been a bit of a coup, but he was very casual about it.

'You can come and play for us,' he said, 'but it's going to be very difficult for you. We've got a lot of good players and we're not desperate for you. It's a decision you've got to make.'

I needed to feel wanted. I'd been with Kolding for so long, he had to really sell Vejle to me. He had to tell me that I was going to be the number-one player and that he would make me captain. He's since admitted that not signing me was one of the biggest mistakes of his career – apparently he still gets a lot of stick from his assistant at Vejle! They were better than everyone else – they won everything – and he thought I should be delighted at the prospect of joining them, but I wasn't. I didn't have to go and play for Vejle to better myself. We were nearly as good as them – certainly at youth level, where I was playing. The senior Kolding side was still in the Third then while Vejle were riding high in the First, but who could have known that it would all change so quickly?

Vejle always made out that Kolding were animals while they were the footballers, so it was nice to beat them 2-0 in the only game that I played against them at senior level.

Then there were teams like Odense and KB Copenhagen, now FC Copenhagen, the pride of the capital, where Michael Laudrup started his career. I suppose it's fair to say that football is the national sport of Denmark, even though it's only played from March to November because of the cold weather. Indoor football, handball, swimming and badminton are very big in the winter but, during the summer, there's only football. Although there are more full-time teams now in Denmark, I'd say the standard in the eighties was better.

Although I'd been a regular goalscorer, I had no problem with my role as sweeper because I had played in that position with the Danish schoolboys' Under-17 and Under-18 teams. It was felt there were enough other players, like Michael Laudrup, to score goals at international level. I'd made my international debut in February 1979 as the youngest schoolboy to play for the Under-16s team.

I then turned out for the Under-21s when I was 17, and while I was in the Second Division with Kolding I was included in a national training get-together. It was East versus West Denmark. The East team was based in Sealand and the Copenhagen area while the West included Kolding. Although the Danish manager Sepp Piontek wasn't in charge, he did oversee the training. He was aware of me long before I made my full international debut against Norway in 1982.

During Kolding's history-making promotion season in 1980–81, I played 27 games and scored 2 goals before signing a full contract in July 1981. There were one or two rumours about other clubs being interested but I was never going to play for anyone else in Denmark apart from Kolding. I lived a bit of a double life – working as an apprentice in a sports shop run by a team-mate and turning out for the football team. When I signed, it seemed the most natural thing in the world to me because I'd always wanted to play the game.

My parents were pleased because they wanted me to do well. Until I was 15, I don't think they realized what it was all about. Then my career and football became the focal point of the family. It figured more prominently in the Molby household because my sister and brothers started playing. My father's pigeons took priority, but if he was away racing them – say, in Germany – my mother was a willing driver for away games. She used to come and watch. Slowly, the whole family became obsessed with football. On match days, supporters used to park their cars near our home and my parents were delighted and very proud that their son was in Kolding's first team. They couldn't believe that, after all the hours I'd spent kicking a ball around, somebody was suddenly paying me for doing it.

My brother Torben was a very good footballer who hasn't really made the most of his talent. He could have been a professional with Tranmere Rovers, or a team in Belgium, but turned them down and retired at the age of 28. He now manages Kolding, who are back in non-League football again. After winning promotion to the First Division in the early eighties, they spent two years in the top flight and then tumbled through the Second and Third Divisions and out of the League altogether.

There's no doubt that I owe a lot of my football success to the start I was given by everyone at Kolding, especially Ernst Nekuta. He was a lovely man who would never shout at you. Instead, he'd put his arm around your shoulders and make you feel special. He'd always spend a little bit of time with me, showing me how to tackle, polishing off my rough edges. Passing was something that always came naturally to me, but Ernst worked on it, explaining the finer points of the game and encouraging me to make decisions. As a sweeper, I was the first line of attack, and it was very difficult for people to pick me up as I came in from behind. I was a good reader of the game – I tried to spot danger before it could happen. I owe a huge debt to Ernst for all the work he put in with me.

When Kolding were promoted to the First Division, we discovered another sweeper and so Ernst moved me up into midfield. We started scoring goals but we also began leaking them. It was so bad that after seven games we were bottom and he moved me back. But my days at Kolding were numbered. I'd already played for the Under-21 team and then I made my debut for the full Danish side on June 15 1982, as an 18-year-old. We lost 2–1 in Norway. I was one of three debutants – the others were Michael Laudrup and Kim Ziegler. Michael scored for us but we conceded two own-goals. I'll never forget how tired I was afterwards. I was an absolute wreck. It was a big step up, the pace was much quicker, but Sepp was pleased with all of us. Ziegler's career never really took off, but Michael and I went on to better things.

After that game, it was then a question of me getting linked with anyone and everyone. I don't think Kolding really wanted to sell me. It was just too good a chance to make some money and improve the team. So, after 13 appearances in my second season – making a total of 40 in all – I played my last game for Kolding just before the six-week summer break.

The main drawback for footballers in Kolding was that the town was nowhere near Copenhagen. All the people who pick or write about the national football team are based in Copenhagen. Nobody really knew about me until we played teams in the capital and then reporters would come to our matches. Obviously, being the star of the local team in a small place made me the proverbial big fish in a small pond. But by the time I left Kolding, I was starting to make an impression nationally. The papers used to give all the First Division players marks out of six after each game and when I left after 13 games, I was top. Michael Laudrup, who was second, then went on to win it.

After we played the last game before the summer break, I went on holiday with a couple of friends. I was being linked with a lot of clubs and I flew to Amsterdam to speak to Ajax. I was pretty relaxed about a possible move. I thought it might or might not happen. It didn't bother me. I was quite happy in Kolding: I loved the place. I was living in a rented house with two of my team-mates and I loved knowing that my old schoolfriends and teachers were watching me from the stands. The local paper made a bit of a splash on a possible move to Ajax but I didn't think it was going to come off. Surely there was no way a player from Kolding could go to Ajax? That sort of thing just didn't happen. But it did – very quickly!

When I came back from holiday for the first day of pre-season training, the club's player-manager and goalkeeper Knud Engedahl called me off the pitch. It was half-past seven on a Tuesday night. Knud said Ajax had been on the phone and Kolding had agreed a price with them. Could I just go and ring them? I went back to the clubhouse to phone the Ajax vice-chairman from the canteen. When I returned to training, Knud asked me what was happening.

'I've got to fly to Amsterdam at eight o'clock in the morning,' I replied, hardly believing what I was saying.

And that's how it happened. That very evening, the club organized a farewell dinner for me downtown. There was a presentation, I was made a life member of Kolding and everyone wished me all the best. I had a few drinks with the boys, met my girlfriend and phoned my mum up at eleven o'clock at night to ask for a lift to the airport in the morning. When she couldn't help because she was working, one of the lads in the house dropped me off at the airport and, with my bag, off I went. Bye-bye Denmark, hello Holland.

At the Feet of the Master

It was the Danish connection which really took me to Amsterdam. I had been linked with a few clubs, like Bruges, Standard Liège and a couple of German teams, and I'd spoken to Ipswich and Hadjuk Split in Yugoslavia, but I just felt that Ajax were right – mainly because they already had two Danes on their books. Although I didn't know Jesper Olsen and Soren Lerby – I had played once with Jesper for the Under-21s – they were the big attraction. Of course, mention Ajax and you automatically think of Johan Cruyff, whom I'd seen playing for Holland in the 1974 World Cup when I was 11. He was a wonderful player and soon replaced Pelé as my hero. Amazingly though, when I agreed to go to Ajax, I didn't think Cruyff was still playing for them.

I didn't pay a great deal of attention to Dutch football. We followed the English game live on TV every Saturday and, when I could, I would get on the ferry and go and watch Arsenal. Danish papers didn't write about Cruyff, but Jesper Olsen, who'd gone to Ajax the previous season. I thought Johan had left and was playing in America.

When I arrived at Amsterdam airport, I was met by the Ajax vice-president, who took me to the training ground. The players were already out so I went to put my kit on and joined in. Some of them must have wondered who I was, but I shook hands with the two Danes and we just got on with it. I'd already arranged with Jesper that I would stay with him for a couple of weeks until the club apartment was decorated, and after training Soren asked us to come to his house for some dinner. It was good to have those two around. I was certainly grateful for their friendship because I didn't make a great initial impression at Ajax.

Soren was playing wide on the left of midfield at Ajax. He was a tough character, a bit like Graeme Souness – someone who could play and put it about a bit. He had blond hair and was famous for having his socks rolled right down – remember, in those days, you didn't have to wear shinguards. So with his socks down and his shirt over the top of his shorts, off to work he went. Everybody in the Ajax side could play but Soren wasn't particularly skilful. There were players there who could do things that we couldn't even dream of. It wasn't until he went to Bayern Munich that he became a playmaker and really blossomed – as I did at Liverpool. He became a really tough playmaker who could score goals as well. He had it all, but he never captained Denmark because of Morten Olsen. I suppose we were nearly all living in the shadow of Cruyff at Ajax, but there was also Gerald Vanenburg, who was probably a better player at 19 than he was later.

Soren and I got on at Ajax because we were Danes, but it never went any further than that. Whereas he and Jesper were really close pals, I never had that type of relationship with Soren. It wasn't until we both left Ajax that we became very friendly. I don't know whether it was because we weren't bumping into each other every day, but we started sharing rooms while playing for Denmark.

I don't think Soren saw me as a rival at Ajax. He saw himself as the experienced Dane who would keep the two youngsters – me and Jesper – in our place.

A couple of days after I arrived, we went off to the training camp. I was terrible. It was as if I'd never played football before – I was that bad. I think it was partly to do with the amount of work we put in: when we were at camp we'd train three times every day and then play every night. I was an absolute wreck. I was so bad that I could have understood the other lads wondering what I was doing there. The Ajax manager Aad de Mos had been to Denmark to watch me a couple of times when I'd played quite well, so obviously he was baffled by my form too. I'd cost him about £75,000 – then the biggest transfer fee ever paid from overseas for a Danish player – and he must have been wondering if the money had been well spent.

As well as the amount of training, there was the problem of working alongside players who were not only as good as me but better. I wasn't intimidated by them – I've never been intimidated by anyone – but things just didn't happen as easily as they used to. To be honest, I did occasionally feel I was out of my league, but the opportunity to play in a team with Johan Cruyff made me more determined than ever to succeed.

Aad de Mos knew he had found a replacement in me for Wim Jansen, former manager of Celtic, who had just retired as sweeper, but Johan pitched up with Leo van Veen. Cruyff picked his own man – he'd played with him in America. Aad wasn't too happy about the move so, right from the start, it was always going to be difficult. When the season got going, Leo played as sweeper and I was in midfield. On that first day, Jesper went over and introduced me to Johan. We shook hands and then we carried on with our pre-season work and he fiddled around with the ball for a while.

Johan wasn't someone who would sit down and talk with you. You would be treated to an audience with the Great Man. He targeted me and Jesper a lot because we were young, but he'd always call a few more players over to listen to him. He was like a king holding court. He knew everything and you couldn't help but listen. At times, you'd want him to shut up, but he wouldn't. People always ask me if it was true that Johan smoked sixty cigarettes a day? It was, but I don't know how he had time to smoke so many because he never stopped talking! If Jesper and I were sitting discussing something with another Dutch player, Johan would come up and ask what we were talking about. We'd tell him and he'd always begin his reply with the words: 'Let me tell you . . .'

When we were about to play for Denmark, he'd ask us who the opposition were. After we'd told him, he'd again say: 'Let me tell you . . .' and then go on to tell us how we could beat them. And that's the way he was. Johan was 37 and still a fantastic footballer. He was right about a lot of things – he was a very clever man – but he was also very hard work. I didn't warm to Johan as a person, because although he was a team-mate, he was such a mega superstar. He had come to expect that he would get his own way. In many respects, he ran Ajax at that time. If there was something he didn't like, he would knock on Aad's door and not ask him but tell him to change it. He always had his say on tactics – I guess after what he'd achieved that was understandable – but he wasn't arrogant.

In the pre-season games, I spent all the time playing in midfield. It didn't bother me because I preferred that position. My team-mates at the time included the new Dutch kids on the block – Ronald Koeman, Frank Rijkaard and Wim Kieft (Marco Van Basten was only training with us then).

It all fell into place for me at Ajax during an annual pre-season tournament in Amsterdam in 1982. It involved Ajax, Spurs, Cologne and another Dutch team AZ67. Big crowds turned up – usually between 30 and 40,000. All our other pre-season games had been against non-League teams and we'd won them 14–0, 17–0 and even 25–0. We were up against our first decent opposition and it suddenly happened for me. I started to perform.

My improvement dated back to the Ajax training. When I arrived there, I was pretty fit. I'd only had a fortnight off because the Danish season runs from March until the end of June. The other Ajax players had finished in May and were just starting to prepare for the new season after seven or eight weeks off. In the first week, there was a lot of running and I did very well, but I was trying so hard to impress in training that I probably burnt myself out within the week. I was bubbling, there was no way I was going to be shown up. But I was trying too hard. The first week was fine but then I became so tired on some days that I would go to bed at half-past five in the evening without even eating! Jesper would wake me up the next morning. He told me he had suffered in the same way when he first came to Ajax and, although I was worried at the time, I've since seen it happening with young players I've worked with. When we got the balls out and started to play, I had nothing to give. My form took a bit of a dive and then I came up for air and it started to happen. My freshness returned when we played in that four-team tournament.

Until then, we'd played a lot of meaningless pre-season friendlies and I wasn't sure that this was what professional football was all about. I wasn't holding back but I was waiting for some decent opposition, which arrived in the shape of Spurs ... Glenn Hoddle, Ossie Ardiles and the rest. I was aware of Glenn at that time but I don't think I realized how good he was until I came to England. I was a great fan of English football and I remember thinking, finally: This is what it's all about! It was also the chance to put one over Arsenal's great rivals – it was great. We beat Spurs 3–2, I had a good game, and it made the other players realize that Ajax hadn't signed a dud. I felt great. The Spurs side included people like Graham Roberts, who said afterwards that I was the hardest youngster he'd ever come up against. For a tough man like Graham to pay me that compliment meant a lot – hardness wasn't something you'd normally associate with my game.

That game against Spurs was a watershed for me. I'll never forget Aad's reaction afterwards. He was beaming. He knew then that we'd both come through what was the ultimate test. It was a turning point for me. The following night we played AZ67. We'd been 3–0 down and came back to lose on penalties, but I played even better than against Spurs. But most important of all, I had won the respect of the lads. Even Johan came up, patted me on the back and said, 'Well done.' That was all I needed from him: I knew I had arrived.

Once the season got going, we made a tremendous start by winning our first game 4–1. I scored the fourth and, in fact, got 3 goals in my first 4 games. Throughout that Double-winning season, in which we lost only twice in the League, I managed 6 in 31 League games. I started off in midfield but, just after the turn of the year, we drew 5–5 at home with Groningen and Aad switched me to sweeper. We met NEC Nijmegen in the two-legged Cup Final, winning 3–0 at home and 4–1 away. It was wonderful to achieve the Double but, at the same time, we were expected to. When we played our last game, Wim Kieft needed five goals to finish top scorer in Europe, so we took care of that. We won the match 8–2 and made sure he got the goals to win the Golden Boot, with 32. It all seemed so natural and, at times, so easy.

There were eighteen teams in the Dutch First Division, and I think twelve of them were on a par with those in the top division in Denmark. The other six – including Ajax, Feyenoord and PSV Eindhoven – were head and shoulders above anything you would find in Danish football. The biggest problem was not the step-up in the standard of football but the training, which was a lot more competitive than the actual games. Ajax got pushed in League matches four times a year – twice against Feyenoord and twice against PSV – but every day in training.

Ajax were so good because they attracted all the good players. It's the same now – any kid with any talent goes to Ajax. When they're aged 6, their names are put on the computer and they become part of the Ajax system – the education programme. The club bring them in from all over Holland, put them up in little villages and give their parents jobs. They don't just pick up nine kids out of ten but ninety-eight out of a hundred. The odd one – like Ruud Gullit – slips through. One of the most important things at Ajax was education – they provide it for the kids while they're teaching them to play football. Having brought them through the system, Ajax then sell off the best players. Ajax obviously want to win things but, if the price is right, they'll let top players go – as they did with Frank Rijkaard and Marco Van Basten. Normally, Ajax would only buy in youngsters – like Jesper and me – although occasionally they did need more experienced players.

We played what was known as total football – where every member of the team could play in virtually any position. I played everywhere apart from out-and-out striker during my time at Ajax. There were never specific players for specific positions. It was a wonderful team to play in – Johan Cruyff at one end of the experience scale and someone like Frank Rijkaard at the other. I never saw

Frank at full stretch – if he'd been a racehorse, he'd have been branded as a non-trier. You'd only get the best out of him if you hurt his pride.

My international career wasn't going quite as well. I played a few times for Denmark that season but we had such a strong side that I just couldn't get in. The manager had his own men and there were a lot of players from big clubs. Soren Lerby had gone to Bayern Munich, Michael Laudrup to Juventus and Preben Elkjaer to Verona. They were all world-class players, the manager Sepp Piontek had a great system, and there was no room for me.

I first came across Preben when Sepp picked a side based on footballers playing in Denmark. It didn't count as an official international, but I was chosen at the age of 17. We played Lokeren from Belgium, and Preben was their star striker. He had moved from Denmark and gone to Cologne where it didn't work out, but he then became known as the Prince of Lokeren. He was the big star, the crowd used to love him and Sepp knew we'd get a good crowd if we played Lokeren with Preben in their side. I was playing at the back in this game at the national stadium and I remember Preben as a fantastic player. He was direct and quick, strong and fearless and, although he scored five goals for Denmark in the 1986 World Cup in Mexico, his main claim to fame was that when he moved to Verona they won the Italian Championship – or, as he put it, 'I took them to the Championship.'

He was a bit of a lad in his younger days and there's a famous story about an incident at Cologne where they were very strong on discipline. Preben had been seen out on the town with a woman and a bottle of either gin or vodka.

'No,' replied Preben when he was hauled before the manager to explain himself, 'that's not true – it was a woman and *two* bottles!'

Later, he changed his lifestyle and settled down when he got married to concentrate on his football. He was a bit like Alan Shearer but not as clinical. He was a fifteen-to-twenty rather than thirty-goals-a-season striker, but ten or twelve of them would be collectors' items. He was a wonderful player, who became involved in Danish television when he retired.

By the last home game of my first season with Ajax against Fortuna Sittard, in May 1983, Johan Cruyff's contract dispute with the club still hadn't been resolved. All the other players knew was that the row was over money. Johan felt that results and crowds had improved since he had returned to Ajax and he wanted what he felt he deserved. We won 6–5, but he came off at the interval – he simply told the manager he was coming off and got changed – to make sure everyone knew that it was the end of his Ajax career. By the end of the game, he was at home having his forty-fifth cigarette of the day and there was uproar at the ground. The fans were so angry about Cruyff being allowed to leave that they stoned all the club cars, including those belonging to the players. It was sad because it was the end of an era. Johan rubbed salt into the wound by moving from Ajax to Feyenoord, which was unheard of then. After he left, I managed to get hold of one of his old number 9 shirts and gave it to a handicapped friend of mine back in Denmark. Johan didn't like wearing number 9 – he preferred 14, the number he wore for Holland in the World Cup and in America. He wore 14 when he came back to Ajax in his first season, but the numbers were then switched to 1 to 11 and he wasn't happy.

When Johan left Ajax, people thought he would either retire or go back to America. We were really surprised to hear he was joining Feyenoord. We played them in the eighth game of the next season at the Olympic Stadium in Amsterdam, in front of 63,000. We had won six and drawn one while they had won six and lost one. This was a big occasion, Johan's first time back.

It was an incredible game – we were 3–0 up after 12 minutes. Feyenoord pulled it back to 3–2 just before half-time but could have been 6–3 up, they missed that many chances. Once we were 3–0 up, we completely froze – we just couldn't handle it. They were all over us. For the first ten minutes of the second half, we couldn't get out of our penalty area – it was non-stop. Then, from nothing, we went up the other end, someone flicked in a long throw-in and that was it – 4–2. After that the heavens opened: 5–2, 6–2, 7–2, 8–2. I didn't score – I was man-marking one of the Feyenoord players – but we ran riot. We finished second in the League to Feyenoord that season, so Johan had the last laugh. Johan and Ruud Gullit won the League for them, whereas we were a younger team who couldn't last the pace.

The biggest thing I learned from Johan was how to pass. He was always stressing the importance of pace – drilling rather than just passing the ball – and there was a lot of emphasis on your first touch. Eighty per cent of the training at Ajax was one-touch football. It was very rare for us to enjoy ourselves in a five-a-side with no restrictions and, no disrespect to the Liverpool players, sometimes you just wouldn't believe your eyes at Ajax. Johan spent time with everybody but, in hindsight, I suppose he may have thought that if I was going to make it in football, I would need something which made me stand apart from everybody else. I didn't have a burst of acceleration and wasn't renowned for being a goal-scoring midfield player so maybe Johan thought he would give me one or two tips on passing.

I was so in awe of Johan that I didn't approach him for the first three or four months at Ajax. Even at 37, his biggest asset was his speed over the first five yards – I had never seen anything like it. With his famous drag-back and that kind of pace, opponents had no chance.

Johan would never congratulate you when you scored. Nine out of ten times, he would provide you with the pass and, as you turned round to celebrate, he would be walking back. You always made sure you acknowledged his contribution with a wave of the hand but when you returned the compliment and set him up, it was then just a wonderful goal by Johan Cruyff! He would celebrate his own goals, never anyone else's, but that's just the way he was.

Heading wasn't one of my strongest points when I arrived at Ajax but we used to play head tennis with a volleyball net. As you could only use your head, that part of my game obviously improved.

After Johan left, the 'new Cruyff' was Gerald Vanenburg, who also played for Holland. I was seen as the 'new Lerby', a hard-working midfield player. I wasn't considered good enough to be the playmaker.

Hard-working really sums up what life was all about at Ajax. It was very competitive there – you had to play for your life and train for your life. You could be in a team which won 5–0 on a Saturday but, if you didn't perform in training during the week, you wouldn't keep your place. It put everyone under tremendous pressure and led to a quick turnover of players. Ajax would take you as far as they could as quickly as they could.

Fourteen of our squad of eighteen were internationals. We were friends and colleagues but we were also rivals – Ronald Koeman saw me as competition because he knew I could play as sweeper. It was everyone for themselves. I could sense it all the time, and it made me a better player. I was stretched as much by the training as by the games. During training at Liverpool, I never felt that I wasn't good enough to be at Anfield, but sometimes at Ajax, if you weren't quite up to it, a whole morning session could completely pass you by. We would train for two hours in the morning, have a break for lunch, and then do another hour and a half in the afternoon. We had special running coaches. One morning a week we'd go to a forest for a really tough run, but the rest of the time we trained with the ball. Every morning we played possession football, eight-a-side in a very confined space (a small square), one-touch, two-touch, with some shocking tackles going in. It was very high-powered stuff. Some of the training sessions were much tougher than some of the games, which we cruised through.

With everything revolving around limited touches, you had to become a very good passer of the ball to survive. Johan Cruyff was responsible for developing my skills in that department. There was one drill in particular which he used to put Ronald and I through. We had to try to hit the corner flag from the halfway line. It sounds impossible, but he would have us standing with our backs to which-ever corner we were aiming for. The ball would be played to us and we were allowed one touch to bring it under control and then put ourselves into a position where we could drive the ball towards the flag. He wanted us to drive everything – and it only counted if you actually hit the flag! It was tedious at times – especially as sometimes it went on for more than an hour – but when Johan told you to do something, you did it.

To be honest, I don't think all those hours spent driving the ball

39

towards the corner flag did us any harm. Having said that, short, crisp passing was just as important at Ajax. When I came to England, where flat back fours were the norm, there was a bit of space in behind defences and I suddenly found that my passing became a weapon. I realized at Ajax that no matter how much natural ability you have, you can always improve by practice. That was the Ajax way – practice, practice and more practice. It certainly paid off for me.

The only player that Johan gave personal coaching to was Marco Van Basten, whom he realized was a bit special at 16. I wasn't surprised to hear how Johan kept trying to sign him from AC Milan when he was manager of Barcelona.

We were all well aware of the pressure to perform at Ajax and occasionally we really felt it. I remember in my second season, we were beaten 3–0 in an away match. When we came in the next day, we were told we were being fined for losing. I'd never heard of this sort of thing before; it seemed our performance was unacceptable. We were fined 500 guilders each – about a quarter of our weekly wage – and although we insisted that we'd tried our best, the club wouldn't accept it. With our captain Lerby at Bayern Munich and Cruyff with Feyenoord there was no one in the dressing room to stand up to the club. They fined us and everyone accepted it.

Off the field, I never really settled in Amsterdam – even though we had a reasonable social life. I didn't know anyone outside the football club and I'm not sure if I ever really gave the city a chance. Some of the players, like Jesper, Ronald and me, used to live in an apartment block, and we'd go round to each other's flats, but I found it too easy to go home to Kolding. I could jump in the car and be there in five hours. After a game on a Saturday night, I'd be on my way home by half-past eight and in the local disco with my mates at three o'clock in the morning. I would spend Sundays with my family before reporting back for training on Monday – having left Kolding at four o'clock in the morning to drive to Amsterdam. Kolding was a place I knew and loved. I had a lot of friends there and, to be honest, the problem was that I never really made the effort to settle in Amsterdam. When I was at home, I played darts with the lads down the local, but in Holland I used to lie on the couch every night watching TV in a language I could hardly understand.

When I was a professional footballer in Denmark, I lived in a house with two of my team-mates and we used to stay up until four every morning playing cards. After a game, the whole team would go out for a beer. One of the side played the guitar and we'd have a sing-song, but during my two years at Ajax we had only two social events. Once we played golf and once we spent the day fishing. The rest of the time we came to work, did our job, and then went home.

Amsterdam obviously had its attractions as an international city, but I don't regret not discovering them. I always had this feeling that Ajax was nothing more than a stepping stone for me. That was the way they did it: they'd bring you in and then ship you out. My closest friend was the Ajax reserve goalkeeper, Hans Galje, and he and his girlfriend did their best to look after me. It wasn't until my last season with Ajax that I met up with a Danish couple, who'd been living round the corner all the time. He was a banker and not interested in football and he'd take me to watch a local baseball team.

I became quite close to him and his wife but our friendship indirectly led to one of the most frightening moments of my whole life. Just before my second year began, we'd been playing tennis and had returned to his house for a few drinks. I hadn't drunk anything for weeks because of a hard pre-season and the wine must have gone to my head. As soon as I got home, I went to sleep in my apartment on the sixth floor of an eight-storey block. For some reason, I then started sleepwalking.

Out of my bedroom door I went, out of the apartment and down in the lift and out of the building altogether. When the bang of the outside door shutting woke me up, I realized I was in deep trouble. I was standing in my underpants in a street just outside Amsterdam at two o'clock in the morning with no way of getting back into my apartment! I knew Jesper wasn't around to let me in so I buzzed a couple of people I knew. At that time of night, they were terrified and refused to answer. I then went through everyone else but still nobody responded. I wandered over to my car, which was locked, but luckily the boot was open. There was no alternative. I would have to sleep in there. I crawled into the boot of my BMW and woke up at about half-past seven.

This time, I managed to get into the apartment building. The problem now was to find a way into my locked flat, the middle one of three on my floor. I took the lift up to the sixth floor, still wearing my boxer shorts. My neighbours on the right were never there and the ones on the left I'd never seen. I rang their bell and although I could hear them behind the door, they wouldn't let me in. I knew I could get into my apartment from theirs via the balcony, so I started to get annoyed and began banging on the door. All I got in return was them telling me to go away.

After half an hour, my neighbour opened the door, but he wouldn't let me into the bedroom. I could see the balcony which led to my apartment, but he said it was out of bounds! Instead, he pointed at a small window and told me I'd have to use that. I argued with him for another ten minutes but, in the end, I had to crawl out of this tiny opening and stand on a very narrow ledge outside before reaching the safety of my apartment. I remember looking down from the sixth floor at the ground below and thinking very nervously about my future. I was terrified. Luckily, I don't think my neighbour knew who I was, but it was still pretty embarrassing – definitely the non-footballing highlight of my time in Amsterdam.

Aad Times in Amsterdam

My one regret while at Ajax was that we didn't have any footballing highlights in European competition. For some reason, we didn't make any impression in the European Cup – largely because of our performances in Amsterdam.

Having won the League Championship the season before I arrived, Ajax were paired with Celtic in the first round in September 1982.

We drew 2–2 at Parkhead in front of nearly 60,000, so really fancied our chances in the second leg. There were nearly 60,000 of our supporters and 8000 Celtic fans in the stadium, but it all went wrong. Charlie Nicholas put them one up at half-time and although Vanenburg equalized ten minutes after the break, George McCluskey popped up with the winner and we were out, losing 4–3 on aggregate.

The following season, again in the European Cup, we drew Olympiakos from Greece and made a real mess of the first leg at home. In front of barely 30,000 people we drew 0–0 and then in their Olympic Stadium, in front of a fanatical crowd of 70,000, there was no score at the end of normal time. In extra time they scored twice. We'd failed to make it into the second round again. Obviously both results were a huge disappointment, but what I really missed was the big occasion – it was fantastic playing in front of such enormous crowds.

We'd done so well in Scotland against Celtic but, even with experienced players like Cruyff, the return leg was always going to be a difficult game, and we just didn't perform. Against Olympiakos everybody had felt it was a formality. But we were just too young and inexperienced to handle such a hostile atmosphere. We were warned when we drew the first leg 0–0 in Amsterdam, but in Greece we reacted badly and ended up having one of our defenders, Ed Ophof, sent off for violent conduct in the second half which, in the end, cost us the game. We had too many youngsters in the team and there was nobody to guide us.

It was hard on the field and Aad off it when the manager started to lose faith in me during my second season with Ajax. We nearly came to blows one day after training and from that moment on, I realized that I would soon be on the Ajax conveyor belt and on my way. During the last six to eight weeks of my second season, when we were chasing the title with Feyenoord, I was hardly involved and spent most of the time on the bench.

It all stemmed from a row in the changing room which almost spilled over into a fist fight. Every Tuesday, we were trained by the Dutch national athletics coach and on this particular day, during a run of bad results, he'd obviously been told by Aad to give us a really tough session. We did two and a half hours of non-stop running before having lunch and then training as usual in the afternoon. A couple of us, myself and Johnny Van Schipp, hadn't been involved in the first team recently and Aad wanted us to play for the reserves that night. We had to meet at the ground at six o'clock.

After training, we were all sitting in the big bath when Aad came in with his towel around his waist. He hung it up and went to have a shower. As Hans Galje climbed out of the bath he picked Aad's towel off the hook and threw it at me. Instead of catching it, I ducked and the towel dropped into the water.

All the players then got out of the bath to have a shower. When Aad came out of the shower, all he could see was his towel floating in the middle of the big bath. Obviously he wasn't happy. He immediately went into the dressing room and started to wring out the towel all over my clothes. He thought I was responsible for his wet towel because he had picked me for the reserves.

When I came out of the shower, the boys told me what had happened. Obviously I wasn't happy. I picked up my towel, threw it in the bath to soak it thoroughly and then stormed off to Aad's office along the corridor. He was in there with a couple of directors. He had just about got his suit on when I barged in and wrung out the water from my towel all over him. I then turned on my heels and walked out.

Aad hit the roof! He was a big man – six foot four and fifteen stone – and he came running out after me, shouting and screaming. When the lads heard all the noise, Frank Rijkaard rushed into the corridor and stood behind me. It looked like Aad wanted to hit me. Frank suddenly piped up: 'Shall we have him?!'

'Yeah!,' I said. For a moment, there was havoc. Pushing and shoving from both sides and more ranting and raving. Nothing materialized though. The directors came out to restrain Aad and we went back into the dressing room. That incident signalled the end of Ajax for me. At the end of the season, I was off to Liverpool and we never got a chance to explain to Aad what had happened.

I played for the reserves that night but not many more times for the first team. Although I'd been a regular, bar one or two suspensions, I didn't figure much in Aad's plans for the rest of the season.

It was frustrating for two reasons. On a personal level, I'd always got on very well with Aad. After all, he'd brought me to Ajax and was delighted when I finally got my game together. There was an incident before I made the breakthrough, when I was playing very badly, when he suddenly remembered my long throw. He'd noticed it when he'd seen me play in Denmark. I think he was so keen to show the other players how good I was that one morning he gave me a piece of desperate advice: 'Try to impress them with your long throw!'

I looked at him slightly bemused, but Aad was serious.

'Show them what a great long throw you've got.'

As he was the manager, I had no alternative but to do as he asked. So, before the training session, he had me launching these long throws from the touchline just to show the lads that I wasn't as bad as they thought I was! I think they were impressed – but only by the long throw. Nice throw, shame that he can't do anything with his bloody feet!

Another time, we had been to Milan to play in an indoor tournament over Christmas. Aad knew that I was a bit of a gambler – not on horses at that point, but I loved playing cards. As we were standing in Amsterdam airport waiting for our luggage to come from the plane, we were all looking for our blue numbered bags with Ajax written on them. Mine was number 9. Suddenly, Aad turned to speak to me.

'What's your number, Molby?'

'Nine,' I replied, thinking no more of it.

'You like a bet, don't you, Molby?'

'Yes,' I said, showing a bit more interest.

'I bet you a thousand guilders that my bag comes out before yours.'

'No problem,' I said, shaking on what I naively thought was a good even-money bet. As we stood there, we could see the blue bags coming round on the conveyor belt. The first one up was mine, number 9. I was chuffed to bits.

'That'll be a thousand guilders,' I said to Aad, and then watched in amazement as four number 25s appeared, one by one.

'What's going on here?' I cried. What I didn't know was that Aad's number 25 was shared by three other members of staff. So there were four 25s and just one number 9.

'I didn't tell you there was only *one* twenty-five,' Aad replied sheepishly, before paying up a thousand guilders – roughly three hundred pounds.

There's another story which Aad himself likes to tell about the time he mistook me for John Sivebaek, the Danish international full-back who went on to play for Manchester United. Ajax were originally alerted to me by Soren Lerby's father. Soren was with Ajax and his father would do a bit of scouting for them. He kept watching me whenever Kolding played in Copenhagen, where he was based, and after his strong recommendation Aad came over to take a look. He chose the local derby against Vejle – the first time the two teams had played each other and, as it happened, my best game ever for Kolding. We won 2–0 in front of a crowd of 11,000.

The next day, the Danish international team were meeting in Copenhagen to fly to Austria and Aad was sitting on the plane next to John Sivebaek. Now John looks very much like me, and during the flight Aad tried desperately to catch John's attention by flashing the match programme in front of his face, making it clear to John that he knew who he was! The trouble was that John was very shy and he didn't bat an eye-lid. As a result, Aad put it about that Jan Molby was a miserable guy who didn't take any interest in the Ajax manager when it was obvious that he'd just been watching him play for Kolding. It wasn't until he came back the next week to see me turn out for the Under-21s that Aad realized his mistake.

So I've got some very fond memories of Aad, which were soured a little by our falling-out over the wet towel. Not being involved in the run-in in my second season was also annoying because I very much wanted to be part of the Denmark squad going to the 1984 European Championships in France. Sepp Piontek had made it clear for a long time that you had to be in your first team to be selected but, somehow, I managed to squeeze into the twenty-two. I soon forgot all about my club troubles once I joined up with the Danish squad.

We played four matches and got beaten in the semi-final on penalties. Sadly, I didn't play in any of them. I was on the bench for every game and didn't get on once. Even so, I had a great four weeks in France, the whole nation was up for it, and not being involved simply whetted my appetite. I couldn't wait to start playing again with Ajax. But when the pre-season games began, I realized that my future lay elsewhere.

Ajax normally played between fifteen and twenty pre-season friendlies and everyone had their fair share of the action. But I just came on every now and then. I hardly got a look-in. It was obvious that I didn't fit into Aad's plans so I approached him about my future. He could see I wasn't happy and asked if I wanted to leave. When I nodded, he asked where I wanted to go. I replied 'England', and that's when my active involvement with English football began.

I'd been brought up on the English game at home. We used to watch it on Danish TV – we had a live game every weekend – and the football magazines we bought weren't Danish or German but *Match* and *Shoot*. I knew every player in the old First Division and, after they beat Liverpool in the 1971 FA Cup Final, I became hooked on Arsenal. At seven, going on eight, I was starting to think for myself and I made up my mind that Arsenal were going to be my team.

One of the greatest moments in my life was watching the 1979 Arsenal–Manchester United FA Cup Final with five United fans as the Gunners won with that late Alan Sunderland goal. I had already visited Highbury with the Danish Under-18 team, who were playing England, and went to see Arsenal take on QPR. That confirmed it. Arsenal were my team. I loved watching players like Graham Rix, Frank Stapleton and especially Liam Brady. He was my third hero behind Pelé and Cruyff, with his vision and his lovely left foot.

I was very disappointed to be going, but when I decided to leave Ajax, an agent, Dennis Roach, started to tout me around the clubs and I sensed a change in Aad's attitude. He put me back in the first team because Ajax needed to sell me, and it was rumoured that people were coming to watch me. Manchester City, Sheffield Wednesday and Crystal Palace were all said to be interested, with City's manager Billy McNeill particularly keen. Howard Wilkinson at Wednesday was the only one I spoke to, though.

When we talked on the phone, Howard said he was very interested, but within a couple of hours I had spoken to Tom Saunders, Liverpool's youth development officer. He said they were looking for a midfield player to replace Graeme Souness. Would I come over for a ten-day trial? A lot of people told me that I shouldn't have to go for a trial. I was 20 years old, playing for Ajax and I was a Danish international. If Liverpool want you, they said, they want you. I said that Liverpool didn't want me but they'd quite like a look. I would go and show them what I could do. I was quite comfortable with that – I felt I'd be able to persuade Liverpool to take me, but even if they didn't their interest might open one or two other doors.

I was excited because the chance to join a club like Liverpool didn't come along every day of the week. And my most recent memory of them was of winning the European Cup in Rome the previous May. Ajax hadn't even reached the second round. Liverpool were the best team in Europe, they had just won the English League three times on the trot, and if they wanted to sign me then I would join them.

As a passer of the ball, I wasn't worried about playing in the English game, where the long-ball ruled. A lot of teams like Watford were using a very direct system and everyone – apart from Liverpool – had a big target man. But Liverpool were able to stand up to the other teams and then let their football take over. I'd not been used to the physical battle and it would take me a year or so to come to terms with it. I'd always wanted to play from the first minute of every game, but Liverpool were to teach me that you had to earn the right to play.

When I told Howard about Liverpool's approach, he said I should jump at any chance to go to Anfield. I flew to Manchester airport, where Tom Saunders was waiting for me. The quizzical look on his face in the arrivals terminal showed me just how much Liverpool knew about their next possible signing. He'd been told I was six foot three and blond! The only way he recognized me at the airport was by the bag I was carrying – it had Ajax written on the side of it. He might have been better off holding up a card with my name on it.

Once we had established contact, Tom took me back to the hotel, where John Wark and Paul Walsh, who'd both just been signed by Liverpool, were staying. I remember on that first night, Ajax played Manchester United as part of the deal which took Jesper Olsen to Old Trafford. We went to the game and it felt quite strange not being involved with most of the players who'd been my team-mates for the previous two years. They wished me all the best, and the next day I started life with Liverpool.

PART TWO

The Adopted Scouser

When Jan Molby arrived at Anfield in August 1984, Liverpool were threatening to dominate not only English but European football.

Bill Shankly's mantle had been effortlessly passed on to Bob Paisley and then Joe Fagan, and at least one major trophy – domestic or foreign, sometimes both – seemed destined for the Anfield boardroom every season. Indeed, the 4–2 win on penalties over Roma in the European Cup Final the previous May, coupled with their third successive First Division title, suggested that this Liverpool side might even outstrip the achievements of the legendary seventies team. A glorious past was in danger of being eclipsed by a fantastic future.

Jan could hardly have signed for a better club at a better time. Even though Graeme Souness had accepted the lure of the lira, the nucleus of the side remained intact. Liverpool were a class act, full to overflowing with internationals, like Kenny Dalglish, Ian Rush, Alan Hansen, Mark Lawrenson and Ronnie Whelan. Having achieved promotion with Kolding and the Double with Ajax, there was no reason to suggest that the 21-year-old Dane would fail to win a trophy with Liverpool.

In his first season though, for the first time for a decade, Liverpool's cupboard remained bare. Whether he liked it or not, Jan was immediately compared with Souness, the strange mixture of strength and skill, who had run the

Liverpool midfield since 1978. With the unusual and almost unbeatable combination of aggression and finesse, Souness had left for Sampdoria in the summer. Alan Hansen, now a much-respected football pundit, recalls the task facing the young Dane.

'Jan had a massive job on his hands because he was replacing a legend,' says Hansen. 'For me, Graeme Souness has been the best midfield player in this country during the last twenty-five years. He and Jan were totally different players but, obviously, with Graeme having just left, there was a void and people automatically saw Jan as virtually a straight replacement. Because we didn't win anything in his first season, the general view was that Souness was irreplaceable, though, in all honesty, it was tough for everybody, not just Jan.'

Liverpool's most capped player, Welsh international striker Ian Rush, was ideally placed to assess the relative contributions of Souness and his successor.

'I can understand why people made the comparison, but Jan was a different sort of player,' recalls Rush. 'Jan would get stuck in, but he was more of a ball-player than Graeme, because of the way he'd been brought up as a Continental. I think Jan was a better passer but Graeme was the better leader on the pitch. When Steve McMahon arrived, he got stuck in to win the ball for Jan, who played it through to me. When they got established, Jan and Steve soon wiped out the Graeme Souness and Terry McDermott era.'

'Jan was a very talented and gifted footballer when he arrived at Anfield,' says Kenny Dalglish, the man who brought out the best in the young Molby when he succeeded Joe Fagan as manager in 1985. 'In his first game for the club in a trial match in Ireland, he scored a great goal. After taking the ball on his chest, he knocked it over an opponent with his knee at the edge of the box, went round another player and then volleyed it into the net.

'I would never compare Jan as someone who was similar in

style to Graeme Souness because they were different players. I thought Joe made a great decision to bring Jan to Anfield and Jan did well under him.'

Alan Hansen recalls the impression made by the new arrival once Joe Fagan had decided to set aside £500,000 to buy Jan. 'You only had to spend ten minutes on the training ground with Jan to realize that his ability was awesome. It shone through right away. It was almost frightening: the two great feet, his passing skills, and a lot of strength. We knew straightaway that we had signed a good player.'

Ian Rush struck up an immediate friendship with the young Dane on and off the field. When Jan arrived, he was put up in a city-centre hotel where the Welsh striker often stayed. They shared a love of horse-racing, and some marvellous moments for Liverpool.

'Jan was simply the best foreign player ever to come to England. He was a naturally gifted footballer and, as a person, I'm just proud to have him as a friend. When he first arrived at Anfield on trial, I tried to help him a little bit because I knew what it was like coming to a big club like Liverpool. He scored that fantastic goal in Ireland and we just took it from there.'

Jan played the first six League games under Fagan before missing a handful and returning as a regular until Christmas. He was then dropped until the last fortnight of the season. Alan Hansen believes Jan received a fair crack of the whip from Fagan, as Liverpool struggled to keep up with their Merseyside rivals, Everton, the eventual League winners.

'Because the team wasn't doing that well, I think Joe just tried to shuffle the pack a bit. When he did that, we would get a couple of decent results and a bit of impetus and it took off from there. As well as that, it took time for Jan to settle, as a foreigner. He had to adapt to different players, systems, supporters and, of course, a different way of life. It wasn't until his second season that Jan really found his feet.

'We had so many good players at Liverpool that it was always going to be difficult in his first season for Jan to come in right away and keep that level of consistency – especially as a foreigner. There's always a bedding-in period for foreigners who come to England.

'I remember watching the Dutchman Arnold Muhren play his first game for Ipswich, against Liverpool, and he didn't know whether he was coming or going. He must have left the pitch and wondered what he'd come to – he got absolutely destroyed! But, in the end, he turned out to be one of the best signings that Ipswich ever made.

'Probably the most talented foreigner who ever came to Liverpool was Avi Cohen, from Israel, but he couldn't adapt to the pace of the game – it was just too quick for him. It's always difficult for foreigners to adjust, and there was a lot of pressure on Jan when he began at Anfield.'

Jan's first, and, sadly, Joe Fagan's last season was a huge disappointment for Liverpool. As well as finishing runners-up in the European Cup and the League, they lost 2–1 to Manchester United in an FA Cup semi-final replay.

The next season, everything fell into place. Jan Molby strutted his stuff from August through to May. From Oldham and Oxford to Brighton and Birmingham, Liverpool swept all before them on their way to the first English Double since 1971. Having won the League, they beat Everton 3–1 at Wembley as Jan Molby became the star turn on the grandest stage of all. Two sublime passes set up goals in the Great Dane's finest hour and a half.

'Jan made a massive contribution during the Double season,' says Kenny Dalglish. 'It's there for all to see, whichever way you want to look at it.'

In scoring 18 goals in all competitions, Jan finished second to his close friend Ian Rush – the biggest beneficiary of his passing skills – who netted 32 goals.

'I had been used to playing with Kenny, and Jan was a quick learner,' says Rush. 'He must have seen the balls that

Kenny was playing in for me and started to produce the same sort of passes. We got on really well off the pitch as well so there was a lot of mickey-taking when we were playing. Jan would put through a ball and I wouldn't be there and he'd give me some stick; and if I made a run and the ball didn't come, then I'd give him some stick. But ultimately he was such a good passer of the ball: he could do anything with it.'

'The beauty of Jan as a player was his versatility,' says Alan Hansen. 'He was as comfortable in defence as he was in the middle of the park. You look at the great midfield players who, when they decide to drop into defence, usually become sweepers.

'I don't think that's an ideal situation. If you're a midfield player, that's where you stay. But Jan was one of the few who could come back and play at centre-back, or sweeper, and get it right. And unlike other true artists, like Glenn Hoddle, he was brilliant in the air, absolutely dominant and strong. In my opinion, too many former midfield players are found wanting in the box because the ball's in the air a lot, but Jan found it very, very easy.

'When I think of Jan, two words come to mind – casual and effortless. I can see him now strolling into the dressing room and playing that way as well. As a midfield player, he had a tremendous shot on him. In the Double season, I have vivid memories of two of the hardest shots I've ever seen in my life: one in the Milk Cup against Manchester United at Anfield, with his left foot; and then an unbelievable one, again with little backlift, against York in the FA Cup. He was also a great penalty-kick taker, very cool under pressure.'

During his Liverpool career, Jan only missed 2 out of 42 spot kicks. His last goal in his last appearance, in March 1995, turned out to be a penalty against Coventry. And it was at the penalty spot that Jan was called upon to rescue Liverpool's 1986 Double hopes towards the end of an FA Cup sixth-round replay at Watford which they were losing 1–0.

'I remember being fouled by Tony Coton just before the end,' recalls Ian Rush. 'Everyone else was nervous but Jan was really cool. If you had to bet your life on someone scoring from the penalty, you'd want that person to be Jan Molby. It was a pressure penalty and Jan stuck it away before I went on to score the winner in extra time.

'That penalty against Watford was crucial,' says Kenny Dalglish. 'I didn't have any doubt in my mind about Jan taking it. He didn't look too worried – it wasn't going to be me taking it, I can tell you that!'

'I was very happy for him to take that late penalty against Watford,' agrees Alan Hansen, 'because I knew he wouldn't miss it. That was the day that everybody else in the team had a nose bleed! His ability with both feet was phenomenal – as good as any player I've ever seen.'

After helping Liverpool to reach the 1986 Final, a bout of food poisoning threatened Jan's place in the Wembley line-up. It wasn't until the same bug laid low Gary Gillespie that Kenny Dalglish finalized his team.

'Jan can wonder all his life about whether I would have picked him for the Final if Gary hadn't gone down ill,' says Dalglish, 'because I would never tell him!'

The Double season was always going to be difficult to top, or even equal – as Kenny Dalglish readily admitted when asked how he could follow it. 'I don't know,' he replied. 'All we can do is try just as hard next season.'

Inconsistency dogged Jan during the following campaign. But his failure either to build on or recapture his outstanding form of 1986 was more the result of a succession of infuriating injuries than a loss of ability. From 1987, his career was bedevilled by bad luck, some of the misfortune self-inflicted. Too often, a purple patch or promising comeback would be halted by a torn muscle or pulled hamstring. Never again – save perhaps for the 1992 FA Cup Final against Sunderland – would Jan dominate centre stage. Injury turned him from a leading man into a bit-part player, forever flitting fitfully in and out of the action, peripheral rather than central, but always involved enough to catch the eye of the more discerning spectator.

Ferry Across the North Sea (via Dublin)

It was a bit of a culture shock when I arrived at Liverpool for the trial. I suppose it had something to do with the fact that they were European club Champions. I was expecting it to be special, but it wasn't, really.

I joined Liverpool on the Tuesday in the build-up to the 1984 Charity Shield against Everton, so I was fully prepared for their training to be limited, but when I took part in the five-a-sides I couldn't believe it! Compared with what I'd been used to at Ajax it was very low-key. There were no flying tackles, nobody was working very hard. Basically, it didn't amount to all that much. Everything was very relaxed. All the staff – Joe Fagan, Ronnie Moran and Roy Evans – were joining in, and I found it difficult to take in at first. It was such a contrast to training with Ajax.

I went down with the squad to Wembley on the Friday. It was a wonderful way to start – my first experience of Liverpool being at Wembley. I was given permission to sit on the bench and I was in my element. Everton may have gained revenge for their Milk Cup Final defeat by beating us 1–0 – Bruce Grobbelaar putting the winning goal into his own net – but it was a great day out all the same.

Afterwards, we flew to Dublin to play Home Farm in a friendly on the following Monday. This was my chance to show what I could do. Again, I was struck by how relaxed everything was. We strolled through the game, winning 3–0, and I scored one, with Ronnie Whelan getting the other two. I played OK but, knowing Liverpool as I do now, I don't think they were looking for me to be outstanding.

They were just concerned with the basics – control and passing. I showed them that I wasn't a greedy player and could work within the system. Of course, they were also looking at my potential, as I was only 21.

After the game we returned to our hotel, and I found myself rooming with Kenny Dalglish – he was my minder – before going to a testimonial dinner for Phil Neal. Some of the evening was spent talking to Roy and Ronnie about Ajax, but I was dying to ask them about my future with Liverpool. They kept avoiding the subject because, at the end of the day, it would be Joe's decision.

About eleven o'clock, I went back to our hotel and ended up in the bar doing an interview with a reporter from the *Liverpool Echo*. The next moment, Kenny barged in and asked me where I'd been! I said I hadn't been anywhere – I was just sitting at the bar. Then, for the first time, I witnessed at first hand Kenny's now infamous suspicion of the press.

'Remember,' he said, 'I'm looking after you. You shouldn't be talking to people like that – be careful!'

I said sorry and went to bed, but I could hardly sleep for worrying about the result of my trial. The next morning the suspense was still killing me, so I asked Kenny if I should speak to Joe about getting the Amsterdam flight.

'No,' said Kenny, 'I don't think you'll be going home. I think they'll offer you a contract.'

When we got to Dublin airport, I asked Joe about the Amsterdam flight anyway. Would I be catching it? His reply was music to my ears.

'Oh no,' Joe said. 'You'll be going back to Anfield. We're going to sign you – we're going to give you a contract.'

I can't tell you how relieved I was – not just because it was Liverpool, but because I was getting a contract. I phoned up my mum and she was all excited. I confirmed that she would now have to switch to English classes (from Dutch).

My dad was less than enthralled. To him, it wasn't a great move. 'I don't think you're that good,' he said. 'You're going to find it very difficult over there.'

To be fair to him, I think he was worried about getting over to England to see me play. When I was at Ajax, he could just pack the twins into the car and drive down to Holland. But getting across to England posed a few problems.

We returned to Anfield on the Tuesday and the next day I began contract negotiations. They didn't amount to much, because you didn't negotiate with Liverpool. The chairman Peter Robinson made me an offer of just over a thousand pounds a week – more than I was getting at Ajax – but money was never the issue. At the time, I didn't realize how fair Liverpool were. I didn't have an agent then, so I just signed the three-year contract. Peter said that if I progressed and became a first-team regular, then I'd be seeing him again. And that was it. Deal done.

I now felt I had arrived. Ajax may have been a great club in Holland but they weren't on the international football map any more. After winning the European Cup three years running in the early seventies, they'd had a bit of a lean spell. I was swapping the past Champions for the present. My transfer was big news in Denmark, as people were slightly surprised. How come I couldn't get a game with Denmark in the 1984 European Championships, yet here I was joining Liverpool, the best club side in the business? I'll never forget the date I signed: Wednesday 22 August 1984. I made my debut in a 3–3 draw at Norwich on the following Saturday.

Teething Troubles

It was a classic wind-up. A bit like being the new boy in the class at school. Jan Molby, the innocent victim of a Scouser set-up.

When we arrived at Carrow Road for my first game, we filed into the away dressing room and I asked Sammy Lee what the form was. We'd already been told the team at the Melwood training ground the day before, but I was wondering what happened now. Sammy told me to get changed. I'd been used to talking tactics before games

– usually for an hour and a half with Kolding and thirty or forty-five minutes with Ajax. We'd go through everything: corners, free-kicks; every player would be told exactly what he had to do. So, just to make sure I'd heard Sammy correctly, I asked Ronnie Moran.

'What do we do now?'

'Just get changed,' growled Ronnie. 'Get yourself ready for the game, son.'

'What time do we go out to warm up?' I asked.

'You don't have to warm up – save your energy!'

I couldn't believe what I was hearing. At Ajax, we spent about twenty-five minutes warming up. As I started to get changed, a couple of the lads said the staff liked the players to have a massage before a game. I should ask Ronnie if he'd give me one. So that's precisely what I did.

'Er . . . Ronnie. Can I have a massage?'

'Fuck off!' shouted Ronnie. 'You earn the fucking right to have a massage! Go out there and play some games and then I might consider it!'

I'd only been at the club a couple of days and I started to wonder what I'd let myself in for. Then I saw all the lads pissing themselves. That was my introduction to the Liverpool dressing-room humour. It was the first, but certainly not the last, example of the camaraderie which kept the team and the club together. From the very first moment I set foot in Liverpool, I was struck by the friendliness of the place. When I arrived that first night for the trial, John Wark and Paul Walsh were at the bar and I went over to shake hands. John asked me if I wanted a drink and appeared most upset when I asked for an orange juice and lemonade. He immediately ordered me a pint of lager instead.

After the Man United–Ajax game, we went back to a wine bar owned by Sammy Lee, and so by the time I went into training the next day I'd already met three of the players, which was a great help. Ian Rush, although he lived in Flint in North Wales, spent a lot of time in the hotel as well. I didn't have a regular room-partner in those days – I was either with Paul Walsh, John Wark or, after a few months, Kevin McDonald – and I became quite close to Dave

Hodgson, now manager of Darlington. In fact, I stayed at his house a few times. Trouble was that after signing me, Liverpool went and sold him!

I felt very much part of it all. At training, all my new team-mates came over and shook hands. I think they were impressed not so much by my Ajax connection but by the fact that I'd played for Denmark. They'd all watched us reach the semi-finals of the 1984 European Championships, where we'd lost to Spain after beating Yugoslavia 5-0 and Belgium 3-2. Everyone had been talking about Denmark, and I think that broke the ice a bit with the Liverpool players – especially as we'd won the group England were in to qualify for the competition in the first place. It stood me in good stead, because Denmark was only really famous for brewing lager and sending butter and bacon over here. Now, suddenly, we had a world-class football team.

It didn't take me that long to adjust to the more relaxed type of training at Anfield. Frankly, the Ajax method was a pain in the backside at times. The Liverpool approach suited me, and I soon realized it also made sense, with the number of games we played every season. In Holland there were 34 League matches, but we would cruise through 20 of them. At Liverpool there were 42 First Division games, and normally quite a few Cup matches, but we could rarely take it easy. We could go away and be two or three nil up but the other teams just wouldn't give in. They'd keep going because their fans would demand it.

After a Saturday match in Holland you could wake up the next day feeling you hadn't played. That never happened with Liverpool. In my first six months at Anfield I couldn't walk after the games, they were all so tough: ninety minutes, non-stop.

The build-up to my first game was typically laid-back. On the Friday we went down to the training ground, sat around having our tea and biscuits, before Joe Fagan came in to tell us the team. He said nothing else. On the Saturday itself, in the dressing room, I was obviously a bit nervous about making my debut so I asked Joe what he wanted me to do during the game.

'Play,' he said. 'Play. Don't do anything silly, just play within the system and remember you'll be in the middle of midfield with John Wark – just play.'

I'll never forget my first contribution to the Liverpool cause on the pitch. It was very early on – in the first minute or so – and Phil Neal had the ball at right-back. I made a run down the right wing and Phil put it over the top. It was set up nicely for me, I had all the time in the world as I saw Kenny Dalglish coming in at the far post. Steve Bruce was making his debut for Norwich in the same game. I lifted the ball in and Steve arrived to score an own goal. That was my – and Steve's – first touch of the game! When we came in at half-time, Joe decided to have a quiet word with me.

'I thought I told you not to do anything silly,' he said. 'Play within the system.'

I knew Joe was joking, but there was a serious point to be made. He was just letting me know that Liverpool didn't expect central midfield players to suddenly shoot off down the wing. We had our system – Sammy Lee down the right, Ronnie Whelan on the left and John Wark and me in the middle – and we should stick to it. Afterwards, Joe told me to be sensible over the weekend because we had another game on Monday, against West Ham at Anfield. We won that 3–0.

My main memory of the Norwich game was the post-match routine. It was so different from Ajax, where we packed up our kit, hopped on to the coach and went home. At Carrow Road, we wandered over to the players' lounge for a few beers. On the way across, a couple of Norwich fans unofficially voted me 'man-of-the-match'. At the time, I didn't think much of it but, to be honest, that was my only good game for a very long time. I struggled from then on.

I basically played until just before Christmas, only missing one or two games (I'd been signed too late to play in Europe). They would put Sammy Lee in my place in midweek and then sometimes keep the same team for Saturday. My problem was that I was too inconsistent. I would have a reasonable game and then a couple of bad ones. When we lost 3–1 at Arsenal, I had an absolute nightmare. It was the first time the London press had seen me and I got slaughtered. People were calling me the 'new Graeme Souness' and although I was never going to be that, they were building up the comparison. It made life very difficult. I didn't play the way Graeme used to; I was an entirely different player. I was looking for a bit of time to acclimatize but the press were looking at my pedigree – the Danish international who'd come from Ajax.

After a couple of weeks without setting the world alight at Anfield, my international career took off when I went back to play for Denmark against Austria. I think Sepp Piontek, the Danish manager, thought he had to give me a game. He threw me in and I had the best game of my 34 internationals. The next day the papers were full of stuff about the way I'd changed since I'd been at Liverpool. One headline read: A STAR IS BORN. It was a great feeling. It was very important for me to let people back home know, to remove any doubt, that I would be making it in England, because there were still a lot of people who weren't sure if I was up to it.

By November I thought I had settled in at Anfield. I was playing better, although I was never really outstanding, and in December I managed to score my first goal, in a 3–1 defeat at Chelsea. I felt I was beginning to understand and work well with our front men, Kenny and Rushie. But after about 20 games Joe Fagan felt enough was enough. He'd just signed Kevin McDonald from Leicester at the end of November and he thought the time was right to play him.

My last game until near the end of the season was on Boxing Day, when we lost 2–1 at home to Leicester. I don't think Kevin was seen as a replacement for me. Joe was looking for someone who was defensively strong in midfield, a good runner and very competitive. There was nobody around to really sit in front of the back four and secure them.

Joe didn't say anything to me – he just left me out of the team when he named it after training. I was a little surprised to be dropped because I thought I was coming to terms with first-team football. What made it worse was that I then played in fifteen unbeaten games for the reserves. It was frustrating because people were saying I should be back in the first team. One day I went to see Joe about a move and he made it very clear that time was on my side as a

21-year-old. He said he would put me back in the first team when I was ready.

I always felt my best position was in front of the back four – dictating things from there. I liked playing there because I was protecting my back line and myself at the same time. I didn't get dragged out to positions where my lack of pace could be exposed, and it was a comfortable place to pass from. I was at the heart of the action and I always felt I'd be a better player, the more I saw of the ball. My lack of pace was rarely exposed because I knew where to go. People used to say I had a problem getting around, but I was always there for ninety minutes.

When Graeme Souness came back to England while he was with Sampdoria, he told me how he'd been asked to play in Italy: 'All I want you to do,' the manager would say, 'is sit in front of the back line and protect them with your life. When you get the ball, put it in the corners.'

The trouble was Graeme had never had to do that at Liverpool. He wasn't that much of a long passer and he couldn't do it with Sampdoria after half an hour because he would be so tired. The passing takes it out of you. Pinging 50- and 60-yard balls all over the place absolutely destroys your thighs. He said it took him a while to readjust, but I didn't have a problem with it. I may have been missing some pace but I never suffered from a lack of stamina. I would be hitting those sort of balls in the 90th minute.

Although I preferred playing in front of the back four, I was quite happy operating wide on the left in the reserves when Joe dropped me.

I was desperate to be involved in the European Cup Final. We'd beaten Panathinaikos 5–0 on aggregate in the semi-final and my adrenalin was really flowing, especially when Mark Lawrenson dislocated his shoulder. I'd been eligible to play from the quarter-finals but had only got as far as the bench. This was the opportunity I'd been waiting for.

Mark's obvious replacement at centre-back was Gary Gillespie, but he was suffering from a hamstring injury, so there was a place up for grabs. We went down for a League game against West Ham in London nine days before the European Cup Final against Juventus and I suddenly found myself back in the first team playing alongside Alan Hansen – the first time I'd been at centre-back or in a flat back four in my career. Joe told me I was in an hour and a half before the game.

'Go and take your chance,' he said.

Alan didn't say anything to me – I don't think he thought it was going to be a problem. We had Phil Neal at right-back, Jocky Hansen and me in the centre and Jim Beglin at left-back. After about 15 minutes, Jocky miscontrolled the ball. As it went up in the air, I was watching it, along with Jocky and Dave Swindlehurst, the West Ham striker. As Dave came in I headed the ball but, as I followed through, I ended up being hit in the face by both of them. I was out cold. I didn't remember anything for about thirty seconds. When I woke up, all I could hear was Bruce Grobbelaar shouting: 'I've found a couple of teeth!'

As well as losing my front teeth, my nose was all over the place, both lips were split, and Ronnie and Roy Evans were by my side. There was no way I could stay on so they escorted me to the touchline and the team went on to win 3–0. So much for taking my chance.

A couple of days later, we were playing Everton at Goodison Park in our last League game of the season. Everton had already won the Championship and were a week away from their FA Cup Final defeat by Manchester United. After the West Ham game I'd been to see both the doctor and the dentist, who told me I'd in fact lost five teeth. (Bruce never was any good at counting.) The dentist said I wouldn't be ready for the Everton game but, after he'd made me a temporary gumshield, I played again at the back alongside Alan, marking Andy Gray. We lost 1–0 but I had a really good game and even the Everton sponsors, Hafnia, named me as the 'man-of-the-match'. I don't know if it had anything to do with them being a Danish company, but I felt great. I had dominated Andy in that match. I won nearly everything that was played up to him in the air, and if he chested the ball down I would come round and take it off him. I also used our possession well from the back. Alan Hansen was great on the ball but he was never a 50- or 60-yard passer from the back. I was able to dictate play from the back. Maybe Everton took their foot off the pedal because they had already won the League by then, but we were really up for the game – we were all playing for a place against Juventus.

My European Cup Final hopes were raised again, as Mark Lawrenson was still struggling with his dislocated shoulder and Gary Gillespie had only just started light training. One week to go to the big day and I was feeling more and more confident of making the starting line-up.

We took a squad of eighteen to Brussels for the Final in the Heysel Stadium. My face was fine, the lips had settled down, my nose was feeling better and I just couldn't wait for the permanent replacement teeth to come through. But once we were in Belgium I realized that I was only dreaming about playing. Mark, who'd dislocated his shoulder twice that season, was starting to pick up in training, so I thought he would get the nod ahead of me. I had taken the precaution of hiring a coach to bring about forty of my family and friends down from Denmark to Brussels for what could be the greatest moment of my career so far. I had to admit, though, it wasn't looking good.

By the time the moment of truth came round on the Wednesday morning, I was in two minds. One minute, I thought I would be in the squad of sixteen and the next, looking around at all our players, I thought I could even miss out altogether. As it happened, Alan Kennedy and Kevin McDonald were the two left out, so I knew I'd at least be on the bench. I really felt sorry for Kevin because, although many people saw us as rivals, I had a great relationship with him. Alan and Kevin didn't take it very well, but there's nothing you can say or do in that situation.

We went training and then Joe picked the team. Mark Lawrenson was at centre-back. I went along with the decision – it seemed fair enough – but after two minutes of the game, Mark went down injured. He fell over and dislocated his shoulder. In hindsight, it's easy to say Mark shouldn't have been on the pitch, but if you've got a player of that calibre, then you try to play him.

Down on the bench, I was rubbing my hands together. I couldn't think of anything else but getting on. The four outfield subs started warming up. I thought my big chance was just about to arrive, but Gary Gillespie was put on instead. Now Gary was a wonderful player but he'd hardly trained because of his hamstring injury. I think the feeling was that I wasn't ready for it. I would have had to play in a flat back four against the likes of Platini and Boniek, so they went for Gary. He had made nearly 200 appearances for Coventry and Liverpool and was a natural central defender but I was very, very disappointed.

I'd really thought I was going to get on because I'd done so well against Everton, but it wasn't to be. It was a huge blow. There was nothing I could do about it – I just went back and sat on the bench and hoped we might have to make another substitution. After that, the rest of the night was a huge anti-climax. Joe put on Craig Johnston, Gary gave away the winning penalty and, after the game, Joe announced his retirement to the press. We had known before the game that he'd simply had enough.

But, as I'll discuss later in this book, we were all aware that something had gone on behind the goal before the game, so the result was never really important. We knew there had been some trouble, but we all agreed that the game had to be played. Juventus were very flat afterwards. They'd won the European Cup but, as we later found out, they'd lost thirty-nine of their supporters. Everyone shook hands, one or two players swapped shirts, and we collected our medals before going back to the dressing room. Joe came in to say it wasn't the way we would have wanted it – to end a long, hard season by getting beaten in the European Cup Final – but, on a night like that, the result was the last thing on everyone's minds.

At the Court of King Kenny

When Joe announced he was leaving, speculation about his successor started straightaway. We knew it was an absolute certainty that the Liverpool board would promote from within. It seemed to be one from four: Kenny Dalglish, Ronnie Moran, Roy Evans or Phil Neal. I was surprised when Kenny was chosen. At the time, I didn't think it was something he wanted to do. He just didn't come across as someone who would like to be a manager. But I had no doubt that once he was appointed, he would make a success of it and that, under him, my career had a much better chance of taking off.

Kenny's move into player-management was never really a problem. Although he had always been one of the lads, he kept himself to himself most of the time. He had one or two very close friends within the game, like Jocky Hansen, but he always kept himself at a distance. If we had a day out, Kenny would be there, but he'd never go the whole way with us. There were two completely different Kenny Dalglishes: the one he allowed the public to get to know, where he didn't say much in interviews, and the one he allowed the players to see. As a player, he was a great one for having fun. There was never a wind-up in our dressing room that he wasn't in on. He was always involved in some way. He had a great sense of humour.

One of Kenny's best wind-ups involved Sammy Lee, just before our European Cup semi-final against Panathinaikos in 1985. Mick Channon, the former Southampton and Manchester City striker, had been very rude about Sammy in an article in the *Sun*. He said Sammy hadn't really been good enough to play for England (he'd actually won 14 caps) and every night, before he went to bed, Mick said Sammy should thank God for his good luck. This article really upset Sammy, who took things like that to heart.

When we arrived at Anfield for the match, there was a letter waiting for him at reception. We all knew what it was about and we watched Sammy perk up as he read it. One or two of the lads asked him what was in the letter.

'Oh nothing,' Sammy replied, dying to show it to somebody he could trust. Five minutes later, he did just that and then explained what had happened.

'I told you Mick Channon wasn't like that,' said Sammy. 'He says in this letter that he was misquoted in that article – he never said those things about me!'

During the game, Sammy had an absolute stormer down the right wing. We won 4–0 – he set up two of the goals. But it wasn't until afterwards that Kenny admitted that he and Alan Hansen had sent the letter. It was a wind-up but also a way of getting Sammy going on behalf of the team. It gave him a real lift. That was typical Kenny. As long as he knew who you were and he trusted you, he was fine. Kenny was always on the edge of things, always one step removed, so he didn't have to change too much when he replaced Joe.

The 1984–85 season was the first time for a long time that Liverpool hadn't won anything, but there wasn't any more pressure inside the club as a result. It was felt there would be one or two changes on the playing side, with people like Phil Neal, Alan Kennedy and Sammy Lee coming towards the end of their time at Anfield. Personally, I felt that by the end of my first season I'd come to terms with English football, and when Kenny took over I thought I had every chance of making my mark. I just hoped he would use me.

The European ban after Heysel meant that our pre-season tour took us to unfamiliar places like Brighton and Bristol. I was a bit frustrated because Kenny was still chopping and changing the team. At Ajax, the side would be settled towards the end of the pre-season games. Although I was playing in midfield, along with people like John Wark, Craig Johnston and Sammy Lee, Kenny could see I was a little unhappy. One day, he pulled me aside.

'This is the way we do it here,' he said. 'You'll play a pre-season game and then I'll leave you on the bench, and then you'll play another one, but don't worry about it. You're very much part of my plans – I want you to slot in behind the front two and just make things happen.'

It was a good piece of man-management. I felt relaxed from then on. But four days before the start of the season, Kenny had to placate me again. We played Everton in Phil Neal's testimonial and I was pulled off after an hour.

'Don't worry,' said Kenny. 'When we kick off the season on Saturday, you'll be in there.'

And I was. I went on to miss only a handful of games through illness in what turned out to be my greatest season with Liverpool. I ended up with 18 goals in all competitions which, for a midfield player, I guess is a good return. People were now seeing a totally different player from the one in my first season. I had been bought by Joe Fagan as a holding player in midfield, but Kenny gave me my freedom. I was able to express myself more by scoring goals and setting them up for the front two. I was really happy in that role, and it meant Kenny finding someone else to fill the holding position behind me (Steve McMahon did so later). Craig Johnston replaced Sammy Lee on the right, Ronnie Whelan was still on the left, with me and John Wark in the middle. Paul Walsh and Ian Rush were playing up front, with Kenny coming in as and when required.

We made an indifferent start to the season, but only because Manchester United seemed unbeatable. They were under an awful lot of pressure, not having won the League since 1967, and they set off at a cracking pace. Eleven successive League wins meant we could only trail in second place. We were doing OK without playing that well. To be fair, we were trying to build a new team. Phil Neal began at right-back before being replaced by Steve Nicol, and Alan Kennedy played a couple of games at left-back before Jim Beglin established himself there. I was a little worried when Steve McMahon was signed from Aston Villa because everyone assumed he was going to take my place. But again, Kenny was there with a quick word. Steve would play with me not instead of me.

We started to pick up the pace, with Paul Walsh hitting a lovely vein of form. He scored 11 goals in 16 League games, but because of Man United's fantastic start, we found ourselves quite a way behind. It all changed in November, when United came to our place, still unbeaten, in the Milk Cup. Paul McGrath gave them the lead before I scored two – the second a penalty – and that was the turning point of the season. United had been beaten and we were on our way.

The first was a bit of a wonder goal – many people describe it as one of the best they've ever seen at Anfield. From what I can remember, I took the ball off Norman Whiteside inside our own half and there was only one man ahead of me, making a run to the right, so the route ahead was clear. I went on a run past three or four United players and then shot with my right foot from about 20 yards. Gary

Bailey, the United keeper, still insists it was the hardest shot he ever faced. It's true that from the moment it left my boot to the moment it hit the net, Gary didn't see it. It was one of those shots that you just know is right when you hit it. I wasn't the only one who was pleased. The next day, Bob Paisley was full of praise for the way in which I'd produced the shot at the end of a 60-yard run, and if you ask any Liverpool fan who watched me during my 12 years at Anfield, they all go back to that goal.

Unfortunately though, there's no official record of it. The game was played during a television dispute, when there was a complete football black-out. But I've got a video of it in Denmark – thanks to the then United manager Ron Atkinson. A friend of his had videoed the game from the stand, and I made a copy of the goal before returning it to Ron. The defeat was a turning point in United's season too because, until then, I think they believed they were unstoppable.

From then on, they started to wobble in the League, while we kept plugging away. But we had a disastrous February, losing two and drawing 1–1 with United at Anfield. By this time though, they'd fallen by the wayside. It had become a straight fight between Liverpool and Everton for the title. They beat us 2–0 at home to take them 8 points clear with 12 games to go.

That draw with Manchester United proved crucial because an injury to Paul Walsh in the game paved the way for Kenny to return. Kenny had been playing the odd game but then featured in 9 of the last 11 in the League. I'm not saying it was simply because Kenny came back but he certainly was a steadying influence as we dropped just one point in our last 12 matches. Nothing could stop us – it reminded me of my days at Ajax.

We hit some tremendous home form. It was all down to confidence. We had stuttered throughout the season. Although we'd reached the semi-finals of both the FA and League Cups, we'd never really got a good run of results together in the League. The run began with a 2–1 away win over Spurs – Rushie and I scored – and finished two months later with victory at Chelsea. It was the snowball effect – it just went on and on. We sensed that we were riding on the crest of a wave – especially at home. We were so far behind Everton that nobody thought we could catch them, so the pressure was off. Everton were favourites to win the Double; whatever we achieved would be great.

I think the most important thing about that run was that everybody was chipping in with goals: I scored in each of our home games against Oxford, Coventry and Birmingham, as we won 6–0, 5–0 and 5–0; Ronnie Whelan notched a hat-trick against Coventry: Gary Gillespie, a defender, managed to get three against Birmingham; and Steve McMahon popped in two against Manchester City. And, all the while, Rushie kept knocking them in – 10 in those last 12 games. It was a real team effort.

It was neck-and-neck right to the finishing line. Merseyside split down the middle as the race between two great rivals reached its climax. Just as Everton were desperate to hang on to their title, so Liverpool were determined to make up for a rare trophyless season. In our penultimate game, we won 2–0 at Leicester while Everton lost 1–0 at Oxford, so we went above them for the first time that year.

It went right down to the wire. If we wanted the title, we had to win at Chelsea in our last game of the season. For me, that match was the start of a week-long nightmare. A couple of the staff had gone down ill with food poisoning after the Leicester win, and I picked it up on the Friday morning. I was really bad. We were leaving for Chelsea in the afternoon and I told Kenny I couldn't go. He told me to get on the bus. It must have been my longest ever journey to London. I was feeling really ill. As soon as we arrived, I went straight to bed – I couldn't eat a thing.

When I woke up on the Saturday morning, Roy Evans came to see me. I had to be honest. Badly though I wanted to play, I just couldn't. I wasn't up to it. Mark Lawrenson was handed my number 10 shirt as I joined the team in the Stamford Bridge dressing room – frustration wasn't in it.

As usual, Kenny didn't say much beforehand. He was a man of few words – especially when it came to team talks. I think he felt that all the hard work had been done on the training ground so he didn't need to go on before the game. We won 1–0 – with Kenny scoring the winner as per the script – but it wasn't quite the same for me because I was feeling so ill. In many ways, it was the worst possible scenario for me. I was made up that we'd won the League – especially by pipping Everton in the last game – but then I had an agonizing wait for a week before the FA Cup Final. Would I get my place back or would Kenny stick with the side that had won the title? They were the longest seven days of my whole career.

On the Spot

I felt I deserved a Wembley place because of the part I'd played in getting us to the Final. I'd stood up to be counted when it mattered and I felt I was owed one.

It all began when Phil Neal, our regular penalty taker, hit a bad run. He scored one against Watford in the League early in September but then missed a couple. When we played Spurs at home, Phil realized that our former keeper Ray Clemence was in goal for Spurs and said he didn't want to take any more penalties. When Kenny asked me if I was interested, I agreed to have a go. Sure enough, in my first game as regular penalty taker against Spurs, we were awarded two. I put them both away, hard and low to Ray's right, and we won 4–1. But then in the New Year, I missed two out of four penalties in the League and Cup, and Kenny decided it was time for a change.

In late March, we found ourselves in a quarter-final replay at Watford. In the first game at Anfield, Kenny had passed the responsibility for penalties to John Wark. As it happened, we drew 0–0 and he wasn't needed. I presumed John would be taking any spot-kicks awarded in the replay. Now it's bad enough being 1–0 down with four minutes to go, but if you're 1–0 down with four minutes to go and you're without your regular penalty taker, then you really are in trouble. When we found ourselves in that position against Watford (John Wark had been substituted) the big question was: who would take the kick?

I looked around me. The ball was lying in the penalty area waiting to be put on the spot and virtually the whole team was walking in the opposite direction. No one wanted the responsibility. Kenny, who was playing that day, just looked at me and said: 'You.' Simple as that, no hesitation. 'You.' No debate either.

As I prepared to take what turned out to be the most important penalty of my career, there was just one thought going through my mind. If I missed it, I would never be forgiven. Never mind that no other bugger wanted to take it! I would be the one to blame for our Cup exit, and the chance of the Double would be gone.

Until that day, I had usually put penalties to the keeper's right. It had worked against Ray Clemence and Spurs and I saw no reason to change the policy. Until, that was, I looked down at the mud in the Watford penalty area. That was my biggest worry as I picked up the ball and placed it on the spot. I had never lifted my kicks off the floor, always preferring to roll them along the ground. But there was so much mud around that if I put it along the floor, the ball might not even make the goalline.

I told myself not to change. Keep it low to the keeper's right. But as I ran up, I did what they always tell you not to do – I changed my mind. Instead of putting the ball to the keeper's right, I switched it to his left. He moved right, the ball went the other way and rolled into the corner of the net. We were level. Phew! The Dane had saved Liverpool's bacon. In extra time, Rushie scored the winner and we were through to the semi-final. The Double was still on. I was obviously relieved but Kenny didn't say anything to me afterwards.

On the Tuesday night of Cup Final week, we played Norwich in the second leg of the semi-final of the ScreenSport Super Cup. This was a competition for those clubs who had qualified for Europe but, because of the Heysel ban, couldn't play. The game was shown live on one of the satellite channels. As I'd missed the win at Chelsea on the previous Saturday, I thought Kenny would give me a game but he left me on the bench. Although I came on against Norwich, scored a goal and we won 3–1, I was still sweating on a place in the Cup Final team.

When we left for the Hilton in Watford on Thursday, I was feeling quite good but, on the Saturday morning, I still didn't know whether I'd be playing. Of course, people like Alan Hansen, Ian Rush and Bruce Grobbelaar knew they'd be in, but most of us were waiting for confirmation. At about a quarter to two, Kenny sat everyone down in the dressing room and announced the team. Most of us put on a front; most of us were cocky. Nobody would admit to being worried about making the line-up, but we all were.

There were three of us vying for one place: Mark Lawrenson, who had staked a claim to play in midfield, Steve McMahon, my room-mate, and me. Nobody knew who was going to be picked. The choice had been made easier for Kenny when the stomach bug which had cost me my place in the title-winning team at Chelsea then struck down Gary Gillespie. Not surprisingly, Mark took over from him in defence and I got the nod over McMahon to play alongside Kevin McDonald – Steve was named as sub.

Kenny never explained his thinking but I suspect I would have played even if Gary hadn't been ill. I had been a regular all season, having only missed a couple of games through illness. I felt there was no way I wasn't going to play but I was still waiting for that confirmation. And when it came, it was great. I didn't say anything to Steve because, although he was obviously disappointed, you either sank or swam at Liverpool – you just got on with your job.

I started getting changed just after two o'clock and did my warm-up for about fifteen minutes in the dressing room. You have to be ready a little earlier at Wembley because of the walk out to the pitch. I'm superstitious so I always like to come out last. It's something I've done throughout my career but maybe I should have come out earlier to sample a little bit more of the atmosphere. By the time I'd walked through the tunnel, there had already been a minute of ninety-odd thousand people screaming their heads off. I remember thinking how great it was but, although I tried to treat it as just another game, virtually everything from that first Cup Final is a bit of a blur. The game was over before it had really begun.

79

It was obviously a special occasion because it was the first Merseyside FA Cup Final. We'd drawn 0–0 in a Milk Cup Final a couple of years earlier, before winning the replay 1–0, but this was the big one. There was added spice because we'd been neck-and-neck with Everton for the Championship and we realized that we were only 90 minutes away from completing our first-ever Double. Everton had finished runners-up to us after being favourites to win the League and were expected to lift the Cup. We were building a new team, and people weren't too sure about new players like me, Jim Beglin and Kevin McDonald. But we had no doubt.

Everton went ahead through Gary Lineker's 40th goal of the season about ten minutes before the interval. Bruce Grobbelaar managed to parry Gary's left-foot shot but could only get a hand to the right-foot rebound. The Liverpool dressing room was very quiet after we'd all trooped in. With Kenny playing, Ronnie and Roy gave us most of the half-time team talk. They didn't mince their words. What was the point of coming to Wembley and playing like we were? We weren't here for a day out but to win a football match, so we should get out there and get on with it. Kenny chipped in with something similar: 'There are forty-five minutes left – let's go and give it our lot!'

For the first fifteen minutes of the second half, we were dreadful. We were all over the place and Everton could have scored again. Bruce Grobbelaar and Jim Beglin were involved in an argument, with Bruce grabbing Jim by the neck. But then, all of a sudden, it changed. We played a long ball into the corner and their right-back Gary Stevens picked it up. But as he tried to play it out of defence, he gave it straight to Ronnie Whelan, who rolled it inside to me.

Everton had tried to hold their back line, I stuck it through Derek Mountfield's legs and Rushie took it around Bobby Mimms and scored. I knew exactly what I was going to do when I got the ball and so did Rushie. It was just a question of putting the right weight on the pass so he could reach it before Bobby. As the ball crossed the line, Craig Johnston dived in to try to claim it because he was desperate to score at Wembley, but it was definitely Rushie's goal.

Craig didn't have long to wait, though. A couple of minutes later we scored again. Rushie chased a ball, laid it back to me just inside the box. I went past Gary Stevens and crossed left-footed for Craig to drive the ball home. All you could hear was him shouting: 'I've done it! I've done it!' It was a great moment. His goal made it 2-1 and I was so delighted that I went off on my own, around behind the net where all our fans were. We then felt it was a case of when rather than if we were going to score again. I should have made it three almost straight away. I was clean through with only Bobby to beat but, instead of placing it, I hit the ball straight at his legs.

Within five minutes it was 3-1. A well-worked move from our own half ended with a pass from Ronnie to Rushie out on the right and his deliberate shot crashed into the corner hitting the camera in the process. Once the third goal went in, we realized that was it – we had won the game and the Double. We felt so confident we were glad there was another twenty minutes to go. We started to relax and stroke the ball around. All the step-overs and back-heels came out. In the end, it could have been 4-1 but Rushie missed a chance for his hat-trick in the last minute. He was put clean through and tried to chip Bobby Mimms – 4-1 would have made it a bit more convincing.

The Final has been described as the pinnacle of my career, but until the first goal I was having an indifferent game. It's true what they say about Wembley being a tiring pitch. I was struggling because I'd been ill with food poisoning and hadn't played for a while. Luckily, we all got second wind and it came right for us in the end. To me, setting up a goal with a lovely pass is as wonderful as scoring a goal itself. To play in an FA Cup Final is one thing, but to make two goals like that, to have such an impact . . . the 1986 Cup Final has to be the greatest moment of my career.

I'd won over the Liverpool regulars with my performances throughout the season and now it was the turn of football fans in Denmark to be impressed. I knew the whole Danish team were sitting back home watching the Final on TV. They'd met up the week before for the World Cup and I was the only one missing. I couldn't be there because I had this one game left. I knew I had a lot to live up to: Soren Lerby had won the German Championship with Bayern

Munich, Preben Elkjaer had helped Verona take the Italian title and Michael Laudrup had done well with Juventus. Five players had won the Double with Anderlecht in Belgium and they were all sitting there watching the greatest Cup Final in the world.

It was the game in which I came of age in the eyes of the Danish people. They saw English matches live on TV every Saturday and we'd been on a couple of times. It would have been nice to turn it on in those games for the people back home, but football's not like that. I hadn't done anything special when we'd been on the box, but then people would read in the paper that we'd won, say, 4–1 in a game not televised and that I'd scored two. They'd begin asking if there was any chance of them seeing me in that sort of form. In the 1986 FA Cup Final, it all came together and I was so pleased to have helped provide Kenny with the Double in his first season as manager.

The Final was probably one of Kenny's quieter games, but, knowing what I do now about preparing a team for Wembley as a player-manager, I bet he was drained by the time he walked out on to the pitch. He's never mentioned it, but that's my feeling now. There's so much to do, you try to please everybody, you interrupt your normal routine and you're shattered by the time you get to Wembley. But it was important for us to have Kenny out there. We had a long spell when we couldn't do anything right and it was crucial that he was with us.

It wasn't until the post-match meal at our hotel that I fully realized what we had done. I was one of the last ones to receive my medal, and after coming down from the Royal Box I posed for a few team photos and then went off on a lap of honour wearing a silly hat. Back at the hotel, it all became too much for me. It suddenly hit home: we had done the Double.

I remember looking down at my two medals (I'd brought my Championship one with me because I was going straight to Denmark to take them both home to my mum). Bruce Grobbelaar gave me one of the many cigars that he used to bring to Wembley, but it didn't make things any better. I was having loads to drink, not a lot to eat, I was smoking this cigar and then I couldn't resist it – I sneaked up to my room to watch the game on *Match of the Day*. After getting undressed, I was lying on the bed with my two medals watching the game when there was a knock at the door. It was a few of my friends from Denmark.

'What's happening?' they asked.

'Nothing,' I said. 'I've had enough. I just want to lie here and watch the game. And then I want to go to sleep.'

'No way!' they replied. 'We've got to go down to Stringfellows!'

As you can imagine, a trip to a trendy nightclub was all I needed – even though it was only five minutes away. When my friends wouldn't take no for an answer, I got dressed again and went downstairs. Waiting in the foyer of the Mountbatten Hotel was Tony Chinn, a Liverpool security man, who was holding the FA Cup.

We made our way around to Stringfellows only to find there was a queue to get in. But you don't queue when you've got the FA Cup with you, so we moved right up to the front, showed the doorman the trophy and went in. All the boys were there – Kenny, Alan Hansen – and I remember having my picture taken with Alex Higgins and the FA Cup before going up into the restaurant with my friends to drink champagne all night. I think I got back to the hotel at about five o'clock in the morning.

As well as missing *Match of the Day*, I wasn't around for the open-top bus tour of Liverpool the next day because I had to fly to Denmark to link up with the national team. At the time, I thought nothing of not being on the bus because I was excited about going home. Looking back though, I would have loved to have been there – especially as the next open-top trip followed the Wimbledon defeat in 1988, which is best forgotten. I wasn't involved in the 1989 Final, when we beat Everton again, and the 1992 trip was a bit low-key because we'd been expected to beat Sunderland. I regret now not asking the Danish authorities for an extra twenty-four hours with Liverpool. I've seen a video of the homecoming and many of the fans who were asked named me as 'man-of-the-match'. I would have loved to have been there but it wasn't to be.

When I arrived at Copenhagen airport, my feet hardly touched the ground. My sponsors Patrick presented me with a golden boot for helping to win the Double, and I was then put on a private plane and flown back to Kolding. There, the local council gave me the freedom of the city out on the pitch at the club's ground. It was an amazing twenty-four hours!

The one question I'm most often asked nowadays is: do I think I achieved too much too early on in my career? I accept that I was only 22 when Liverpool won the Double, but what else can I say? There wasn't a great deal I could do about it. If you have the opportunity to do well, you take it. I was lucky to be successful with Ajax and then Liverpool, but it's not something I thought about or planned at the time.

It was always going to be hard to repeat the success I experienced in the 1986 Double season. We had set ourselves very high standards and it was almost impossible to meet them again. So I understand why people say that I never really reached those heights again, but then you don't stay at Anfield for nearly twelve years without having something. Liverpool are famous for unloading players who they've no further use for. During my time at Anfield, I had one or two crucial injuries which restricted my appearances, but, like Denmark, Liverpool had a lot of good midfield players. Look through the team sheets and you'll see that I was in pretty good company.

The Double season was remarkable because we were in the middle of rebuilding the team. And yet, in a strange sort of way, achieving the Double with Liverpool was similar to winning it with Ajax, because everyone at Anfield also expected success. As a result, nobody in the team said anything special to me about my part in the Final. We had a great team spirit, everyone just got on with their job, and although managers can do much to generate the right mood, if you haven't got the right characters in your team you're fighting a losing battle.

First and foremost, as he was number one, we had Bruce Grobbelaar, who was completely in control of the dressing room. I had to laugh when the match-fixing allegations were made against him. It's one thing to try to forecast games, and another to try to fix them. Bruce wouldn't get involved in anything like that. I didn't play in the infamous Newcastle game but I remember watching it on Sky and there was nothing at all wrong with Bruce's performance that night. He wasn't to blame for any of those goals.

Bruce was an eccentric character, who let in silly goals from time to time – like the one that Kevin Ratcliffe, the Everton captain, scored from 35 yards, which went through his legs – but that's just the way he was. It's true that he often complained about the wages Liverpool were paying him but he always signed his contracts. I'm sure Bruce wouldn't try to supplement his income with bribes and I wasn't at all surprised when the jury at Winchester Crown Court agreed by returning their not guilty verdict.

Alan Hansen was our leader. At times, a silent leader, but also the team joker. Jocky the jocular. He didn't say that much but he loved winding people up.

Someone like Steve Nicol would have been meat and drink to Jocky. He was an easy target: you'd always have a laugh and a joke with him, people were always trying to take the mickey out of Steve. For instance, there was the time when a group of Scots in the team were on their way to an international on a cold and wet day. As they were driving along the motorway, Steve Nicol asked Graeme Souness why he wasn't using the windscreen wipers. Souness said they weren't working and asked Steve to pop out and see what was wrong with them. As soon as he was out of the car, Souness drove off leaving Steve standing in just tracksuit bottoms and a T-shirt on the hard shoulder in the freezing cold. But they came off at the next turn-off to pick him up. Mark Lawrenson was very quiet, normally on the fringe of things, and he probably had more friends outside of Liverpool than inside. That's not to say he was disliked: Mark was very popular and a hell of a player.

Rushie and I were very close both on and off the pitch. When I arrived at Liverpool, I struck up a friendship with him straightaway, and we spent a lot of time together, mainly in the hotel where I was staying. We bought our first horse together, and our families got on well. Our friendship was very light-hearted – it wasn't the type where we'd sit down for a heart-to-heart.

On the field, it was uncanny the way we clicked. Rushie had a good relationship with Kenny and although I wasn't the same type of player as Kenny, I think I could spot the same openings. We just seemed to know what the other was about to do. It was great that Kenny and Rushie got back together at Newcastle – Rushie ended up at Wrexham, though I would have loved to have had him down at Swansea, but he'd have had to have taken an 80 per cent pay cut.

At Liverpool, Rushie would be involved in all the wind-ups, but he was never the brains behind any of them. People didn't pull any tricks on players like Rushie and Mark Lawrenson because they were well respected in the dressing room. Sammy Lee was the resident singer. Whenever there was a dull moment, he'd start up, mainly doing Beatles songs, because he was Liverpool through and through.

Ronnie Whelan was a rival, but a real friend. It wasn't until I was injured and Ronnie moved into central midfield that people realized what a good player he was. He'd already done so much out wide on the left by scoring great goals, winning three League titles and the European Cup, but he really came into his own when he moved inside. Ronnie wasn't given his full credit because he wasn't a head-line grabber.

Alongside him, we had another fantastic player, Steve McMahon, a fierce competitor, who was a bit like Graeme Souness because he could play as well as tough it out. It seems strange that the three of us went into management (at Swansea, Southend and Swindon), because back in the eighties Jocky Hansen and Mark Lawrenson were thought the players more likely to go down that route. Mark had a go at managing Oxford and then coaching with Newcastle but, like Jocky, he's now realized that the easy money is to be made in a TV studio on a Saturday night rather than in a dug-out on a Saturday afternoon.

Then there was Kenny. What a start for him in his new role! I think he was successful in his early days as manager because he was guided by the Liverpool backroom staff – the boys in the Boot Room, Ronnie Moran and Roy Evans, must take a lot of credit for what he achieved. But Kenny still had to make some difficult decisions.

When he was appointed to succeed Joe Fagan, Phil Neal was very upset. He'd fancied the job himself and there was also the problem of him, and Alan Kennedy, coming towards the end of their careers. Phil had been a real Anfield stalwart and Alan's goals had won Liverpool two European Cups, so they were almost permanent fixtures at Anfield. Somebody had to say when it was time for Phil and Alan Kennedy to be moved aside, and Kenny proved himself a good man-manager. Kenny was shrewd enough to realize they needed replacing but he didn't just kick them out. He eased them out gently by bringing in Steve Nicol and Jim Beglin in their places. Phil and Alan both played the first six to a dozen games of that season and, if they'd continued, we probably would have been just as successful. But Kenny was looking to the future. He felt Steve and Jim were at least as good as them and, with experience, they would be better. As players, I don't think we were aware of what Kenny was doing at the time. But he did show a pretty mean streak in replacing Phil with Jocky as captain. Phil eventually went off to Bolton and Alan returned to his home town of Sunderland.

Tactically, Kenny was very aware. Even in those days, he was looking abroad. He would spend a lot of time studying the way they were doing things in Italy. He was always watching Italian football on the TV and he'd bring videos of the games on to the coach when we travelled away. There was even a spell when he came to watch me play for Denmark three or four times, because he just wanted to see what was going on outside Britain. Kenny felt we should try to take that one extra tactical step, but he understood that it couldn't happen overnight. With Liverpool banned from Europe, he wanted to keep in touch with, and then take on board, some of the European ideas. Even though we couldn't compete, Kenny wanted us to be aware of what was happening elsewhere.

One of the funnier memories of that season is an incident on the flight back to Liverpool after the Cup Final. There was always fierce rivalry on the pitch during Merseyside derbies and this one had been no exception. Afterwards though, we were usually all back to being friends – not just the players but the fans as well – and the two clubs were sharing the plane home on the Sunday.

During the flight, there was a light-hearted disagreement between the players about the amount of room on the plane.

'Move your fat arse!' the Everton and Wales full-back Pat Van Den Hauwe shouted at little Sammy Lee.

'Sorry,' replied Sammy, 'but what do you expect? I've got two bloody medals in my back pocket!'

Bringing Home the Bacon?

Everything in the garden was rosy. Liverpool had won the Double, I was in the Danish party for the Mexico World Cup finals, and it looked as if I would be in the starting line-up. My squad number was 7 and, although I was a little disappointed not to be given the number 10 I'd inherited at Liverpool, I felt confident of being picked for the first game.

When I arrived at Anfield, there was no recognized number 10, so I took the shirt – partly because of the Pelé connection and partly because I'd always worn number 10 as a kid anyway. I really wanted that shirt. Nobody objected, maybe because the number doesn't have the same significance in England as it does abroad where it's worn by the playmaker, the man who makes everything happen. Number 10 plays but only when his team has got the ball.

We'd had to work hard to reach the finals, with our last two qualifying games being away against Norway and the Republic of Ireland. Just before the Norway game, Joe Jordan of Southampton gave me a hell of a whack on the ankle and it was touch and go whether I was going to make it. But two other players were injured and Sepp Piontek wasn't happy about fielding three half-fit players, so he left me on the bench.

We were 1–0 down at half-time. I came on for the second half and we won 5–1. A lot was made of me changing the game, but the truth was I didn't. I don't remember making any contribution to the win, but I played the whole game against Ireland, which we won 4–1, so, not unreasonably, I thought I was going to be in the team for the first match in Mexico.

I'd never been a regular in the Danish team, partly because of the pedigree of the players who were already there and partly because of circumstances. When I was breaking into the side, the Danish sweeper Per Rontved was about to retire. But Sepp decided not to throw an 18-year-old into such a crucial position, so I was kept in the squad – along with Michael Laudrup, as it happens – without playing too many games. Instead, Sepp went for Morten Olsen, a midfield player who had to play sweeper for one game in an emergency and ended up making the position his for the rest of his career. He became one of the greatest sweepers of the eighties by accident, and played his last international when he was 42.

Sepp saw me as a playmaker but Soren Lerby was already well established in that role, so that basically took care of that. I think people have to remember that Denmark were a very good team; many weren't aware of just how good players like Lerby, Laudrup and Sivebaek were.

Denmark had players at all the top clubs all over Europe and, at that time, I simply wasn't good enough to get in the team. John Sivebaek, even before he arrived at Manchester United, was one of the best right-backs in the world. He was pacy, put good crosses in, and chipped in with one or two goals. I remember Michael Laudrup being described as the best player in the world after we'd beaten Uruguay 6–1 in Mexico in 1986, although he perhaps never went on to fulfil that promise. He was the one who would always catch the eye, but you had to play with him to fully appreciate how fantastic he actually was. Soren Lerby was always out on the left of midfield and never made it into the middle where he really wanted to be. Even a player with the pedigree of Ajax, Bayern Munich, Monaco and PSV Eindhoven couldn't make that spot his own. It was taken by Jens Jorgen Berthelsen, a hard-working midfielder who never wasted a ball. He was the exception to the rule in that he played for clubs in Denmark, Holland, Belgium and France but never for one of the top sides. Despite that, he was someone Denmark couldn't do without. I was just one of a number of good players who had all done well with their individual clubs all over Europe.

I also think my versatility worked against me – a little like it affected Steve Nicol at Liverpool. He was his own worst enemy because he could play anywhere. He should go down as perhaps the best left-back Liverpool ever had, but he won't, as he kept popping up all over the place in the team. I was certainly aware of the 'jack-of-all-trades-master-of-none' danger when playing for Denmark. It was a bit of a handicap. I think I'll be remembered as a midfield playmaker, because that's the role I filled most for Liverpool.

The eighties were exciting times for Danish football – a revival was just starting to take off. We'd done well in the European Championships (knocked out in the semi-finals on penalties), we'd come through a tough qualifying group against teams like Norway, the Republic of Ireland and Russia, and we beat Poland 1–0 in a final warm-up match in Denmark before flying to Colombia to prepare for the high altitude of Mexico.

We had a couple of games against local teams, but I wasn't playing particularly well – I think I was waiting for the real stuff to begin. I was tired. It had been a long season, after all. We knew we had a job on our hands in Mexico because we'd been drawn in one of the most difficult groups, the one that's always called the 'Group of Death' – Scotland, Uruguay, Germany and Denmark.

As our first game against Scotland drew nearer, I began to realize that Sepp was going to leave me out. It always suited Denmark to play British teams because they employed a flat back four. We didn't put two up front through the middle but instead used the pace of two wide men to get in behind the back line and then have midfield players pouring into the box. We'd done well against England and the Republic of Ireland, so it was nice to start the World Cup against Scotland. In view of our record against British teams, we felt if we could begin with a win we might have a chance of reaching the quarter-finals. We won 1–0. I came on for the second half and didn't contribute much. My memory of that game is Graeme Souness suffering from the heat. He was coming towards the end of his international career and the altitude was a problem. Some of the media had billed Denmark against Scotland as Molby against Souness, but that never really came off – I didn't even speak to him during the game.

We took very well to the heat of Mexico. We'd done a lot of hard work with masks back in Denmark to try to get used to the altitude. We spent a fortnight in Colombia then arrived in Mexico four or five days before our first game, so we were very well prepared.

In the next match against Uruguay Sepp kept the same team, and we won 6–1, with Preben Elkjaer scoring a hat-trick. They were a dirty team, who had decided that they'd have to kick us off the park to stand any chance of beating us. We were happy with that so we stood up to them and eventually played them off the park. It was 2–1 when I came on in the second half and set up goals for Preben and Jesper Olsen.

I started our third match against the Germans and, after we'd won 2–0, I thought I was going to be more involved. We were top of our group and had qualified to play Spain. If we hadn't beaten Germany, we would have met Morocco, but there's such great rivalry between us and the Germans that we just had to beat them! There were all sorts of suggestions in the press that we should throw the game, but the players weren't ever interested in such an idea. A lot of us had been internationals for a while – some for as long as eight years – and hadn't yet played Germany: when were we likely to get the chance to play them again? There was no way we weren't going to give it 100 per cent. I remember senior players, like Morten Olsen, saying that we had to go and beat Germany to show them that we had arrived on the world scene and to put them in their place.

I played at right wing-back which wasn't ideal but it was nice to be involved. Jesper Olsen scored our first from a penalty and then, with Frank Arnesen, I helped set up our second for Johnny Eriksen. It was a bit of a nasty game which boiled over in the last minute when Frank was sent off for a second bookable offence when he fouled a German. It was a blow losing him for the next game because he provided us with a bit of flair. He had a great change of pace in the Cruyff mould.

I felt I had done enough to keep my place against Spain but when the team was announced on the morning of the match, Sepp left me out. I was very disappointed when I looked up at the team he'd written on a flipchart, but I couldn't really complain: he could have picked any of the twenty-two. Other players had done just as well as me against Scotland and Uruguay. If you play your football in Europe as opposed to England, you're perhaps more used to the squad system. There was a good spirit in the camp, we were coping well with the heat and we played and trained hard.

Everything was going well in our quarter-final match against Spain. Again, Jesper gave us the lead with a penalty and then turned from hero to villain a minute before half-time. Our keeper threw him the ball in the right wing-back position. I'm not quite sure what Jesper was doing there but, as one of the Spaniards closed him down, he decided to roll the ball back to the keeper. He thought if the ball was in the keeper's hands, he could see out the half. Unfortunately, it was a case of 'nice pace, shame about the direction'. Instead of rolling the ball back to the keeper, Jesper pushed it square for Butragueno to nip in and put it between the keeper's legs. So it was 1–1 at half-time and that was the turning point of our World Cup.

Sepp didn't say much at half-time because there wasn't a great deal wrong. We had dominated the first half and he wasn't going to admit that their goal would change the game, but Spain took the lead early in the second half – the signal for me to go on. Sepp told me to get ready and, as I was taking off my tracksuit, Spain scored again.

'Go on, Big Man,' said Sepp, perhaps with his tongue in his cheek, 'go and show us what you can do!'

Great, I thought. Thanks, Sepp.

We weren't too worried when we went 2–1 down because, at that stage, we thought we were invincible. We'd won all three group matches, including one against Germany, and we were some people's favourites to lift the World Cup. The problem was, after deciding to go after Spain with forty minutes left, we lost our shape. I think it was a mistake to go chasing them. If we'd carried on playing, we would have got back in the game. We left ourselves open at the back and the score went from 2–1 to 5–1.

Just after I came on, I played a one-two with Preben Elkjaer and, although my shot was from a bit of an angle, I should have scored, but their keeper parried it. That would have made it 3–2, but within thirty seconds, Spain went up the other end and scored their fourth. Back in the dressing room, we were obviously gutted. We'd won three games we didn't have to win and lost the one we couldn't afford to lose. Sepp didn't blame anyone – it was just the end of our World Cup.

I actually had a very good relationship with Sepp. Although he was a German and very much into discipline, he was a very humorous man. He turned Danish football around. Before he came, internationals were looked upon as a bit of fun. We would go back to Denmark for three or four days, see a few relatives, buy some Danish food to take back with us, and then play the game. Sepp changed all that. His was a strict regime – with curfews and very hard training – but we accepted it, especially when we started to win. When you're winning, players will put up with anything.

The Mexico World Cup wasn't all work and no play though. After we'd beaten Uruguay 6–1, there was a mile drive from the ground to the hotel. The hotel had brought in a Mexican band to welcome us back and we could hear the noise as we approached. As I looked out of the coach window, who did I see, joining in with all the Danish fans, but Steve Nicol and Charlie Nicholas! The Scottish party were staying in our hotel and those two were leading the singing:

> We are red, we are white,
> We are Danish Dynamite!

They were both there in their Danish T-shirts, ready for the party. They knew we were sponsored by Carlsberg, so there'd be no shortage of beer.

Sepp Piontek always involved me from the time I was 17. In 1982, we were very close to qualifying for the World Cup, and he included me in his squad of twenty-five which would have gone to the finals. It was a vote of confidence which I didn't find out about until later.

Sepp always liked the way I was playing but, because of the class he had in midfield, it was always going to be difficult for me to force my way in. Apart from Michael Laudrup, who was a sensation, they were all a bit older with more experience – players like Lerby, Frank Arnesen of Anderlecht, Klaus Berger from Roma, and Jesper Olsen. Sepp always felt that, at 22, I had time on my side.

After Spain, it all started to fall into place for me with Denmark. I played a couple of games where I was just finding my feet and then, towards the end of the 1987 season, I went through a spell where I just couldn't stop scoring. After a 0–0 draw in a friendly against Liverpool at Anfield, we beat Finland 1–0 away and I netted the winner; I got another in a 2–0 win over Verona from Italy, and then my goal in a 1–1 with Czechoslovakia took us to the top of the European Championship qualifying group.

I was now the Danish playmaker. But when I broke a bone in my foot in pre-season training with Liverpool, my career with Denmark was never the same again. I remember going to Ninian Park in Cardiff to see Denmark get beaten 1–0 by Wales – Mark Hughes scored the goal – with my leg in plaster. When I came back for Liverpool, I picked up another injury in a reserve game against Everton, and was out for four months so I missed virtually the whole of that season. By the time we qualified for Euro '88, I had only managed four League games for Liverpool.

I went to play for Denmark in Hungary – we drew 2–2 – and although I thought I'd done OK, Sepp didn't agree, and left me out of the squad. In 1989, he resigned to manage the Turkish national team and I played for another year under his successor Richard Moller Nielsen.

I thought I was going to get on well with Richard. When I was 17 he'd made me captain of the Under-21s. After his appointment as national manager he asked me if I wanted to play as sweeper or in midfield. In September 1990, I came on at half-time against Wales and we won 1–0 through a Brian Laudrup goal, and then I made my last international appearance against Yugoslavia in Copenhagen. I played for 78 minutes before being substituted when the score was 0–0. We ended up losing 2–0.

I suppose my one regret was that I never became a regular in the Danish side. During my time as an international, Denmark became established as a world-class footballing nation but, for a variety of reasons, I never quite brought home the bacon.

After the Lord Mayor's Show

How do you follow the Double? That was the question everyone in football was asking at the start of the 1986–87 season. Perhaps with the Treble? Maybe with another Double? After all, no team had done the double Double in the history of the game.

There was a feeling at Liverpool that it would be difficult to repeat our success but we were made favourites for the League, having won it with so many new players. It was felt we could get even stronger. As it turned out, we did achieve a sort of double – finishing runners-up in the League to Everton and losing to Arsenal in the Milk Cup Final at Wembley.

Personally, I think I eventually suffered because of the World Cup. I figured in all four of Denmark's matches – mainly as a second-half substitute – and took part in all the training. I wasn't rested, and I got back to Denmark after the World Cup seven weeks after the FA Cup Final at Wembley. So my summer holiday lasted about a fortnight. For the first three months of the season, though, I was on fire. I came back from Mexico raring to go and because of my natural fitness, I was playing well. I scored 6 of my 7 League goals in the first 17 games, but then I started to fall away. The World Cup had caught up with me and I just couldn't get my game together. Kenny kept picking me in the hope that I could turn it around and start performing again, but I think he knew I was tired.

I remember once when he put me in the reserves for a midweek fixture against Aston Villa.

'Go and get your confidence back,' he said. 'Start running at people and having a few shots.'

I had a reasonable game and afterwards Kenny was pleased. 'That's it,' he said. 'That's what I want in the first team.'

But it didn't happen regularly enough. Although I started 34 of the 42 League games, it was very much an in-and-out sort of season. I did turn it on in a couple of matches – like the one against Norwich at Anfield at the beginning of November. They were top, we were third, and we beat them 6–2.

For me, it was one of the most complete Liverpool performances during my time at Anfield. I didn't score but it was a game where nearly everything we tried came off. We were 2–0 up at half-time, Rushie got two and Paul Walsh picked up a hat-trick. When I went to Norwich on loan in the 1995–96 season, one or two of their players had been in their team on that day nine years earlier, and it was the first thing they mentioned to me.

It's a game I'll never forget but it was a gem in the middle of a pretty dull season.

For the second successive season, our final League game was down at Chelsea. The result didn't matter to either side. There was nothing at stake. The pressure was off because we couldn't win the League. It was a stroll in the sun. We drew 3–3, after being 2–1 down at the interval, and afterwards Kenny said that if I'd played like that all season, we would have won the League. I didn't feel guilty about his remark. He was right, but I was tired.

It was great getting to Wembley again for the Littlewoods Cup Final against Arsenal. We took the lead in the 20th minute, when Rushie rounded off a move involving me and Steve McMahon, and we thought that was that. We'd had this incredible record of never losing a match in which Rushie had scored so we thought it was going to be our day. But then Charlie Nicholas took a hand with a couple of the luckiest goals I've ever seen. The equalizer came almost immediately, and just before the end Perry Groves came on as sub and his fresh legs provided the cross for Charlie's winner. Arsenal deserved to win because, once we went ahead, we lost a little of our aura and they became the better team. We thought we could enjoy ourselves but it backfired on us. That defeat was one of four in a nightmare period which decided the Double.

Losing the Rushie record in the Final was a bit of a blow – until then, we'd gone 144 games unbeaten in the matches in

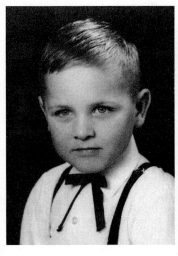

All ready for dance class, aged 4 (above left); the Molby family portrait (above right); and the kids from Kolding (below) – Jan is on the back row, first from the left.

(Above) Discussing post-match plans with a young Frank Rijkaard; (above right) Three great Danes go Dutch. Soren Lerby leads the way at Ajax, Jan and Jesper Olsen follow.

Jan on duty with Denmark (right, Stewart Kendall/*Sportsphoto*) and having a drink with his mate Michael Laudrup (below).

Celebrating the Championship and FA Cup Double in Jan's second season on Merseyside (left, Popperfoto); action from the 1986 FA Cup Final triumph over Everton – Jan's greatest game in a Liverpool shirt (Colorsport/Popperfoto).

A big thank you from the boss – Kenny Dalglish celebrates with Jan, who supplied the cross for the second goal against Everton (left); the party begins (below, both Colorsport).

(Above) Denmark celebrate after beating Germany 2–0 in the Mexico '86 World Cup; (below) back to matters more prosaic – Liverpool overcome Watford 1–0 at Anfield (both Popperfoto).

Scandinavian-like conditions on Merseyside...
(Stewart Kendall/Sportsphoto).

which he scored. And then in the very next match he bagged a goal at Norwich, but we lost 2–1 and slipped down to second place in the League. It was our third consecutive League defeat and it effectively handed the title to Everton. I remember being locked in the dressing room for an hour after the Norwich game as Kenny and Ronnie took us apart. They said too many of us hadn't been pulling our weight. I hold up my hands, because I was as much to blame as anyone.

We had lost the Littlewoods Cup Final and the chance to win the League, and there was no spirit in the side – we couldn't even play for pride. It was just one of those things that happen. We had known the Double wasn't on since January, when we lost to Luton in a second FA Cup third-round replay. We drew 0–0 at Kenilworth Road but when Luton became stranded in a snow storm on their way to Liverpool, the replay at Anfield was called off two hours before kick-off.

We had met up in a hotel where all the players, apart from Alan Irvine, were told about the postponement. Alan had just signed for Liverpool so was staying at the hotel and had disappeared up to his room to put on his suit for the game. Once it was called off, we stayed in our tracksuits and hopped on the bus to go back to Anfield to pick up our cars. Suddenly Alan Irvine arrived smartly kitted out in his suit. Everybody twigged that it was time for a wind-up.

'Why are you all wearing tracksuits?' he asked.

'It's a club rule,' said a couple of the lads. 'When we're playing in the FA Cup, you can wear what you want – you don't have to put on suits.'

That satisfied new boy Alan and he sat down at the back of the coach. Up at the front, Kenny and Jocky Hansen were putting their heads together. Alan had made his debut as a sub against Charlton just before Christmas but hadn't started a game since coming down from Scotland. His two fellow countrymen decided it was time to set him up. The cards had just been brought out at the back of the coach as Kenny called Alan down to the front.

'Keep it quiet,' he confided to Alan, 'I haven't announced the team yet, but you're in. Don't tell anyone.'

Alan returned to his seat at the back beaming all over his face. 'What's the matter?' asked a couple of the lads.

'Nothing,' said Alan.

But when he was pressed, Alan couldn't contain himself.

'I'm playing!' he blurted out. 'But don't tell anyone!' And with that, he sat down, pleased as punch.

When we arrived at Anfield, the place was deserted. Normally, for an FA Cup replay, it would be buzzing.

'There's no one here!' cried Alan. We assured him that, because it was a midweek game, most of the crowd were at work, but they'd be arriving later. No need to worry. The place'll be packed by kick-off. We went into the dressing room and sat around the table as Kenny announced the team. Alan was in. Everyone wished him all the best on his debut.

'Go and do yourselves a favour now,' Kenny then said to us all. 'Sort out your complimentary tickets and then come back in here and let's go for it!'

Whoosh! Off went Alan straight to the players' lounge to ring his wife with the good news.

'Get up here!' he screamed down the phone. 'I'm playing!'

A couple of the lads had gone down to eavesdrop on the conversation but they were back in their places when Alan returned to the dressing room. Almost immediately, he picked up a programme and went to the toilet. That was the moment we'd been waiting for. We all steamed out and switched off the lights. Alan was left there sitting on the toilet trying to read the match programme in total darkness.

I don't know how he found out that he'd been set up. I went off to fetch my car and go home. I presume he left the dressing room and bumped into a steward in the corridor who told him the bad news. Alan turned out once more for Liverpool – again as a sub, against Southampton, at the end of February. He never made that elusive full debut, after all.

Unfortunately, it wasn't so funny on the pitch when we finally got round to playing Luton. We drew 0–0 again at Anfield, and then got smacked 3–0 on the Astroturf at Kenilworth Road. It was always going to be difficult against Luton, because they were more familiar with the pitch. I had the technical ability to cope with controlling a ball but, as far as passing was concerned, I couldn't put much in front of our strikers because as soon as the ball hit the deck it went out of play. I think the games we played on artificial turf at Luton, or QPR, evened themselves out in the end – we won as many as we lost.

The one bright spot in the 1986–87 season was provided by those games I played for Denmark against Verona and Czechoslovakia, in which I scored. I felt I was over the bad spell and I was on the way back.

I wasn't particularly worried about my future at Liverpool, but Kenny felt we needed to do something, so during the summer and early part of the next season, he bought Ray Houghton, John Aldridge, John Barnes and Peter Beardsley. Aldo was a replacement for Rushie, who'd gone to Juventus, and Peter was the new Kenny, the man who would set up chances for Aldo and score a few goals himself. It went completely against the traditional Liverpool way of bringing in new players – normally youngsters – and sticking them in the reserves for a few years before introducing them into the first team.

I thought the new signings were great. I didn't see any of them as a direct threat: Ray played on the right, John on the left, and the other two were strikers. I assumed the middle of the midfield was going to be occupied by Steve McMahon and me. Until, that was, I suffered the most crucial injury in my whole career – I badly injured my left foot in pre-season training.

The incident happened during a practice game being held on a Saturday at Melwood to get everyone back into the swing of things. As I went into a tackle with John Wark he caught me on my left foot. It was an accident – John would never do anything malicious – but I knew something was wrong straight away. I stood up, limped off the pitch and Ronnie Moran told me to put my foot under the cold water tap in the changing-room bath. It was too sore even to do that. I managed to climb on to the bus to take us back to Anfield, but I could hardly walk.

When I got into my car to drive to Walton Hospital, I realized I couldn't use the clutch – my foot was killing me. One of the stewards at Anfield had to drive my car instead. I went into the hospital in agony and came out in plaster. I'd broken a bone in my foot, which meant I would miss the seventeen-day pre-season tour to Germany, Denmark, Norway and Sweden – the longest one Liverpool had ever had.

Kenny told me not to worry – in reality, I'd probably solved a selection problem for him! – and he soon let me know I wouldn't be forgotten. I was pretty depressed when I hobbled off home on crutches and the team went off on tour. I was living in a house by myself at the time, and it wasn't much fun being laid up. In fact, I was having real problems getting around. But then, at the start of the next week, the phone went. It was Kenny, ringing from Germany.

'We're flying from here today,' he said. 'But we're not going to Denmark, Norway and Sweden without you. I want you to come out here now – we need somebody to speak the lingo.'

So I made it on to the tour, after all. It was a bit awkward with my crutches, but Peter Beardsley was my minder, carrying my bag and generally looking after me. I really enjoyed my fortnight away – it was nice to be part of it, even though I was on crutches.

When we came back, Kenny decided to send me to Lilleshall to help my recovery. At that time, the centre was being run by a guy called Graham Smith. He was a bit of a tough character who liked to put his charges through their paces. But I was keen to get my fitness levels up while my foot healed, so I went along with it all. I was working hard in the swimming pool and on the exercise bike and it was all going well until I fell off the bike and broke the bone again. It meant I was in plaster for eight rather than four weeks.

While all this was going on, Liverpool were making a fantastic start to the season, with an amazing twenty-nine-match unbeaten run in the League. The trouble was, I wasn't part of it. It wasn't too bad being away at Lilleshall for two months, just returning to Liverpool at weekends. If I'd been back at Anfield all the time, it would have been harder to swallow, seeing all the boys bouncing off the walls with so much confidence and not being involved. I managed to get to the home games and I still thought that when I recovered,

I would be back in the team. In my absence, Ronnie Whelan had moved into the middle to partner Steve McMahon, with Ray and John the wide men.

My comeback began when I started playing for the reserves towards the end of October. Everything had healed well but, not surprisingly after such a long lay-off, I was pretty awful for the first couple of games. Then I scored a hat-trick at Leeds and popped in a goal against Everton at Goodison. I was doing well and feeling fine when John Ebbrell caught me on my left foot again. I thought I'd broken my leg, never mind my foot! My whole ankle swelled up like a balloon. Luckily, it was only badly bruised, but it took me a long time to get over it. The swelling wouldn't go down for weeks, and I couldn't get back to playing. In January, I went back to hospital, where they put me out and broke up the swelling, but I didn't return to the first-team starting line-up until the beginning of April. I was on the bench four times before being picked as part of a five-man midfield for the 2–1 defeat at Nottingham Forest – only the second time we'd lost all season in the League but our second defeat in three games.

Ten days later, I had a bird's-eye view from the bench as we demolished Forest with some superb football in a 5–0 thrashing at Anfield. Kenny must have been delighted. He'd been criticized for his tactics in the earlier 2–1 defeat at Forest. He described the 5–0 win as 'a great exhibition of football' and that just about summed it up.

It was such breathtaking stuff that a video of the game was quickly rushed out. Everyone wanted a permanent reminder of a fabulous night of football. My only regret was that I didn't play a bigger part in the game. I came on as a late sub for Steve McMahon. That performance was our biggest of the season and we took the title by a mile. I didn't get a medal because I hadn't played enough games.

As the season drew to a close, the Double was on again. In between our 2–1 defeat and the 5–0 thrashing, we beat Forest 2–1 in the FA Cup semi-final at Hillsborough to reach the Final again. I'd not been involved at all in the run, but I returned after a spell out of the squad for our last-but-one League game, at Sheffield Wednesday in early May. We won 5–1, I came on as sub for the second half and had a great game at the back.

I couldn't play in the last game against Luton at Anfield because I was in Hungary with Denmark, but my hopes of making the Cup Final team against Wimbledon were raised by an unfortunate incident in that fixture. Nigel Spackman and Gary Gillespie collided with each other and each had to have thirteen stitches put in head wounds. Four days to go to the Cup Final and my fingers were crossed. I certainly felt I deserved a break after the season I'd had. In the event, Nigel and Gary both played with protective headbands. I was quite pleased to be named as sub.

It was a nice way to end what had been a miserable nine months for me but a wonderful season for Liverpool. Our biggest regret was that despite winning the League in some style we didn't perform for the showpiece occasion at Wembley. Obviously Wimbledon's manager Bobby Gould and his assistant Don Howe had done their homework, and they were a team of hard-workers: they managed to stop us playing.

The day had got off to an eventful start when Craig Johnston announced his retirement from football in a big splash in one of the newspapers. He was going back to Australia to look after his seriously ill sister. I wasn't really surprised because, when I arrived at Liverpool in my first season, I was told that although Craig was on the Anfield staff, he wouldn't be around for a couple of months. He was staying Down Under until his wife had given birth to their first child. I couldn't believe it, but that was Craig: very single-minded, very honest and also someone who, while on the pitch, never stopped working for the Liverpool cause.

He was so enthusiastic and determined to do well that he used to ruffle a few feathers along the way. Controversy seemed to follow Craig around, especially when Joe Fagan was manager, and he nearly walked out of Anfield after being dropped for a European Cup match in 1983.

Craig was one of the most creative characters I've ever met. A couple of years earlier during one of Sammy Lee's testimonial dinners, he'd said that he had four or five things lined up which would make him more money than football. Players often don't think that there's anything outside their world, and at the time we thought he was talking rubbish, but he was right. He'd already helped make the 'Anfield Rap' record, and when back in Australia, he became involved in photography, sports commentating and dreaming up TV quiz shows. He even invented a new type of football boot.

'The Anfield Rap' was Craig's idea. He wrote it with one or two of his musical friends and then designed the video to go with it. He sorted all that out. The players started off thinking it was a bit of a laugh, just another football record. We went into a studio in Liverpool to record the song, with a few beers and a buffet. I don't think we ever thought it was going to be as big as it turned out to be – we hadn't dreamt of selling all those copies with the record getting into the charts. Craig showed he had a real talent for designing things and we weren't at all surprised when he arrived back at Anfield with his new boot.

On the field, I think Kenny would have preferred someone more predictable. Half the time Craig didn't know what he was going to do, so what hope was there for his team-mates? Craig's announcement didn't have any effect on the rest of the players, or Kenny, who put him on the bench against Wimbledon. A lot of managers would have sulked about Craig retiring and left him out, but Kenny felt it was right for the team to name him as sub because Liverpool might need him some time during the match. As it was, Craig did come on but he couldn't turn it round. Nor could I when I left the bench for the last thirteen minutes. The game was long over by then – it just wasn't going to happen for us that day.

I suppose the 1988 FA Cup Final will be remembered for two incidents – the winning goal and the missed penalty by John Aldridge. When Lawrie Sanchez flicked home that Dennis Wise free-kick in the first half, the Liverpool bench thought it was just what we needed. The goal would give us a kick up the backside to get us going. But we couldn't get out of first gear.

The penalty miss – or rather the save by Dave Beasant – was a real sickener. I'd been out for virtually the whole season, so Aldo had become the recognized penalty-taker and, in fact, I don't think we'd ever been on the pitch at the same time. When his shot was saved, everybody on the bench just looked at each other. It was going to be one of those days.

I remember Kenny standing for the whole 90 minutes in the boiling heat in his Liverpool coat. It was a tradition that he wouldn't take it off because he felt it brought him good luck. On that day, tradition, or rather superstition, let us down. But, to be honest, we let ourselves down.

After the game, Wimbledon claimed they had psyched us out by their behaviour in the tunnel before the teams walked out. Vinnie Jones had written a newspaper article in which he said he was going to rip off Kenny's ears and spit in the hole. As we were waiting to walk out, the Wimbledon players kept shouting, 'In the hole! In the hole!' But no games are won and lost in the tunnel, and the majority of our players had seen it all before.

We lost because we didn't perform on the day. We felt we had a perfectly good goal by Peter Beardsley disallowed early on – when the referee awarded us a free-kick instead of playing advantage – but you can argue about decisions like that until you're blue in the face. It doesn't matter. The referee blew up – end of story.

You have to give a little credit to Wimbledon. They had a plan and they stuck to it, but we were very disappointed as we trudged off the pitch at Wembley. I think they felt they had to stop us getting round their back four, so they doubled up on our wide men, John Barnes and Ray Houghton. Their main plan of attack was to stop John – he and Ray always had two men marking them. We should have been able to counter this tactic but, at the time, we didn't think there was a lot wrong with the way we were playing. We probably thought it was only a matter of time before Barnsey got the better of his markers but it just didn't happen. When they went 1–0 up, Wimbledon's plan was strengthened – it was slightly easier to stick to and they didn't have to alter anything. Liverpool weren't renowned for changing things, we believed in what we were doing, so we stuck with it. For the second successive season, we'd fallen at the final hurdle at the Twin Towers.

After staying overnight in London, we went back to Liverpool for a very low-key open-top bus ride around the city. There weren't many people on the streets to welcome us.

I felt most sorry for John Aldridge and Peter Beardsley – one foiled by a goalkeeper and the other by a referee. Some people described Aldo as a poor man's Ian Rush, and it's true he was bought to replace Rushie and he did look quite a bit like him. But although he wasn't as prolific a scorer as Rushie, he did end up with more than 60 goals in a little over 100 games. He was a very important part of the 1988 Championship-winning side – one of the best ever produced by Liverpool – and the following season, he was often picked ahead of Rushie, who'd returned from Italy.

When Kenny brought Aldo to Anfield, he was playing dream-maker, because John had been rejected by Liverpool as a 14-year-old trialist. He was one of the most committed players ever to pull on a red shirt, and I think he was sold too early by Kenny. Real Sociedad paid a million pounds for him in September 1989 after he and Rushie had together seen off Everton in the FA Cup Final the previous May.

His last game for Liverpool was a very emotional occasion at Anfield. Aldo and I were on the bench as we walloped Crystal Palace 9–0. We were 3–0 up at half-time in front of nearly 36,000, and in the second half Kenny showed why he is such a great manager. In a lovely gesture, he invited Aldo off the bench to score a penalty and then, on the final whistle, Aldo threw his shirt and boots to the Kop. He had been one of them and it was right they should have a memento of his time at Anfield. Sadly, because of my foot injury, we didn't have the chance to strike up the kind of relationship I had with Rushie.

Despite what a lot of people thought, Kenny and Peter Beardsley had a good relationship. Kenny bought Peter to replace himself and the two never had a problem. During the 1990–91 season, Peter would often find himself on the bench as Kenny fiddled with his formation. It depended on who we were playing – sometimes we would field five or six defenders – but, to the best of my knowledge, Peter and Kenny never rowed about it.

PART THREE

Much More Important Than That?

Bill Shankly had been dead for nearly four years when his oft-quoted observations on the significance of football first returned to haunt his beloved Reds.

The 1984 Heysel disaster left thirty-nine Juventus fans dead and Liverpool, along with the rest of the best English teams, out in the cold. They had lost 1–0 in the European Cup Final but, for once, the result didn't matter. When a group of their supporters were involved in rioting across a terrace, a wall collapsed killing many of those Juventus fans caught up in the mayhem.

Four years later, alleged police incompetence at Sheffield Wednesday's Hillsborough ground led to ninety-six Liverpool supporters being crushed to death at the Leppings Lane End before and during their FA Cup semi-final against Nottingham Forest. For once, Shanks had got it wrong. Football was not much more important than life or death. Heysel and Hillsborough made sure it would never be so again. In imposing their ban on English clubs taking part in Europe for five (or in Liverpool's case six) years, UEFA simply reinforced the new order.

Jan Molby was 21 when he experienced the horror of Heysel. He was 25 when Hillsborough changed the face of British football for ever. Between those two tragedies, Jan underwent his own personal disaster as a result of youthful exuberance.

During his time on Merseyside, he had been involved in a

number of brushes with the law, mainly for speeding. He was breathalysed once and received three penalty points for going through a red light. Jan was also banned from driving for six months for speeding on the M25 on his way back to Liverpool from London. In February 1988, he was arrested after an early-morning high-speed car chase from the outskirts of Liverpool to his then home in Chester. Six months later, rave notices in the sports pages were replaced by garish tabloid headlines when Jan was jailed for ninety days for reckless driving. With good behaviour, he served half his sentence at three different prisons in the North-West – Walton, Kirkham and Preston.

Mandy Molby first met Jan at a housewarming party of a friend of her mother. She had been seeing him for about fourteen months when he was jailed.

'I couldn't believe it, because nobody had been expecting it,' she recalls. 'A hefty fine and a big ban, maybe. But not prison. I was working in my mum's clothes shop at the time and I didn't bother going to court. I thought he would end up with a suspended sentence. When I heard, I didn't think it was real.

'Jan shouldn't have been driving so fast, but I think they made a prime example of him because he was in the spotlight at the time. The sentence was a bit strong, but if the law says you've got to go to jail, you've got to go to jail.'

During his six weeks in prison, Jan Molby's future lay on the line. After Kenny Dalglish had met with Liverpool's eight-man board of directors, chief executive Peter Robinson emerged to announce, in effect, a suspension of judgement in a prepared statement:

'The board and the manager have decided for the moment to withhold payment of Jan Molby's weekly salary because he is obviously unable to fulfil the terms of his contract.

'No other action will be taken at present,' the statement continued. 'The whole matter will be discussed with him when he is able to report to Anfield again.'

Liverpool's decision not to place their protective arm around their imprisoned Dane meant that nobody from the club – director, manager or player – went to see him in gaol. Perhaps this latest transgression was considered one too many for a football club whose proud reputation had already been tarnished by indisciplined behaviour off the pitch.

First-team players Paul Walsh and Sammy Lee and reserve John McGregor were accused of inflicting grievous bodily harm on a 17-year-old youth outside a Liverpool nightclub before eventually being cleared, and Walsh was banned for six months for driving up the M6 at 100 m.p.h. After another court case, John Aldridge was cleared of threatening a club bouncer and swearing at a barmaid. Liverpool had stood by all these previous miscreants before allowing Walsh to move on to Spurs. Now the club appeared to be about to wash their hands of Jan Molby. In the meantime, he would be left to stew in jail – without an estimated £10,000 in wages.

'I only went to see Jan in prison once because after the first time he didn't want me to go again,' says Mandy. 'It was a big circus at Kirkham. It was strange, everything about it was weird. I had to give them my visitor's order, they checked in the book, and I had to wait around. I didn't spend long with Jan – it was difficult to know what to say. It was hard.

'Liverpool's attitude while Jan was inside perhaps doesn't seem very caring, but that's the way they were. Life goes on. Jan says that in training, when you were injured nobody talked to you. When you were nearing the end of your injury and you were getting better, they started talking to you again. When you're injured you have no significance at all so you're pushed aside and they give their time to the people who can play. Obviously Jan couldn't play, so nobody was interested in him at all.'

Kenny Dalglish had been Liverpool's manager for more than three years when Jan was jailed. He was to play an important part in the Dane's rehabilitation at Anfield: 'As far as I know, there was no policy from the board or me about going to see Jan in gaol. I would have thought the players were free to go and see him. I don't remember saying anything, or anything being said other than that. Prison's not the type of place I would like to visit.'

On his release, Jan's immediate future was inextricably bound up with Dalglish. He and his wife Marina took Jan under their wing and arranged for him to stay in a flat in Southport. The manager wanted Jan to return to Liverpool and accompanied him to his hearing in front of the board.

When the board had delivered their verdict, Jan used a prepared statement to outline his future: 'I have served my sentence and now face the daunting prospect of regaining my self-respect before the eyes of thousands of fans.

'My ambition is twofold. Firstly, to regain and secure my first-team place at Liverpool Football Club. Secondly, to represent my country again at international level. I know I can expect no concessions from any quarter, but I am determined to achieve my aim with as much dignity as all sections of the public will allow.'

As far as Jan and the board were concerned, the incident was now closed. His determination to rehabilitate himself at Anfield was rewarded with a return to the first team within a month.

'I don't know how close Jan was to being sacked,' recalls Dalglish. 'You can imagine if someone's been given a jail sentence, it doesn't reflect too well on the club or the individual himself. But everyone's entitled to a second chance and I think that's what was in Jan's favour. That was the only concern – that he got a second chance. There was embarrassment for everyone, but most of all for Jan's family.

'I don't think Jan Molby was made to suffer in any way, shape or form – apart from the time he spent in prison. I don't think that went against him and there was no change in attitude towards him as far as the football side was concerned. He certainly wasn't left out of my teams because he'd been in prison. What other people thought of him being put in prison I don't know.'

After spending three weeks in the gym at Kirkham and then undergoing a strenuous workout for an hour a day at Preston, Jan emerged from jail a wiser and fitter man. His time inside had produced a transformation which astounded his team-mates. Captain Alan Hansen remembers returning to Anfield from a session at the Melwood training ground.

'I was the first one to walk into the dressing room that day. Jan was sitting at the table but I didn't recognize him! He was twelve and a half stone and he looked completely different.'

'He looked magnificent when he came out,' recalls Kenny Dalglish. 'He was in great condition.'

'We were made up,' says Jan's room-mate Ian Rush, 'because he came out looking the slimmest I'd ever seen him. Within a month, Jan was back in the first team and he was magnificent for us. I think he had something to prove.

'Nobody took the mickey when Jan came out of prison because everyone knew what he was really like. He was a good lad and we didn't give him stick because we knew it would affect him. We wanted to get the best out of Jan. We knew that, really, he shouldn't have gone to jail. It was unfortunate that the judge wanted to make an example of him.'

Mandy Molby noticed the change in her husband after his spell in prison. 'I think he came out a little bit more sensible than when he went in. He was just a kid, really. He wasn't street-wise. I think he put the whole six weeks down to experience and just wanted to get on with his life and not talk about it. It obviously wasn't a very pleasant experience, otherwise we'd all be queueing up to go. I think he was starting to grow up then anyway. He'd been with the club for a few years and he was starting to settle down, find his feet a little bit and get some new mates.'

Ian Rush also believes that prison had a sobering effect – as did fatherhood. Jan's son Kingsley had been born the previous July and the Molby family was completed by the arrival of Karina nearly six years later.

'Everyone's happy for Jan now because he seems to have learnt from his time in prison. It's even worse when you get into these situations and you don't learn from them. He's calmed down a bit and he's learnt the value of people and life. He was a lot more caring when he came out. I noticed he was a lot more responsible. He became a better person for it.'

Kenny Dalglish also noticed a marked difference in Jan's attitude: 'There was the initial change, in that his spell in prison wasn't going to be repeated. He came out full of remorse and regret and he never ended up back inside.'

Within months of successfully overseeing Jan's return to the fold, Dalglish found himself engulfed by the Hillsborough tragedy.

In 1971, Dalglish was in the Celtic party (but not the team) when sixty-six fans were killed towards the end of an Old Firm derby at Ibrox; he had been present at Heysel as part of the Liverpool side beaten by Juventus; Hillsborough was his third football tragedy. With the support of his wife and the backing of the club and its players, Dalglish, almost single-handedly, set about the task of comforting the bereaved with a dignity which was to make and, eventually, break him.

Jan Molby could not help but be caught up in the aftermath of Hillsborough. During his five years on Merseyside, he had settled down in the area with a local girl and become an adopted Scouser, unique accent and all. Along with most of the Liverpool players, he attended funerals and talked to relatives – both at Anfield and in their homes. Mandy Molby believes the tragedy put Jan's recent personal problem into perspective.

'Hillsborough was shocking, devastating, unbelievable – Jan's prison sentence was nothing in comparison. It makes me sick just thinking about it. It was hard on Jan, because he'd only been to one funeral before – his grandfather's. He didn't know how the relatives felt.

'The ninety-six who died should have justice – that's all I can say. They put up a shrine at Anfield, but that's not enough. They need to get to the bottom of what happened on that day. My dad was at Hillsborough – in the stand not in the pen – but it could quite easily have been him. I would have felt so bitter now had he been killed.'

Ian Rush accompanied Jan to some of the Hillsborough funerals as the players rallied round. 'Jan was seen as a Scouser because of the way he just got on with people in Liverpool. I think the full impact of Hillsborough didn't sink in until later with both us – we were a bit young at the time.

'When we went to the funerals together, we got an idea of how hard it was for the families of the victims. Liverpool is such a close-knit area that everyone helped each other. We felt we had to do the same to keep everyone going.'

In a Foreign Field

When we arrived at the Heysel Stadium for the 1985 European Cup Final against Juventus, there was no hint at all of any trouble. We turned up an hour and a half before kick-off, and as we didn't normally start getting ready until an hour before the match started, we went for a walk around the ground.

The Liverpool supporters were in good spirits as we indulged in a bit of banter with them. They kicked a ball to us and we kicked it back. There was a good atmosphere in the ground. We did notice that some of the Liverpool fans were jam-packed into a section in the corner to the right of one of the goals next to what should have been a neutral area for fans from Belgium. We could see that some Juventus supporters were in this section, but most of the Italian club's fans were at the other end of the ground. The segregation didn't seem brilliant but we thought nothing of it because everything was good-humoured. We'd always had a good rapport with the fans and that night seemed to be no different.

What we didn't know was that as we sauntered around the ground, stones were already being thrown by Juventus fans at the Liverpool supporters. A year before, they had been on the receiving end when Roma troublemakers pelted them with missiles – bricks and stones – before and after our European Cup Final win. Now it was happening again.

After we'd walked around, one or two of the players went out to warm up. Everybody was looking forward to the game starting. We'd been back in the dressing room for a few moments when we were told that the kick-off had been delayed, but nobody knew for how long. We all had an idea that something was wrong when one of the players warming up came back in and said there'd been a little bit of trouble on the terrace.

Since Heysel, there's been a lot of speculation about whether the players knew that anyone had died before the kick-off. Most of us weren't clear what precisely had happened. At the time, I don't think anyone was completely aware of how serious it all was. It was obvious that something had gone on behind the goal, but we didn't see anything. The dressing rooms were very low down in the stadium and you had to go outside if you wanted to take a look, but the officials wouldn't let us.

Players like Mark Lawrenson and Craig Johnston have both made it clear in their autobiographies that we didn't know, although the then Liverpool captain Phil Neal has admitted that he was aware that some people had died before the game started. On his way to make an appeal for calm via the public address Tannoy, he had seen some of the bodies. Kenny Dalglish, who was about to take over from Joe Fagan, has always said that he knew nothing of the deaths until after the game, and I'm sure he didn't. I seem to remember him not being well – I think he had the flu – and during the delay, he was resting in the treatment room away from the main area.

During his team talk, Joe mentioned the delay caused by crowd trouble but he told us to keep our minds on the game in hand.

'You're here to do a job,' he said. 'And that is to win a football match. Don't let what's happened affect you.'

At that time, it made sense – as did the decision to play the game. Things might have gone from very bad to worse if it had been called off. Joe, Roy and Ronnie kept talking about football all the time. We were expecting to beat Juventus, even though they had some world-class players like Platini and Boniek. Unlike Ajax, Liverpool had that invincible air about them in Europe and we just didn't feel there was anyone who could beat us.

By the time we came out for the game, all the bodies had been cleared from a line in front of the main stand where they'd been put to be identified. The Final itself was a huge non-event with all the Liverpool players just going through the motions. You didn't need to be a genius to know that something had happened – a football match wouldn't be delayed for that amount of time if it hadn't been serious. But we didn't know just how serious.

From what I can remember, we were the better team on the night, even though we lost 1–0 through a disputed penalty. At half-time, I stayed out with the other subs to give our young keeper some shooting practice (Bob Boulder had broken his leg two weeks before). I could see the area behind the goal was empty but everything else seemed OK.

In light of the deaths, I just didn't feel it was right to watch the game again, and I haven't to this day. People go on about the penalty – which probably shouldn't have been awarded because the foul was outside the box – or the one we didn't get when Ronnie Whelan was brought down, but who wants to argue? I don't think anybody has been bothered to sit down and say 'we were robbed!', because thirty-nine people lost their lives. The suggestion that a referee made a wrong decision was never important.

Back in the dressing room after the game, it was very flat. Players are naturally nosey and we wanted to know what had happened. It was a perfectly understandable reaction but Joe, Ronnie and Roy wouldn't tell us anything.

I actually found out people had died when I left the dressing room and was met outside by the Danish press. They asked me about the tragedy, but in the end they had to tell me what had happened. My first thought was: Is it all worth it? It's only a game of football. All these people have died – surely it can't all be worth it. Everyone wanted to know what we thought about the incident, but it was very difficult to give a point of view straight after the game when we weren't sure what had happened.

There was a post-match meal, which our wives and girlfriends came to, and then we went back to the hotel. It was only when we boarded the bus the next morning that we realized that the Liverpool fans were being blamed for the deaths. Italian supporters were banging on the side of the bus as we left for the airport with a police escort and Belgian people in the street were screaming 'English bastards!' at us.

When we arrived back in England, I dived into my car and drove straight to Harwich to return to Denmark for my summer holiday, so I missed the majority of the aftermath of Heysel. The press couldn't get hold of me for a couple of weeks in Denmark, and I didn't arrive back in England for another seven weeks after that. It figured pretty prominently in the Danish papers because they had always made a big thing out of English hooliganism. They really went to town on the Liverpool fans and, at the time, because it was my club, I didn't agree with what they were saying. Again, though, it was difficult to argue against because I didn't really know what had happened. If I'd had to make a public statement about Heysel then I would have found out the facts but, for a long time, perhaps a year to eighteen months, Liverpool put up a smokescreen and the players didn't discuss what had happened publicly.

At pre-season training, we were still talking about Heysel because the majority of Liverpool fans felt they were hard done by. They were being blamed for the deaths and were trying to tell everyone they were innocent. I didn't make a judgement then but now I think it was a bit of both – bad behaviour and bad organization. I think the Liverpool supporters came over the fence either because they were being stoned or to try to create a bit of space for themselves – there were so many of them. It was difficult for the Liverpool fans, because if you get put in an enclosure you've got no right to climb over the fence. But if you're having stones thrown at you, for the second European Cup Final running, what are you supposed to do?

There's no doubt that the Liverpool fans terrified the Juventus supporters. They jumped over the fence and chased after them. Although they didn't get hold of that many, everyone ended up getting squashed against the wall. The stadium was old, the wall couldn't stand up to the pressure and it collapsed and people were crushed to death.

By deciding to scale the fence themselves, the Liverpool supporters were probably in the wrong but I'm sure everything could have been organized better. As well as my friends from Denmark, there were people from Liverpool who, to this day, tell me that they didn't have to produce a ticket for the Final – they could just walk in. The

Belgian authorities assumed everyone outside the ground would have a ticket, so they didn't bother checking and people were walking in whether they had a ticket or not. That's probably why the crowd wasn't segregated properly. Some of my friends still have their tickets intact. I'm sure it could have been dealt with better.

By the time I came back to Liverpool, people had stopped pointing the finger. Kenny Dalglish was firmly installed as the new manager and Liverpool issued a statement that stressed the need to deal with the tragedy and then move on. The club felt it was important to be as positive as possible, and got the same message across to the players. We were unhappy that Liverpool fans were being blamed for the ban on English clubs playing in Europe – nobody really thought that it was entirely their fault: the poor organization and the appalling state of the stadium played their parts. We all felt that the ruling was harsh, but obviously UEFA had to do something, and English clubs paid a very harsh price with a five-year ban. Liverpool received an extra year.

Since then, ground safety and supporter segregation have improved – it's just sad that something like Heysel had to happen before anything was done. Was it right to penalize the players by banning them from Europe for the violent behaviour of a small section of their supporters? I don't know. There's only so much responsibility that a club's board, manager and players can have for the way their fans behave. After all, we're employed to kick a ball around.

Nowadays, as football becomes more like big business and more high profile, I accept that we have certain responsibilities to improve the image of the game. Back in the eighties, I'm afraid I didn't set a very good example in my own personal life.

Life in the Fast Lane

I have to be honest, I didn't have the best of track records when I ran into trouble with the Merseyside police in February 1988. During my three and a half years with Liverpool, I'd already picked up four driving convictions – mainly for speeding – but, even so, I think I was a marked man as far as the boys in blue were concerned. They were out to get me by hook or by crook and, in the end, they succeeded. I was convicted for reckless driving and spent 45 days in jail in what turned out to be the worst six weeks of my life.

The incident in question came at a doubly frustrating time for me. The team was doing really well in the 1987–88 season but I was injured. I was struggling to recover from my foot injury which had kept me out from the beginning of the season. Now when you're not involved, you want the team to win, say, 1–0 but not to play well. Unfortunately for me, this wasn't happening. The team were winning comfortably and playing out of their skins. Liverpool were such a high-profile club that people were constantly reminding me of how well they were doing without me.

As a result of being injured, I had a lot of spare time on my hands. It meant I could have a pint on a Thursday or Friday night, which I couldn't when I was fit, but, although I had my fair share of nights out, I wasn't really getting up to anything. I've no doubt that one or two police officers were looking for me that night. I was a young footballer who had a nice sports car, a BMW M3, which was worth a few quid. I'm sure the police saw me as a good catch.

On that night, I was acting as a chauffeur for some friends and we'd gone to a nightclub in the centre of Liverpool. I'd only had a couple of pints because I was driving and, as I walked out, I saw some policemen use their walkie-talkies. They were standing alongside a couple of police cars parked near by and as soon as I drove off, on came the blue flashing lights.

I realized I was on the drink-driving borderline as I started the twenty-mile drive home to Chester, so I just put my foot down. That car could really move. There was no way the police were going to be able to keep up with me. I was frightened but I just thought that if I drove home as quickly as possible, I would be OK. It was about half-past midnight and I screeched through a couple of roundabouts – I didn't pay them the respect they deserved but I didn't go over them. The roads were clear and, within two minutes, I couldn't see the police cars any more. I drove home, got up the next day and then went training.

For the life of me, I can't explain why I did it. In court, my defence counsel called it 'two minutes of madness' and I can't think of a better description. I think the implications of getting done for drink-driving were in the back of my mind. Having been in trouble with the police four times before, I was worried that Liverpool would see another brush with the law as the last straw. I feared they would sack me if I was convicted for drink-driving. Once I had decided on plan A – to get away – I had to go for plan B: to make sure I got away. It was all about self-preservation.

The next day, I thought I'd got away with it – I couldn't believe the police hadn't picked me up. In the event, I think they caught me by chance, by sheer fluke. In the evening, I parked my car outside a pub and went inside for an orange juice. The police must have spotted my Danish number plates because suddenly eight of them rushed in, asked me if I was Jan Molby, dragged me from the bar and took me outside. It was a bit heavy-handed, but I expected it of them. I had been nicked and started to fear the worst.

At first, I was going to deny that I was driving the car but I thought better of it after speaking to my solicitor, Kevin Dooley from Southport. We decided that I should plead guilty. We expected a hefty fine and a long ban but not a prison sentence. By the time my case came to Liverpool Crown Court, the police had really gone to town on me. They had piled smear upon smear upon smear.

I remember standing up, saying my name, pleading guilty and then sitting down to hear the prosecution outline their case. They claimed I had driven at a hundred miles an hour during the run home, but my defence argued that it wasn't possible for me to have been going that fast – unless I'd been on an aeroplane. I'd been seen by so many police officers that I just didn't have a leg to stand on. Apparently, I was driving so dangerously that three police cars had to abandon the chase, but there were no near-misses – in fact, I can't remember seeing another car. When the prosecution had finished, one or two people spoke on my behalf, including a Liverpool director who's since died. It was nice of the club to send someone along. The court heard all about the charity work I'd been doing and then it was down to the judge. He asked me to stand up before reading me the riot act.

'It is only by the grace of providence that you did not kill or maim somebody,' he said.

When I heard those words, my heart sank. The judge then said he was giving me a custodial sentence of ninety days. I couldn't believe my ears. I thought Jeremy Beadle was going to appear and tell everyone it was a wind-up! It was completely unexpected. I just didn't think I would be going to jail. A five or ten thousand-pound fine would have been hard but it wouldn't have surprised me. But a jail sentence? It seemed as if my previous convictions had come back to haunt me.

I was completely shell-shocked. I just felt numb. The year-long ban from driving and the £320 costs didn't register. All I could think about was going down. I glanced at Kevin, who returned my look of amazement, and two officers took me from the dock. As we went down in a lift to the cells, they said they thought I'd got the rough end of the stick – like 90 per cent of the people I discussed my case with.

Once I was in the cell, the nightmare really began. I had to stay there until the end of the court's business that day. I kept hoping it was all a bad dream. Every time the door went, I thought somebody would come in and say they'd changed the sentence. But they didn't. A prison officer told me I would have to serve half of my sentence, which, by my calculations, meant I would be inside for about six weeks.

Kevin came to see me and, after talking it through, we decided not to appeal. He said if we appealed, I could be taken home straight away, but we'd have to come back. I don't think an appeal would have changed anything. Kevin was visibly shocked because he hadn't expected me to be jailed either.

My immediate concern was Liverpool's reaction. What would they say? Would I have a future with them or would they sack me? I started to work out my release date – December – and I knew I wouldn't be playing football again until at least the New Year. I began to picture all the headlines in the papers. At least I could escape from the press in prison – nobody could get to me inside, could they?

I couldn't see forward to the end of the forty-five days at that stage. There was nothing I could do. I was also worried about the effect my sentence would have on my family, the shame and the embarrassment. All in all, it wasn't a very pleasant experience sitting in a police cell for five and a half hours until the court proceedings were over, but worse was to come.

Handcuffs were put on me and, along with about twenty other men, I went on a bus to Walton Jail. I suspect most of them had been inside before. It was horrible. As we left the court, all the press were there, the traffic had stopped and the man in charge threw a blanket over me. I half-expected to have something put over my head but I didn't think the blanket would be as big as it was. I took it off during the fifteen-minute journey and I think most of the other prisoners recognized me.

As we approached Walton Jail, we could see the place was crawling with cameramen and photographers so, just before we arrived, the blanket went back on. It was in the police's interests not to turn my arrival at Walton into a big circus. Deep down, I was quite pleased to be under that blanket. For a final few moments, I was just another prisoner. I knew there'd be no hiding place once I was in prison.

The Inside Story

I'll never forget my first few moments actually inside Walton Jail. I went into reception, took off my clothes and checked in with the doctor. Then I picked up my prison uniform – a shirt, jeans and a pair of big black shoes – and made my way to my cell. When I walked into the wing, everyone was looking at me and muttering my name.

I couldn't wait to get into my cell to be alone, but I was paired with another prisoner. It was obvious he didn't know who I was. He offered me a cigarette and asked what I was in for, but I wasn't very communicative. In fact, he was lucky that I wasn't in for murder! He sat up all night cutting whatever he was going to smoke and coughing every thirty seconds. It was terrible – he was doing my head in! So when they moved me the next day, I was absolutely delighted. I now had a corner cell for two prisoners, but I was by myself. As I was lying there, grateful for a bit of peace and quiet, someone shouted out to me:

'Hey, Molby! What's it like to play at Wembley?'

Before I could say a word, another prisoner piped up in my Danish-Scouser voice:

'Well . . . it's a lovely experience. I've been there so many times now.'

I couldn't believe what I'd just heard. It was so like me, it was uncanny! Whoever it was had answered for me so convincingly that other prisoners started shouting out their own questions:

'What do you think of Everton?'

'Well, they'll never be as good as Liverpool!'

'What are you going to do in jail?'

'I have to serve my sentence like everybody else. There's nothing else I can do.'

The questions just kept on coming. They must have gone on for at least half an hour. I was howling. The men kept asking questions because they thought it was me answering back. I slept much better that night. The warder on my wing at Walton was a season-ticket holder at Anfield and, the morning after the floor show, when all the other prisoners were either at work or locked up, he opened my cell door to let me walk around. One of the other men who was cleaning them came up to me.

'Did you enjoy the show last night?'

'What do you mean?'

'The question-and-answer session.'

'Yeah, that was brilliant.'

'That was me,' he said proudly.

It was great to come face to face with the Grand Impersonator.

As I was talking to him, another warder came up and said he wanted to strip-search me. He'd heard that I was going to be taking drugs to Kirkham Open Prison where it seemed I was being moved the next day. He stripped the whole cell and I had to take off all my clothes – it was pathetic, but I had to do it. A couple of hours later, another prison officer told me not to worry about the warder involved – he apparently wanted to make a name for himself by humiliating me in front of everybody.

My two days at Walton were terrible. I couldn't begin to describe the food, but luckily I didn't feel like eating. I slopped out along with everybody else when I went to wash in the morning. I just wanted to get out of there. I'm quite good on my own – I'm not somebody who needs company – but I don't think I could have stood forty-five days in Walton.

We left Walton on a half-full bus and called in at Strangeways Prison in Manchester to pick up some more men on our way to Kirkham Open Prison, which was halfway between Preston and Blackpool and apparently more suitable for the crime I'd committed. I was much happier at Kirkham simply because the cells had been replaced by barrack rooms. Twenty-four of us shared twelve rooms and although we were locked up at night, we could move around. There were toilets and baths – it was a bit like being away at camp – and it was a lot more civilized. I felt I could cope with life in Kirkham.

Not long after I arrived, the officer in charge of the Sunday five-a-side competition asked me if I fancied a game. They played between two and five o'clock, with three or four teams. The winners stayed on.

I turned up just before two on the Sunday to find the whole place packed. Eighty-odd prisoners, fifteen teams, it was a fiasco – they'd all come because they knew I'd be there. We had our fair share of games and I enjoyed the run-out but I remember that day because of a bit of an incident with this long-haired fella from Manchester. He'd never been to the five-a-side before, he couldn't play football, and as he came running towards me I nutmegged him. As I tried to run around him, he ran straight into me and pushed me up against the wall. Before I could do anything, a couple of Scousers who were watching from above slipped down the wall and took care of him as the game was going on! He got a real working-over.

I also spent a lot of my time during the early part of my stay at Kirkham ducking and diving out of the way of a couple of other lads staying in the same barracks. This was the deal: they said they'd been offered £500 by a paper to take some pictures of me and, if I agreed, they'd split the money fifty-fifty. I told them where to go, but they kept trying to snap me.

I remember lying on my bed one Sunday afternoon when they came in and tried to take a picture. I put the pillow over my head so they couldn't see my face, but they were very persistent. Eventually, they gave up – although I'm not sure if they weren't caught with the camera by the authorities.

On another Sunday afternoon in Kirkham, there was a live football game on TV. We had to be in our cells by four o'clock for the count by the warders. Every prisoner was back in barracks but one – that was me, the prison's most famous inmate. Nobody could find me, so they started to search the place. All hell broke loose! The alarm bells were ringing and warders were rushing around looking for me. I hadn't done a runner – I was in the governor's house having a cup of tea and a biscuit in front of the TV! I should have gone back at half-time, but we both forgot about the four o'clock rule and I'd just carried on watching the game.

'Don't worry,' said the governor, when he was told about the prisoner on the run. 'He's in here with me.'

How nice to have friends in high places!

Before I went to prison, I'd heard all sorts of stories about the way celebrities are sometimes treated inside. They can be given a difficult time by some of the more hardened criminals, but nothing like that happened to me. I became quite matey with Ronnie Stretch, the brother of the Wigan boxer Gary Stretch. It was nice to have him around as company. We played badminton and did circuit training together.

To be honest, I was never worried about getting hit by some nutter. I was big enough to look after myself and I could give as good as I got but deliberately kept myself to myself anyway. Pretty early on at Kirkham, I came across a fella called 'Scouse'. I was in barrack number 1. One day a prisoner arrived at my door.

'Scouse wants to see you,' he said.

'Who's "Scouse"?'

'Never mind. Barrack eleven. Bottom room.'

I walked down to find this huge man, about eighteen stone, with a big beard.

'Hello, Jan,' he said. 'When you're in here, I look after you. I'm in charge of this place. Are you hungry?'

'I'm starving!'

'What do you want?'

He pulled out these two big boxes from underneath his bed. There was everything you could dream of in them. Biscuits, bananas – whatever you wanted was there in those boxes.

'Whenever you're hungry,' he said, 'you come up here. I'll look after you.'

It was the one and only time I ever visited 'Scouse' – and that was because I was told to. I never went again. I didn't want to get involved. I wanted to keep myself apart from the other prisoners – just do my time and then get out.

My routine during the twenty-one days I spent there never varied. We were up at six o'clock to have a shave and put on our uniform – a pair of jeans, a shirt and a tie – and then after breakfast, we'd go to work. I started in the clothes exchange department. The seven hundred prisoners would bring their dirty clothes into us and we would put them into skips to be cleaned. When they came back, we'd place them into compartments for the men to collect. The fellow in charge was a big Manchester United fan and we used to have a bet on games, with a Mars Bar as the stake.

I'd only been working there for four or five days before I was transferred to the hospital wing. This was the best job in the prison because I was moved out of the barracks and into the wing. I lived the Life of Riley, if that's possible when you're inside. There were three of us altogether – two other prisoners in charge and me – but no patients. All I did was a bit of cleaning. I had so much spare time on my hands that I'd be in the prison gym for six or eight hours a day. I would have lunch with the kitchen staff, work in the gym in the afternoon, and then play badminton and do circuit training in the evening. I was working harder at keeping fit than when I'd been at Anfield!

I was quite happy at Kirkham but the governor thought my presence put a lot of strain on the prison in security terms. There were photographers waiting outside all the time and people were passing cameras over the fence to try to take pictures of me. One day, two Scousers approached me and said some lunatic had just given them a camera and offered £200 for a photo. They'd gone into the greenhouse for half an hour, taken a few pictures in there, given the camera back and taken the money. It was crazy.

So after twenty-one days of relative luxury at Kirkham, I was moved to Preston Prison, just down the road, for another three weeks. In one sense, it was worse than Walton because I was locked up in my cell for twenty-three out of every twenty-four hours. On the other hand, I was in the hospital wing, so it wasn't as grotty as Walton. All the officers told me I shouldn't really be there. But I was, and it was awful.

To be fair, I was lucky to find a sympathetic prison officer. He used to finish his shift at four o'clock in the afternoon and take me down to the gym for a session. He'd put me through a fifty-minute circuit at the only time of the day the gym was free. Although he was a big Manchester United fan, he didn't hold my Liverpool connection against me. I was very grateful because he helped me in his own time, day after day, and, thanks to him, I kept myself fit. I'd never been one for hard training but he really put me through it. I actually looked forward to the session.

For the rest of the day, I read, listened to the radio and slept. My solicitor once brought me ten books. I finished them in two days. They were all about Liverpool – books on Bill Shankly, Bob Paisley and Emlyn Hughes. It was pretty quiet on the hospital wing – I only saw the warders and one other prisoner, who had a broken leg. He had been jailed for murdering his wife, in a classic crime of passion. He'd come home one day to find her in bed with another man and had completely flipped. He'd then blacked out and said he couldn't remember what he'd done. He was a lovely fella, and I'd spend ten minutes chatting with him every day. After fourteen years inside, he was six months away from release and about to start a new life down south. Perhaps he had mellowed over time, but I just couldn't believe he was a murderer. In a way, I felt sorry for him. He'd certainly paid for his moment of madness – and I felt that I was paying for mine.

My solicitor Kevin, and Mandy, came to see me, and although my parents wrote asking if they could visit, I didn't want them to. I just read and looked forward to five-past four every day.

As time went by, I was starting to worry more and more about the prospect of facing Liverpool Football Club, and the world in general. I knew it wasn't going to be easy after the club's reaction to me being jailed. When I was sentenced, Kevin rang Kenny Dalglish to tell him, and Liverpool issued a statement saying they would deal with the situation when I was released.

Nobody from the club came to see me when I was locked up. I think Kenny might have wanted to but didn't feel it was the right thing to do. It would probably have turned into a media circus had he arrived at the prison. I was disappointed that nobody from Liverpool wrote to me, especially as I received some personal good-luck messages from the Danish squad. It was almost as if Liverpool had decided to wash their hands of me until I'd served my time.

As my release date drew nearer, I was becoming really worried about my future. Kevin couldn't give me any reassurance. He said that when I came out, I'd have to go in front of the board for them to make a decision on my future. But although I was worried, I was more than a little relieved to be released. The events of that day are still pretty clear in my mind.

I was woken up as usual at about six and had a bath and a shave. The officers' shift changed at seven, and because there were so many media people waiting outside I had to leave prison in secret. Just before seven o'clock, a convoy of cars carrying prison officers swept through the gates of Preston Prison with me tucked away in one of the boots. Very secretive, and very exciting.

131

We drove down the road for a few hundred yards, I hopped out of the boot and jumped into Kevin's Mercedes. I lay down on the back seat and he whisked me away to his home in Southport. An hour later, when everybody else was released, the reporters and photographers were still outside the gates scratching their heads and looking for yours truly.

I must admit to allowing myself a slight chuckle when I was in the car boot – it was nice being able to give the media the slip because at the time I hated them. Some of them were having a right dig at me but, at the end of the day, nobody had been injured by my action. Despite what some people were saying, there was no drink-driving conviction and I thought I'd more than paid for what I'd done. I felt I'd had a raw deal from both the police and the press.

Some of the coverage of my case was very unfair – other reports were a disgrace. The *Daily Mirror* was the worst. One of their reporters had a right pop at me under a headline KICK HIM OUT! The story said there was no place for thugs like me in football. Whatever I'd done, it wasn't worthy of comments like that. I don't want to harp on about it, but I do feel that I was made an example of by the police and the press because of who I was. On my release, Liverpool's chief executive, Peter Robinson, told me he was very sorry for the treatment I'd received. He said it could only have happened in this country.

When I arrived at Kevin's house, I was looking forward to a really big breakfast. In prison, I'd been used to starting my day with cereal and then having mashed potatoes and some kind of pie or chicken for lunch and dinner. Kevin's wife had made everything – fried eggs, sausages, bacon, the works – but I just couldn't eat. I don't know whether it was because I was excited but it was the best breakfast I never had. I'd been lying in my cell dreaming of eating this huge English breakfast on the day I was released, but unfortunately it didn't quite work out like that.

Later that day, Kevin drove me to Anfield. To avoid the media waiting in reception, I went into the club's souvenir shop and then under the main stand and into the dressing room. I bypassed reception altogether. Kevin was in charge of things, and this was the way he wanted to do it. The players were out training, so I did some work around the pitch. After a while, they came back from Melwood to find me sitting in the dressing room waiting for them.

At first, they didn't know how to handle my return – they didn't know what to expect. Would I be the same or had prison affected me? It was a bit uncomfortable for them and me. Nobody asked what prison had been like. I remember Ray Houghton's reaction. I was never that close to him but he was absolutely made up to see me. After a few moments, Kenny Dalglish said it was time to go and we drove back to his house for lunch.

Waiting to know my fate was as bad, if not worse, than waiting for Kenny to announce an FA Cup Final team. I just didn't know what his or Liverpool's reaction was going to be now that I was out. Kenny put most of my fears to rest by telling me what I desperately hoped to hear. He said he wanted to keep me but we would have to face the board the next day. At least I had him on my side – that was a start. It was a huge weight off my shoulders, but I knew there was another hurdle to clear.

I wanted to stay at Anfield, even though during my six weeks inside I'd been linked with almost every club in Europe. The prison staff had told me what the papers were saying about possible transfers to teams like PSV Eindhoven and Hamburg, and everybody seemed convinced that Liverpool would sell me when I was released.

Now I was out, the press couldn't help themselves. They couldn't get a photo of me while I was inside so it was time to have another go. As I was chatting to Kenny and his wife Marina, she pointed to a photographer in the garden.

'Watch this,' said Kenny, as he picked up the telephone.

Within two minutes, the photographer had been dealt with by the Southport police. Kenny was delighted. He told me that was the way to deal with people like nosy photographers.

We then went to an apartment in Southport, which was to be my bolthole for a couple of days. Liverpool had just signed Dave Burrows from West Bromwich Albion and he was staying there. I'd obviously never met him, and it was uncomfortable for both of us for a while, but we got on OK.

The next day, Kenny picked me up and we drove to Anfield. The media circus was well and truly in town. The car park was packed. There were reporters and photographers and cameramen all over the place – it was a relief to get inside the boardroom! I went in with Kevin and Kenny to hear Liverpool's chairman Sir John Smith outline the background to my case. He then had a go at me by asking what I was going to do about my drink problem.

Kenny stepped in to correct the chairman.

'Jan doesn't have a drink problem,' he explained. 'If he did have one, he wouldn't have been at this club as a player.'

When my turn came, I apologized for what had happened and said I would like a second chance. I was then told to go outside and wait until the board had reached their decision. My hearing lasted twenty minutes, but it was another three hours before I knew my fate. It was a very long three hours. We just sat around outside until Kenny called us back into the boardroom and Sir John delivered the verdict.

'We've decided to keep you on as a Liverpool player,' he said, shaking my hand. 'Nice to see you back.'

A huge wave of relief washed over me. Looking back, I realize that if Liverpool had sacked me, I would have become a free agent and they would have lost quite a lot of money. Then I could have gone wherever I wanted to. But what I really wanted was to stay at Anfield.

Liverpool had prepared a press statement for me to read and drawn up a contract which meant I couldn't discuss the whole incident in public while I was with the club. I signed the contract despite some very tempting offers for the story of my time in jail. My solicitor spoke to the *News of the World*, who offered £8000 for an exclusive mocked-up picture of me climbing out of the boot of a car! A weekly magazine in Denmark also contacted Kevin, but I wasn't interested. I just wanted to forget about it and get back to playing football for Liverpool.

The worst moment of all was having to read the prepared statement to the press. We walked into the trophy room at Anfield and sat down at a table. It's a huge room, and it was full of reporters.

They'd come from Holland, Norway, Germany and Denmark as well as England. It was unbelievable! Everywhere I looked there was a camera lens or microphone or notebook at the ready. There was nothing else for it. Without looking up once, I read out the statement in thirty seconds flat, got up and got out. The reporters had been told there'd be no opportunity to ask questions.

Kenny took me back to Southport and the next day I played for the A team in front of my mother and sister. And that was it – I was back into the swing of things. I had the feeling that Kenny was dying to put me back into the first team, and after playing a couple more A games I came on as a sub against Manchester United at Old Trafford on New Year's Day, 1989 – a month after my release. A New Year and a new start. We lost 3–1, but it was great to be back.

Our next opponents were Aston Villa at Anfield. I had a good game in defence in a 1–0 win. I then had my best spell since 1986 but, almost inevitably, just four games later, the injury jinx struck again during our 2–0 win over Charlton at Anfield. I ripped a thigh muscle and that was the end of my season.

Looking back on the whole prison affair, I'm convinced more than ever in hindsight that the police wanted to make an example of me. It happened in February 1988 but the case didn't come to court until October. During that period, I was stopped in my car about twenty-five times by the police. On a couple of occasions they even asked me my name, knowing full well who I was. They were just being awkward.

As for Liverpool's attitude towards me, I must admit to having mixed feelings. At the time I thought it was fine. It was a new experience for one of their players to go to jail and perhaps they weren't sure how to deal with it. The eyes of the nation were on me and the club. Then, I felt they behaved in the right way, but now I think they probably could have handled it differently.

I feel their original statement about dealing with me when I was released left a few questions unanswered, and gave the media plenty of ammunition. So, not surprisingly, there were headlines like KICK HIM OUT! in the papers. A more supportive statement from Liverpool would probably have made it easier for me.

Since then, there's been much more sympathy shown towards jailed footballers. Tony Adams of Arsenal, for example, was convicted of drink-driving. Tony knew what the future held for him because Arsenal said they would stand by him. He wasn't punished financially while inside, whereas Liverpool stopped my wages. I would have loved to have had the same support that Tony received from Arsenal. They publicly backed him as they did Paul Merson when he ran into his drink, drugs and gambling problems. I wasn't worried about my wages being stopped, but it would have been nice if Liverpool had put their arms around me and said: 'Don't worry, Jan – we'll be here waiting for you when you come out.' Nevertheless, they were within their rights as I had obviously breached my contract with them.

At least I received that emotional support from Denmark. The national team manager Sepp Piontek and his squad were on their way to an international and they all sent small notes of encouragement to the prison. I have a feeling that the Liverpool players were told not to contact me while I was inside. I'm not sure, but when I returned to the dressing room, there was no stick at all. Nobody has mentioned it to this day. Footballers are normally quite prepared to take the mickey and they can be pretty cruel at times, but I think they felt this was different. They could see that there'd been enough written and said about the incident, so they decided not to jump on the bandwagon. I was grateful for that.

Opposition supporters weren't so kind. As well as receiving the usual chants of 'You fat bastard!' and 'Who ate all the pies?', I was now known as 'Jailbird', but it didn't affect my game at all. After six weeks inside, I could easily cope with a bit of teasing from the terraces.

It's difficult for me to say how prison affected me as a person. I think it changed my ways a little, hopefully for the better. Going to prison made me determined not to put myself into positions where I could get into trouble again – and that's basically what I've done. I was more careful after that. Perhaps in the past, I'd occasionally got away with having a pint or two too many before driving, but I'd never been a criminal.

I've come to realize that once you've been to jail, it's difficult to shake off your past. Since being released, I've been breathalysed by the police a few times. I remember being stopped on my way home from training a couple of years ago. This officer had gone down a dual carriageway, spotted me and reversed back up before starting his blue light flashing and pulling me over.

'I've caught you!' he said, triumphantly.

'What do you mean you've caught me?' I replied.

'You're banned from driving!'

'I was banned from driving seven years ago!'

The policeman must have remembered my court case and was obviously delighted to have picked me up. He later apologized, but it was pathetic. I don't know why the police have this attitude, but it seems that nicking somebody who's famous gives them more pleasure than catching ordinary members of the public.

Generally, I've been successful in putting prison out of my mind. At first, though, there was always the former prisoner called 'Red' to remind me of the bad times. He was a fanatical Liverpool supporter and he always followed me around like a little lapdog inside and then outside jail. I'd been out for about six months when he was released. He'd started to watch Liverpool again, and at virtually every away game 'Red' would be there. I first came across him when we were getting off the bus at Highbury. I suddenly heard this voice booming out:

'Jan! Jan! Any chance of any tickets!'

'Who are you?' I said, not knowing him from Adam.

'Don't you remember me from Kirkham?'

You can imagine how I felt. There I was, trying to forget my time in prison and here was this Liverpool fanatic reminding everyone that I'd been a jailbird wherever I went! 'Red' was the only ex-con I met outside, until I went into the boardroom at Tranmere Rovers one day. A man was standing there in a club blazer and he wasn't at all embarrassed by our connection.

'Do you remember me?' he asked.

'Yes, I do,' I replied, racking my brains, trying to remember where I'd seen his face.

'Kirkham,' he said.

My six-week spell in prison was the worst time of my life, not just my career. It was something I vowed never ever to put myself, my family or my friends through again. I'd committed a crime, I'd served my time, but I couldn't change what happened.

They'll Never Walk Alone

Prison may have been a personal tragedy for me but within six months Liverpool Football Club, indeed the whole nation, were involved in a far more serious disaster. I watched Hillsborough unfold from the main stand. Although my thigh muscle injury had put me out for the rest of the season, I was in the Liverpool party for the FA Cup semi-final against Nottingham Forest.

After my successful post-prison mini-comeback, I was obviously disappointed not to be part of the squad, but it felt good to be alive on that Saturday afternoon. It was a lovely sunny day and we were top of the League and favourites to reach our second successive Cup Final. I'd had the usual build-up to semi-final day. Everybody wanted tickets and I'd done my best but, in the end, I couldn't satisfy the demand.

I remember thinking about the allocation of tickets as I sat behind the dug-out looking out towards the Leppings Lane End. It was weird, because I noticed that all the Liverpool fans were in the middle section but the two sides were virtually empty. My first reaction was a purely personal one. Why, I thought, couldn't I have had some more tickets, with all that room – there's nobody in there! In retrospect, I realize how significant those empty spaces were.

Pretty soon after the kick-off, Peter Beardsley's shot skimmed the Forest crossbar and there was a surge behind the goal at the Leppings Lane End. We just thought the fans had rushed forward in response to Peter's effort. The two side sections were still far from full and the next thing I noticed was that people were climbing over the fence.

The referee then took the players off but, from where Barry Venison, Nigel Spackman and I were sitting, it just looked like a little bit of bother. We didn't go down the tunnel with the players, and the next thing I remember was everybody screaming and shouting that people were being squashed down there. One or two said that some were even dying.

We didn't know what to think. Ronnie Moran came out and called us into the dressing room. We knew there was something wrong because we were next to the medical room and it was being used to treat the injured as they were ferried in from the pitch. One or two rumours started to circulate and then people began talking. Kenny called us all together. He said we should forget about any rumours we might hear about people dying. He didn't want anyone letting their imagination run wild and worrying other players. He said there were people next door fighting for their lives and until we were told differently, nothing had happened. It just went on and on and on. All we knew was that the game had been delayed for the time being. Then, just after four, we heard it had been abandoned because people had died.

We were stuck in the dressing room for the whole time, just sitting, talking and drinking tea. There was a slight feeling of *déjà vu*. Like Heysel, we wanted to know what was going on, but there was no information being given out. We didn't leave the dressing room until after five o'clock – more than two hours after the tragedy began.

I was one of the first to arrive in the players' lounge because I didn't have to get changed. All the wives and girlfriends were crying. I realized then how serious things were. By watching the television, we started to learn more about what had happened. My mind didn't immediately go back to Heysel because that was more of a tragedy for Turin than Liverpool.

Gradually, the other players came up to the lounge and the picture became clearer. As soon as we were all ready, we got on the coach and drove back across the Pennines to Anfield. The coach was very quiet. Nobody could really take in what had happened. Back in Liverpool, we didn't know what to do, so we all went home. But one person did know what had to be done. From that moment on,

Kenny Dalglish came into his own. He became a true leader of men, the person who, with the help of his wife Marina, organized everything.

The next day, all the players received a phone call telling us to report to Anfield. We were told that we were also expected to attend a memorial service at the Catholic cathedral in the evening. It was then that the real horror of Hillsborough dawned on me. I remember walking through the Shankly Gates and being overwhelmed by it all. Flowers, rosettes, banners and scarves wherever you looked – and so many people! Families, friends, the players, all having come to pay tribute to those supporters who had died. I couldn't understand what had happened.

If somebody had said there'd been fighting or rioting like there was at Heysel then maybe it might have been easier, but there'd been no trouble at all. Those supporters who were in the front at the Leppings Lane End – having arrived nice and early – were the ones who paid the price. It was almost impossible to take it all in.

All the players were devastated, but it was especially hard on local lads like Steve McMahon and John Aldridge. They were from the city, from the sort of families who were now counting the cost of supporting Liverpool. On the Monday morning we went to the two hospitals in Sheffield where the survivors were being treated. We sat and listened to their stories and heard about the horror first hand. It was gruesome stuff but there was no alternative. We had to, and wanted to, help in any way we could.

During the next ten days or so, Anfield became both a shrine and a sanctuary. Grieving relatives and friends were able to lay their flowers on the pitch and make use of the offices. Coffee and biscuits were provided and the players were on hand to talk and listen to the victims' relatives, trying to help them through. It was difficult, simply because some of us were just young footballers with very little experience of death or grief. I was 25, and I admit I found it hard.

I would sit with a family who'd just lost somebody and I wouldn't know what to say. So I'd ask them what had happened to their relatives, but we'd end up talking football. Who was his or her favourite player, and did they go to many games? These were the kinds of thing we'd ask them. All the families were urging us to go on and win the Double because they said that's what the victims would have wanted. 'Go and win it for them' was the clear message from the bereaved to the Liverpool players.

The club rightly issued a statement saying that a past or present player would attend every funeral. I went to eight, and they were pretty harrowing. Before Hillsborough I'd only been to my grandad's funeral. I found it difficult, but we were there as ambassadors of Liverpool Football Club. Sometimes I went to the house first, sometimes straight to the church.

John Barnes and I attended one funeral at Warrington, where half the Manchester United side and Alex Ferguson were present – that was typical of the way it touched everybody. Players from Everton, Tranmere and Manchester City also attended funerals in their area. John and I went to another funeral in Birkenhead for two young brothers. We called in at the house first and the family were hysterical. The boys were only 18 or 19 – they hadn't even started their lives. They died for something as meaningless as football. I must admit it was difficult for me to get my head round it.

I found it impossible to put myself in their place, to try to imagine what it was like to lose a relative. Perhaps, though, it was slightly easier for me than some of the other players to understand, because my son Kingsley was nearly two years old. Like everyone else, becoming a parent changed my life. All of a sudden, Kingsley became the most important thing in it – he gave me new responsibilities. When Kingsley was born, Mandy and I weren't living together, but once we were settled in our house, we built a nice, solid home base for Kingsley and then Karina. Football became not just a career for me but a means of looking after my family. Mandy has been a tower of strength over the years, and I've been accepted as a member of the wider Merseyside family.

In the aftermath of Hillsborough, I tended just to listen. If the families wanted us with them during the early stages of bereavement then that was fine, but often words didn't make it any better. Sometimes they can only make it worse. Although I spent a lot of time with the relatives, I didn't make any lasting friendships with any of the families – unlike Kenny and some of the players.

At the time, I don't think we appreciated what Kenny was doing. Having been a manager myself for a couple of years, I'm more aware of the responsibilities he had then. Football clubs are often owned by individuals or companies but, at the end of the day, the manager is at the helm. Kenny felt it was his football club and he took it upon himself to make sure that he comforted as many of the families as possible.

He dedicated himself to that job because their relatives had died supporting Liverpool. They had given their time and money and ultimately their lives to following his team. Kenny knew this was the right thing to do and he and Marina took it upon themselves to do their best.

On some days there were as many as ten funerals being held, and Kenny attended as many of them as he could. He spent every hour of the day at Anfield talking to the bereaved families. During the grieving period, we players had a choice. We came into Anfield in the morning but we could go home when we'd had enough. Kenny came in and stayed until there was no one else left. Like the ground itself, Kenny was available to anyone at any time. If there was still a family at Anfield at ten o'clock at night, Kenny would be there with them.

Whatever bill he had to pay, he was prepared to pay it later. As he was still quite a young man, Kenny probably thought he could handle it. I think even if he'd known the effect Hillsborough would have on him, he would have done it anyway, simply because he felt it was right. It was something he just had to do.

Anfield was an open house for about ten days. Relatives and friends kept coming to the ground to lay their flowers. It came to an end because it had to. At some stage, we had to get back to playing. For a start, we had the semi-final against Forest to finish. Kenny was very annoyed about the Football Association's obsession with a deadline for the Forest game. Eventually, nearly a fortnight after Hillsborough, we resumed training in preparation for our first match back, the next day. Because of the close links between the two clubs, it had been decided that we'd play Celtic at Parkhead with all the proceeds going to the Hillsborough Fund. Our first competitive match was against Everton in the League, in front of 46,000 at Goodison on another emotional occasion.

It was unbelievable that the two clubs most affected by Hillsborough should face each other in our first fixture after the tragedy. The camaraderie between the teams had been strengthened by the Everton players attending many of the funerals, and the game gave their supporters the chance to show the world how deeply they'd been affected. Before the kick-off, the crowd sang 'You'll Never Walk Alone', but once the whistle blew, there was a game to be won. In the event, it turned out to be a typical 0–0 draw with very few chances. It didn't have the normal passion of a Merseyside derby because everyone, players and fans alike, was scared of stepping out of line. Liverpool had had a rough time in the media over Hillsborough, so we were all on our best behaviour. It was a huge relief to be back playing, and it was nice to return in an away game which was in effect at home in the city of Liverpool.

The aftermath of Hillsborough leaves a very bad taste in my mouth. I'm very unhappy about the way everything has been handled and I fully support those relatives who feel that justice just hasn't been done. What really annoys me is the way that compensation has been paid out to the police officers who were allegedly traumatized by the tragedy but the needs of the relatives have been ignored. It's not really about financial gain – it's about right and wrong.

Maybe people have been a little bit too scared to point the finger. I don't know all the details but there has been enough criticism to suggest that, on the day, things weren't quite as they should have been. Lord Justice Taylor, in his final report, said that 'the main reason for the disaster was the failure of police control', yet disciplinary charges against police officers on duty at the ground were later dropped.

The relatives obviously feel so strongly about it that they want something done. I think we would all like to know what happened. It's all very well saying, as the *Sun* did, that Liverpool fans arrived late and some of them were drunk, but that's been disproved. The *Sun*'s reporting of the tragedy was, as the evening paper the *Liverpool*

Echo said, 'a disgrace to journalism'. Under the headline 'THE TRUTH', it ran the following outrageous claims: 'Some fans picked pockets of victims; some fans urinated on the brave cops and some fans beat up PC giving kiss-of-life!' It also quoted the chairman of the South Yorkshire Police Federation as saying that there was mass drunkenness among the 3000 fans milling around the Leppings Lane entrance. Not surprisingly, the coverage became a big issue on Merseyside – it was us against the world. Liverpool people felt very strongly about it – and I was one of those people.

Hillsborough isn't something you want to be reminded about all the time because it was such a terrible tragedy, but you can understand why the people directly involved don't want it to be forgotten – they want to make sure it never happens again. They want justice and they want to know the truth. What actually happened on the day? Why were ninety-six Liverpool supporters crushed to death? Their relatives have a right to know why their loved ones died.

At least there will now be a permanent memorial at the scene of the tragedy (not at the Leppings Lane End but in a prominent position near the main entrance to Hillsborough). I'm amazed that it has taken ten years for the relatives to be provided with a place to visit to remember the dead and injured. I'm delighted that Liverpool, Sheffield Wednesday and the Hillsborough Family Support Group have finally come to an agreement over the memorial – it's long overdue.

PART FOUR

The Show Must Go On

It was always going to be difficult after Hillsborough. Much though they might have wanted to end their season there and then, Liverpool knew they had to carry on – if only for the hundreds of their supporters who had lost relatives in the tragedy. After a reasonable and respectful period of mourning, the team resumed playing and were swept along on an understandable tide of emotion.

When Nottingham Forest were eventually overcome in the restaged FA Cup semi-final, the scene was set for another assault on the coveted Double. Three League wins before Wembley then propelled Liverpool towards the top of the table alongside Arsenal. After the heartbreak of Hillsborough, it was asking a lot of Liverpool to pull it off. It was a tribute to the club, their players and their supporters that they so very nearly succeeded.

Jan Molby watched the climax to the most emotional season in Liverpool's history from the sidelines. Injured again, he was a mere spectator as Liverpool won the second Merseyside FA Cup Final but then failed to complete their second Double in three years. He watched in amazement from the tunnel as Michael Thomas dashed Liverpool's Championship hopes in the final seconds of an astonishing game.

Managerial tactical whims disrupted Jan's next season, and then life under Dalglish's long-term successor, Graeme Souness, turned out to be just as unpredictable.

After the first three years of his Anfield career, Jan was involved in an almost constant battle with his weight. So easy to put on, the extra pounds were so hard to take off . . . especially when injuries intervened. It had not been a problem when he played for Ajax.

'If you look at team photos from Jan's time in Amsterdam,' says Frank Rijkaard, 'he wasn't that heavy. It was just his physical make-up – he was a strong guy. He weighed more than the other players but he was much lighter than he became in England.'

At the height of his weight problem, Jan was taunted from the terraces about his size. The Great Dane was indeed a big man. Team-mates, as well as opposition supporters, appreciated his predicament.

'Both Jan and I were aware of his problem,' recalls Kenny Dalglish. 'But it's only the person involved who can do something about it. He should have done more and he himself would feel he should have done more – I think he would openly admit that.

'The discipline comes from the player himself. As a manager, you're not going to baby-sit people, are you? If they're not responsible enough to do it, then that's up to them. Unfortunately, we bore the consequences, and so does Jan, because he regrets that there are a lot of things which have gone unfulfilled in his career.'

'Maybe the pints in England have more calories . . . I don't know,' jokes Frank Rijkaard. 'Seriously, if Jan was drinking too much, he wouldn't have had such a successful career.'

Ian Rush disputes the theory that Jan was a big drinker. 'He may have been seen with a pint in his hand but he didn't put back any more or less than someone like me. He did try to diet, but it was just unfortunate that he seemed to put weight on very easily.

'It was funny . . . I would eat a bar of chocolate and it wouldn't affect me; Jan would have one and put on two or three pounds. It was down to his metabolism. It was hard for

Jan to cope with, especially when he was playing. But he was such a good player that he could still perform in the Premiership with that weight.'

'Right up to the day that he left Anfield,' says Alan Hansen, 'you knew that whenever he was on the ball, it was going to go to a red shirt . . . no matter what his weight was. He's probably the only player who was sixteen stone but could play so well. The problem was he couldn't get up and down, so he'd stand in the middle of the park and be given the ball. Then he'd play.

'People said he was slow. In actual fact, he was quick, but if you're carrying fifteen and a half or sixteen stone, there's no way you're going to be quick for a hundred per cent of the time. If he had been playing at fourteen stone, or something, then I think we'd have been talking about the best of the best.'

Mandy Molby observed her husband's fight for fitness at first hand. 'It was heart-breaking watching Jan cope with his injuries. He would decide to lose loads of weight and he'd do sit-ups in the garden, work out on the exercise bike and run for miles on the treadmill. Then he'd go and play a great game but be injured again the next match. But he always thought that the next season was going to be his year. His heart was there but his body just wasn't always willing.'

It is often said that Jan Molby peaked too soon and achieved too little. He was, after all, only 22 when the FA Cup and League title returned to Anfield together for the first time. Those two medals represented precisely half his achievement at Anfield.

'In all honesty, if you were critical at all of Jan,' says Alan Hansen, 'you would have to say that he has underachieved – because of the talent he had. I don't think there's any doubt about that. He won two Championships and two FA Cup medals, which was great, but it's a poor return for someone who should be looked upon as an all-time great because of his high level of ability. In my view, he was one of the top three as far as talent was concerned at Liverpool.'

Ian Rush disagrees with the view that Jan promised much but never really delivered. 'People say that Jan underachieved as a player, but his main problem was injuries.

'I don't think there's a right time to be successful. You can't say Jan was too young to win the Double at 22. Remember Pelé was helping Brazil win the World Cup when he was 17! When you're achieving success when you're young, you don't think anything of it. At Liverpool, we felt we would win the League and make another trip to Wembley the next season, so we didn't really appreciate it at the time.

'Not many players have achieved what Jan has. I think he was lucky in that he found the right club in Liverpool, and he's done very well for himself.'

'I don't think he achieved from his career what a person with his ability should have achieved,' maintains Kenny Dalglish. 'It was not entirely his own fault, but he made a contribution. He was successful – the medals he's got testify to that – but he wasn't as successful as he should have been.

'Jan was a very, very talented player, with a great knowledge and appreciation of how to play football, but he was also someone who never got as much from the game as he should have done. To be fair, he also picked up a couple of problems with his ankles and his foot. But that's the sixty-four-thousand-dollar question. Were the injuries down to bad luck, or bad living? Or was it just fate? I don't know.'

Four years after winning his last major honour at Anfield, and with loan spells at Barnsley and Norwich behind him, Jan Molby reluctantly bade farewell to Merseyside.

The Boot Room may have disappeared to make way for bigger and better press facilities, but its principles remained. When Roy Evans – whom Kenny Dalglish has described as 'one of the guardians of the Boot Room philosophy and tradition' – succeeded Graeme Souness as manager in 1994,

Liverpool returned to one of their own. Jan knew the rules and had always been prepared to abide by them. He realized that when Liverpool had no further use for you, it was time to go.

After being omitted from a European game squad in October 1995, Jan accepted that his future lay further afield.

The Friendly Final and the Unfriendly Finale

Although we hadn't played a League match for nearly three weeks because of Hillsborough, I don't think the delay had taken the edge off our game. We might have been drained emotionally, but what kept us going was the response from the relatives of the Hillsborough victims. They not only wanted us to win the Cup for those who'd died but the Double as well.

After beating Celtic 4–0 at Parkhead, with Kenny opening the scoring, our first League game after Hillsborough was the 0–0 draw with Everton at Goodison. It was a rather disappointing result but at least we hadn't lost and we were all relieved to be back in business. We then beat Forest 3–1 in the replayed FA Cup semi-final at Old Trafford to reach our third Final in four years. This was the game we had to win. We needed a big stadium because there was a lot of interest, and we were really up for it. After our lay-off we were ready to take on Forest, and we were much too strong for them. It was more important to reach the Final than win it. The chance of doing the Double was still on. Before the Wembley date with Everton, we narrowly beat Forest, Wimbledon and QPR in the League to keep in touch with Arsenal at the top. We knew it was going to be very tight but everyone was desperate to go one better than last season.

By the Cup Final I was building up my torn thigh muscle, doing some gentle jogging. It was the first time, apart from that first Charity Shield in 1984, that I'd been to Wembley with Liverpool without being involved at all in the action. I noticed that members of the overall party didn't get the same treatment as the squad players. We were dropped off outside the stadium and walked up Wembley Way through the crowds before making our way to the dressing room. Although I think we saw more of the build-up to the Final through not being in the squad.

In the aftermath of Hillsborough, the game became known as 'The Friendly Final' – Liverpool versus Everton, another Merseyside head-to-head and the first game where the fences were taken down since the tragedy. It was the day that Liverpool came to London, Gerry Marsden led the singing of a very emotional 'You'll Never Walk Alone', and it turned out to be a great occasion, if not a great game until the final stages. Post-Hillsborough it was fitting that two Merseyside teams were in the final.

I suppose really it was a game of two subs – Ian Rush, who came on to score two goals for us, and Stuart McCall, who popped in a couple for them. After John Aldridge had put us ahead early on, nothing much happened until the very last minute when Everton equalized through McCall to force extra time. Kenny was canny enough to have held on to Rushie until then but now was the moment to bring him on. He soon made it 2–1, although McCall equalized again before Rushie popped in the winner.

We were delighted to have won, but we still had two games to play in the League, against West Ham and Arsenal, both at Anfield. It was fantastic to lift the Cup because of what it meant to the club and our supporters, but mainly to the bereaved families. Hillsborough had put extra pressure on us, but we'd managed to deal with it. Now we wanted to go all the way and complete the Double.

The situation facing us then was pretty clear: we needed to win our last two games. For the West Ham match, Kenny preferred Rushie to Peter Beardsley and we romped home 5–1 in front of nearly 42,000. The glut of goals not only sent West Ham down; it meant that all we had to do to achieve the Double was not to lose to Arsenal by more than one goal. Personally, I was pleased that the last game was on a Friday night, because my sister was getting married the next day. I had it all planned: I'd celebrate our Double success and then catch the first flight to Denmark in the morning. But what do they say about the best laid plans of mice and men?

Looking back, I'm not sure whether those five goals against West

Ham did us any favours. If we'd needed to beat Arsenal, we might have approached the game differently. At least Arsenal knew what they had to do. They were three points behind us and they had to win by two clear goals to nick the title from under our noses. They could be positive, whereas we had to be defensive. They had to win – and we couldn't afford to lose – by two clear goals. The most important thing was to convince our players to go and win the game rather than play Russian roulette with goal difference.

As at Wembley on the previous Saturday, I was on the Liverpool bench just behind the dug-out. From what I remember, we took the game to Arsenal for an hour, but their opening goal proved the turning point. At half-time everything seemed to be going according to plan. There was no score and the message of Kenny's team talk was obvious. If we kept it tight, the title would be ours.

The first goal came seven minutes into the second half from an indirect free-kick on the left side of our defence. Nigel Winterburn floated the ball over to the far post with his left foot and it ended up in our net. We were unhappy about two things: a challenge by David O'Leary as the ball came across and then what initially appeared to be a wrong decision by the referee. We thought the ball had gone straight into the net from Winterburn's foot but the referee ignored his linesman's flag and ruled that Alan Smith had got the final touch to turn the indirect free-kick into a goal. After a lot of Liverpool protests, the referee did consult his linesman but stuck to his original decision. We were behind.

The implications immediately hit home. Arsenal realized that if they got one more, they could take the title. I think the goal affected the result because, perhaps understandably, we became more defensive.

As the game wore on, I remember Ronnie Moran telling those of us who weren't playing to go and get changed into our kit. I had made enough appearances to pick up a winner's medal and we would all be taking part in the victory celebrations, including a lap of honour. We were just on our way down to put on our tracksuits when Michael Thomas scored Arsenal's second goal in the very last minute.

We were waiting in the tunnel just wanting to catch the final few seconds of the game when Michael made up for a miss fifteen minutes earlier by striding through our defence and sweeping the ball past Bruce Grobbelaar. Thirty seconds later the final whistle blew. We'd blown it. We'd been denied the Double in successive seasons by a single goal, but this time in the most dramatic of fashions.

There surely can't be a worse way to lose a title – by a goal in the last minute of the last game? And that at the end of one of the most traumatic seasons in British football. It might have made fantastic viewing for the fifteen million people sitting at home in front of their television sets, but down on the Liverpool bench nobody could believe it. You get these moments in football when you just can't take in what has happened. There was no shouting or screaming or grabbing other people by the throat. Kenny was horrified. He just looked at Ronnie and Roy. They, too, couldn't believe what had happened.

We had played 42 League games, and as we went into the last one I don't think anyone in their wildest dreams thought we were going to lose the title. Despite Hillsborough, I think the supporters had enjoyed the season. We'd played some good football and won the FA Cup, but after Michael's goal went in there was total silence on the terraces and in the stands. The Kop was quiet. They couldn't believe it either. It was pretty subdued in the dressing room too until Ronnie Moran, as usual, reminded us how many days there were left until pre-season training and told us to go and enjoy our summer. Kenny was no different to normal. He said little apart from making it clear that he couldn't fault any of the players – they had given their all – and he didn't blame anybody for the winning goal.

It had been a pretty harrowing season all round for me. The shock of spending six weeks in prison was followed by yet another long-term injury and then Hillsborough. The tragedy put everything into perspective. The elation of beating Everton in the Cup Final was soon replaced by the despair of Arsenal's snatch-and-grab victory at Anfield, but the next day I went off to Denmark for my sister's wedding. It was the start of a rare summer free from football. My number one priority was to get fit – and get my career back on track.

Normal Service Resumed

By the time pre-season began, I was pretty well back to full fitness. Liverpool's eighteenth League title was to provide me with my second Championship medal but 1989–90 turned out to be a funny sort of season. I was in and out of the first team depending on Kenny's tactical thinking at the time.

I didn't make the first-term squad until the 9–0 hammering of Crystal Palace at Anfield in September, when I was on the bench. It was our fifth League game after a disappointing start, and John Aldridge's last for Liverpool before he went off to Real Sociedad for a million pounds. After the Palace game I didn't come back into the reckoning until November, again as sub, and then I played in all but one of the next nine games.

There followed another period out of the squad before I returned in April, first as a sub and then in the starting line-up. I found myself playing more in away games than those at Anfield. Kenny explained his plans to all of us and when I was in the side I was happy. Ronnie Whelan and Steve McMahon had struck up a good partnership in the middle and I was pleased to play anywhere. I always felt that Kenny would try to find a place for me somewhere in the side.

My first reaction to not being in the team was to work a little bit harder. I never knocked on Kenny's door to ask him why I wasn't playing because I could see sense in his thinking. More and more, he would look at who we were playing and then pick his team accordingly. He would choose players whom he felt would perform best against the opposition, and it usually worked.

There was no point in sulking because you knew that once Kenny had made his mind up, that was it. I remember how it worked in a game against Millwall, who, in those days, were a very direct team, with Tony Cascarino and Teddy Sheringham up front. We knew to expect an aerial bombardment, so Kenny stuck me in as a sweeper.

157

He'd played three at the back with me as the spare man. The tactic worked well and we won 2–1, but then I was left out for the next game when we beat Arsenal 2–1 at Anfield. I wasn't even on the bench, but then I played in midfield against Sheffield Wednesday and we lost 2–0. It was always frustrating when I wasn't playing, but whether I was in or out of the team, I didn't ask questions. The majority of the players at Anfield were bright enough to know what Kenny was trying to do and respected his decisions. We accepted the squad system and just got on with it.

Personally, I was happy wherever Kenny wanted to play me. I was wide on the left at Manchester City, then right-back against Villa at Anfield, wide left at Chelsea and then in the middle of the park at home against Manchester United. I had to be realistic: I wasn't a regular, I only started 12 League games, and when my frustration got to me I would look at the players around me. I then realized that it was no disgrace being in the squad and, more often than not, Kenny would at least use me.

And I wasn't the only one who was affected by his tactical whims. Peter Beardsley and Ray Houghton also suffered, with Peter often sitting on the bench when Kenny put the accent on defence. Everyone was disappointed to be left out, but you had to be man enough to encourage the rest of the team, and when your chance came you had to take it. Mind you, sometimes you did just that and Kenny would still leave you out for the next game. I suppose I could have become a regular somewhere else and improved my chances of playing for Denmark, but I never thought about moving on. Every now and then I would get linked with one or two clubs but I thought that if Liverpool didn't want me, they would come and tell me. Until that happened, I was happy to stay put.

After beating Everton to win the FA Cup, we quite fancied our chances of making it a hat-trick of Wembley appearances. Swansea paid the price for holding us to a 0–0 draw at the Vetch Field in the third round when we walloped them 8–0 in a replay at Anfield, and then we beat Norwich, QPR and Southampton on our way to the semi-final against Crystal Palace at Villa Park. The Twin Towers were beckoning and the result seemed a formality as we'd already beaten Palace 9–0 and 2–0 in the League. I wasn't included in our squad of thirteen so I watched what one of the tabloids later called 'the biggest FA Cup semi-final upset in history' from the main stand.

In many ways, it was very much like the Wimbledon defeat at Wembley two years earlier. The hot favourites against the no-hopers. We felt we had the better of the draw – the other semi-final had paired Oldham with Manchester United – and although we had the psychological edge over them through the two League wins, on the day Palace played out of their skins. At the time, we were being criticized for the way we defended at dead-ball situations, and it was true that Palace scored three headers from long throws and corners. They may have pinpointed what they thought were our weaknesses on the day, but I never felt it was a problem.

Jocky Hansen took a lot of stick afterwards and while he might have lost his fair share of headers in that semi-final, if you'd have played the same game with the same amount of balls coming in on another day, they wouldn't have scored. Palace were a little bit more fired up for that semi-final and they put a lot of quality balls into the box for big people like Mark Bright, Eric Young and Andy Gray. We had played plenty of teams with direct styles, like Millwall, Wimbledon and Palace, and it wasn't the norm for us to let in three or four goals. It was just one of those days. I don't think Alan was losing it at all. Nobody in the club attached a great deal of blame to Alan for that defeat. People outside may have been looking for excuses, and one of them was that Jocky couldn't deal with high balls, but it wasn't true. Palace felt that this was the way to get at Liverpool and there was always one team who managed to do it every season. It wasn't something which happened on a regular basis. But on the day they did score – four to our three over 120 minutes – and they deserved to win. So, once again, for the third successive season, we were denied the Double – this time at the semi-final stage.

Whenever we were beaten in important games during the late eighties and early nineties, we didn't worry because we knew we'd be back the next season. We always felt that we would make our mark – especially in Cup games. We were very difficult to beat in one-off situations and we always felt we would win – even if it took

159

a replay. We did slip up in a number of crucial games but, then again, if we had won them, our success rate would have been ridiculous. We would have completely dominated English football (apart from 1987, when Everton easily won the League and Coventry beat Spurs in the Cup Final). We would have won the Double so many times that it would have been unreal. No one could dominate football like that, although I accept that Manchester United are doing it at the moment.

We clinched the title by beating Derby 1–0 at Anfield as Aston Villa, our nearest challengers, drew 2–2 at home. That game will always hold a special place in my memory because I came off with 20 minutes left so that a little piece of history could be made. I'd broken my nose in a clash with Geraint Williams and Kenny insisted that I leave the field. He then brought himself on for his very last game for Liverpool. I was disappointed to be substituted so that Kenny could have a final run-out but, after all, I had broken my nose and Kenny was the boss. Kenny later claimed that he'd swung the game because it was 0–0 when he came on! I'm not sure I remember it quite that way, but helping to win the Championship in front of his adoring fans at Anfield was a fitting way for Kenny to achieve what turned out to be his last major success with Liverpool.

Our final game was away at Coventry who, for once, had nothing to play for. With the temperature in the nineties, we thought we'd take it easy, and nobody really wanted to bother until Coventry scored early on. The goal stirred something in us, we felt under a bit of pressure, and we went on to win 6–1. John Barnes scored a hat-trick and 'Rocket' Ronnie Rosenthal got two. He was still on loan then, having scored three on his full debut against Charlton to become a real favourite with the fans.

Looking back at that run-in, Ronnie Rosenthal was probably the reason we won the title. He scored seven goals in eight games, which meant Kenny had to pay a million rather than £600,000 to buy him from Standard Liège. Ronnie wasn't quite as sensational as David 'Supersub' Fairclough, but he would unsettle opponents with his running, robust style and amazing ability to hang on to the ball. People outside Liverpool used to mock Ronnie a little – partly because of his style but mainly because of all the amazing sitters he used to miss. Probably the most famous one was against Villa when he took the ball around the keeper and then somehow managed to hit the crossbar! I think he felt he had his part to play – he was really a natural sub. If he started a game, he'd more than likely be taken off, and if he came on as a sub he'd more than likely score a goal or two.

There might have been rumblings in the media about the way Liverpool were playing, but you'd never hear players whispering about either Kenny's tactics or each other in the corridors of the ground itself. Not all the media men got on with Kenny; they couldn't get through to him, and this was their way of getting back. When we lost games, they blamed his tactics, but within the football club everyone was 100 per cent behind him. It was in everybody's interests for the team to do well. It was all for one and one for all during that season. Everyone in the squad wanted to be in the first team, but we all felt that we would benefit from being at a successful club. And in winning the title again, Liverpool had shown that they were a very successful club.

It's true that we hadn't become Champions with the same style as in 1988, and many more of our opponents were ground down rather than swept aside, but the club had shown great spirit in bouncing back from the Hillsborough tragedy and that dramatic last-minute defeat by Arsenal at Anfield. Apart from the FA Cup semi-final upset, it had been normal service resumed for Liverpool. As it turned out, it was merely the calm before the storm. There was more drama just around the corner.

His Master's Voice

When I came back for the 1990–91 season, I was raring to go. Denmark hadn't qualified for Italia '90 and a summer away from the game had whetted my appetite. My batteries were recharged, I felt fighting fit and I couldn't wait to pick up where we'd left off the previous May.

We made a terrific start. Eight straight wins in the League and only one defeat in our first eighteen games. I played in the opening match at Sheffield United but was injured and missed a couple of games before returning for the 2–1 win at Wimbledon in early September. I was then in and out of the team before settling in the middle of midfield from the New Year. But towards the end of October, my Liverpool career suddenly looked to be coming to an end.

Under Kenny Dalglish, I'd had the privilege of learning from one of the greatest players in British football. Suddenly, right out of the blue, came the call from the Master, Johan Cruyff. He was now managing Barcelona and it looked as if another country was about to be stamped on to my passport.

It all began when I received a message to ring Tony Slot-Brown, whom I'd known as the reserve-team manager at Ajax. I wondered what he could want? I hadn't seen Tony for six years. What I didn't know was that he was now assistant to Johan at the Nou Camp. After quickly exchanging the usual pleasantries, Tony explained Barcelona's problem.

Ronald Koeman, their sweeper, whom I'd played with at Ajax, had snapped his Achilles tendon. He could be out until the end of the season and they needed a replacement. The penny took a moment to drop. Tony then said that, as they'd been discussing Ronald's injury, he'd run through a few names with Cruyff. When mine came up, Johan had stopped him: 'That's who I want,' he'd said. Tony then made the phone call to Merseyside.

I was a bit shocked at first because I couldn't remember saying fifty words to Johan in our year together. I remember him filling my head with millions of words about various things, but I suppose I must have made some sort of impression for him to want me. He obviously remembered me playing sweeper for Ajax and I saw his interest as a great compliment. As Ronald had only been injured the day before, I was probably the first player they had approached. When Tony asked me if I was interested, I said he'd have to deal with Liverpool, but I was obviously attracted by the prospect of teaming up with Michael Laudrup at one of the world's greatest clubs, under Johan Cruyff.

I explained to Tony that our next game was away at Manchester United in the third round of the Rumbelows Cup the following Wednesday, and when I went into training the next day Tony was there in the office with Kenny. He seemed keen to get it all wrapped up. I didn't have a great game against United in a match we lost 3–1. Then on the Sunday, we were at Spurs in a televised live match on the BBC. Tony was watching again and this time I played well in a 3–1 win. The game had also been shown live in Spain. Negotiations were under way.

I don't think that Kenny particularly wanted to sell me, but he felt that every player had his price. I was led to believe that Liverpool had agreed a fee of £1.6 million with Barcelona, and Kenny felt that as I wasn't a regular in the first team it was a fair return for the club. I don't know whether I was seen by Barcelona just as a six-month replacement for Ronald, but I didn't really care. My aim was to get into the first team and make Ronald fight to win back his place.

On the following Thursday, we agreed my terms with Barcelona and two days later I played what should have been my last game for Liverpool, against Luton at Anfield. I scored a penalty in a pretty comfortable 4–0 win in front of 35,000. Afterwards, I went up to Peter Robinson's office to sign a registration release document and then flew to Denmark to prepare for the midweek international against Yugoslavia. As far as I was concerned, the deal was done and dusted. To all intents and purposes, I was now a Barcelona player.

The next night, I was lying in my hotel room in Copenhagen watching television at about eleven o'clock when the phone rang. It was Radio Barcelona wanting my reaction to the news that the transfer had been called off! The reporter brushed aside my doubts and said he didn't know why the deal had fallen through. Then Kenny rang to confirm it.

'Whatever the reasons,' he said, 'I'm afraid it's off. It's not going to happen. So play the game for Denmark and then come back to Anfield.'

When I put the phone down, I was in a bit of a state. My dream move to Barcelona had been called off for reasons beyond me and beyond Kenny. I had all my gear with me and I'd sold my car in England. I'd given up the house we were renting: I was all ready to go. I was very disappointed – as was Michael Laudrup. He'd found a house for me near his, with room for a pool table. Apparently, you couldn't go out at all in Barcelona because of their fanatical supporters, so Michael had it all planned. The women would mind the children and we'd spend all day playing pool!

Rumours were rife that the deal fell through over the way the money was due to be paid. Liverpool wanted it all up front because they claimed they'd had one or two bad experiences with Barcelona in the past, and it just never happened. I've since found out that Liverpool wouldn't agree to Barcelona's request to take me on loan. I've always believed that what is meant to happen will happen.

Although I was a bit depressed, it wasn't a big problem going back to Liverpool. They were still one of the best clubs in the world. I'd been half-set on the move, though. When Rushie went to Juventus in 1987 I remember being linked with clubs like Real Madrid and Hamburg, but I was playing well at Liverpool and didn't want to leave. But Barcelona in 1990 really appealed to me and, looking back over what they've achieved since then, I suppose I could have been part of a very successful team if I'd signed the four-year deal.

When I returned to Anfield, I had to put up with a lot of mickey-taking from the other players. It was fair enough, but one or two of them knew that I was a bit upset. In fact, it was one of those weeks. Two days after the Barcelona deal had fallen through, Denmark lost 2–0 to Yugoslavia in what turned out to be my last international game. I was never in the squad again.

After my rather traumatic week, Kenny left me out of the Liverpool set-up for the 1–0 win at Coventry, but he seemed pleased to have me back. He said he'd never really wanted me to leave. As I settled down to life in Liverpool again, my feeling was that I was coming towards the end of my last contract with the club. It had only a year to run, and Liverpool had already shown their hand by trying to sell me. Little did I know that it would be Kenny rather than me who'd be leaving Anfield before the season was out.

The King is Dead . . . Long Live Champagne Charlie

When Kenny resigned as manager of Liverpool on Friday 22 February 1991, he stayed true to form. He had always been a man of few words, and when he came into the Anfield dressing room that morning, shoulders hunched, he didn't say much. He looked drained, his eyes were bloodshot. We could see there was something wrong. His comments were brief and to the point.

'Thanks for everything you've done, boys,' he said. 'I've got no complaints in the years I've been here as manager. I wish you all the best for the future, but I'll no longer be in charge – I've had enough. I'm not prepared to do the job any more. I'm resigning.'

And with that, after shaking hands with everybody, he left. For a moment or two, nobody said anything. We were too stunned. I remember glancing around the dressing room. There were looks of disbelief on every face. Then Roy Evans confirmed it: 'We've all spent the last twenty-four hours trying to talk him out of it,' he said. 'But he's made up his mind.'

And everyone knew it was the end of an era. Kenny Dalglish was a man of his word. His decision to resign took everyone by surprise – the supporters, the board, the backroom staff, and especially the players. We knew that he'd been criticized during the season – particularly over his tactics and his treatment of Peter Beardsley – but when he decided to leave, we were gobsmacked. We were three points clear of Arsenal in the League and still in the fifth round of the FA Cup. We had everything to play for, but the unthinkable had happened. Kenny Dalglish, my mentor and the man who had made my career, had walked out of Liverpool. At the time, I wasn't aware of any build-up of the pressure which Kenny has subsequently blamed for his resignation. In hindsight, it's easy to look back and say that maybe there were one or two little tell-tale signs.

After the Barcelona deal fell through in November, I was in and out of the first team for a couple of months as we led the table. For once, I benefited from an injury problem instead of suffering from one. For the second half of the season, we were without both Steve McMahon and Ronnie Whelan, so I had a regular place in midfield from the start of 1991. Jocky Hansen missed all the season through injury, which meant we weren't at our strongest in defence.

But the only major hiccup in the League was our first defeat of the season in early December against Arsenal at Highbury. They'd just been walloped 6–2 at home by Manchester United in the Rumbelows Cup, but they bounced back to beat us 3–0. Some people later suggested that this was the moment that Kenny decided to leave Liverpool. Others pointed to our 3–1 defeat by United at Old Trafford in the Rumbelows Cup in November.

As I've already admitted, I had a poor game against United, but then so did nearly everyone else. At half-time, Kenny gave us some stick, before being on the receiving end himself as the press laid into the team – the first of many attacks on what were perceived as his negative tactics during the season. Because it was the Rumbelows Cup and not the League, I don't remember too many people in Anfield making too much of that defeat.

Liverpool also had this knack of bouncing back from very poor performances. After the Man United humiliation, we played Spurs at White Hart Lane in a televised game. They were going well – unbeaten and third in the table – and Kenny chose an ultra-defensive team. He dropped Peter Beardsley and Ray Houghton and brought in me and Gary Ablett. This was the way Kenny often operated. He would tell thirteen players that they'd be involved but wouldn't say who was actually playing until forty-five minutes before kick-off. He was trying to keep the opposition in the dark, but maybe this was a sign of the pressure he was starting to feel. Kenny would pick a team to do a particular job on our opponents rather than put out the best Liverpool eleven. It worked against Spurs – my old flat-mate David Burrows kept Paul Gascoigne quiet and we won 3-1.

Then we demolished Luton 4–0 to end the mini-crisis. But three League games later, Kenny's team selection was being blamed for that defeat against Arsenal. The press had done their usual job of hyping up the match, and after their mauling by Man United Arsenal were really under pressure. Kenny went back to a six-man defence to protect our six-point lead at the top of the table, and Peter was left out of the squad altogether.

We fell behind to a disputed goal just before the break, then Arsenal were awarded a very debatable penalty and eventually ran out 3–0 winners. It was the first time we hadn't scored all season and our heaviest defeat for more than a year. It was said we'd been punished for being too cautious, but we'd gone to Arsenal in the past and absorbed their pressure before catching them on the break. On the day, we were bad and they were very good. Arsenal never gave us the chance to play, they overpowered us. We knew what Kenny wanted to do because he'd told us before the game. We could see it all made sense, but it just didn't come off. If things had come off every time, then we'd all have a lot more medals in our cabinets. Whatever pressure Kenny himself may have felt under, we never had the feeling that he was losing his grip on the team. He always seemed to be in control of what he was doing before and after games.

But for the first time anyone could remember, Kenny then had a go at us in public after the Arsenal game. He just let rip. He said we hadn't done ourselves justice and wouldn't have won even if we'd had twelve players to Arsenal's eleven. But again, although we were embarrassed by the shocking way we'd played, nobody in the dressing room picked up on his public criticism.

I think Kenny sometimes made things too complicated – and I think he might now agree with that. He's got such a fine footballing brain, and he was busy trying to create the Kenny Dalglish style. The idea of choosing certain players for home games and different ones when you're away was used abroad, but I don't think players in Britain were ready to cope with it. Maybe now, with managers like Gianlucca Vialli in charge, it stands more change of working but, at the time, it might have been better to stick with 4–4–2 and let the opposition worry about us.

Picking a side to match a particular opposition certainly made sense to me because I'd been brought up like that at club and international level in Denmark and with Ajax, but it was very unusual for a British team to do that. Liverpool had always followed the philosophy of letting the opposition worry about us, but Kenny wasn't your average guy – he wanted to do things his own way. Over the duration of the season, I think we would be more successful with 4–4–2, but on the odd occasion you could change the formation and get away with it. But I think that players rather than systems win you games. You develop a system that suits your players. A manager probably prefers to have a big squad where players are regularly interchangeable, but footballers see being in the first team – rather than just a member of the squad – as the best thing in the world. Flexible players are a godsend to a manager. You can change the course of a game by using your substitutes but if you have flexible players already on the pitch, it gives you more options and you might not have to use your substitutes. In those days, if Liverpool wanted a new right-back, they'd go out and buy the best one available. They didn't look for flexible players. Steve Nicol was a rarity because he could play in more than one position – as players have to do more these days – but most of the squad then were specialists.

I think Kenny was a little too far ahead of his time. He didn't have the players to put his theories into practice, and he was getting frustrated. One of the things I really admired about Kenny was the way he managed to keep so many players happy. Occasionally somebody would have a dig at him but most of us were pleased to be involved in his flexible formations because, in those days, it really meant something to be at Anfield. Nowadays, I feel footballers don't worry who they play for, but we wanted to play for Liverpool – if not one week then maybe the next.

Our form in the New Year was disappointing compared with the way we'd started the season, but we were still there or thereabouts at the beginning of February. David Speedie, signed from Coventry for nearly £700,000, was a breath of fresh air. He scored on his debut in a 1–1 draw at Old Trafford and then bagged two as we beat Everton 3–1 at Anfield. I scored the other – the first of eight before the end of the season, seven of which were penalties.

It was our performance in the FA Cup fifth-round replay against Everton three days later which appeared to push Kenny over the edge. In fact, he'd already decided to leave Liverpool before the game – regardless of the result. The first meeting had been a drab 0–0 draw at Anfield, in which Steve McMahon's challenge on John Ebbrell left him with torn knee tendons and Liverpool without his services for the rest of the season.

Back at Goodison on the following Wednesday, one of the most amazing matches in the history of Merseyside derbies took place, when we drew 4–4. For what turned out to be his last game in charge, Kenny again shuffled the pack. Peter Beardsley came in for Speedie, who was on the bench.

It was a game which should have been beyond Everton. Four times we were ahead, but they kept coming back. They hardly had a kick, we had loads of chances; but every time we scored, so did they. Peter put us ahead just before half-time only for Graeme Sharp to equalize straight after the break. Then a wonderful solo goal by Peter made it 2–1 midway through the second half but, almost immediately, up popped Graeme with Everton's second equalizer! When I crossed for Rushie to head us in front again about five minutes later, we all thought it would be the winner.

But Everton refused to give up and, in the final seconds, substitute Tony Cottee took the tie into extra time. Kenny was beside himself. I remember him shouting from the dug-out like a man possessed. Near the end of the first period of extra time, John Barnes made it 4–3 with a beautiful chip, before Cottee grabbed the final Everton equalizer after Glen Hysen and I were involved in a bit of a mix-up. Goodison Park went mad and, I suspect, so did Kenny. On the bench, there were similar looks to those I'd seen when Arsenal pipped us for the title two years before. As we trooped off the pitch to the dressing room, the gloves were about to come off.

It might have been an exciting game for the spectators but, for

169

Liverpool, the result was a disaster. I'd played in some high-scoring games with Ajax, though for Liverpool to be involved in a four-all draw was very unusual. We should have buried Everton and we knew it. And Ronnie Moran made sure we knew it.

Post-match rows were nothing new in the Liverpool dressing room, but this was bad. It was eyeball-to-eyeball stuff. The worst one I can remember. Ronnie and Roy Evans were having a go at the defence for conceding the two late goals, and so were the forwards. As soon as they were scoring goals, the defence was letting them in! Everyone was shouting at everyone else, Ronnie had a huge argument with Bruce Grobbelaar. It was all very nasty. At one stage I thought it would end in a fight. But that was the Liverpool way. We wanted to win so badly that it didn't matter afterwards whom you'd upset or whose toes you'd stood on – people just wanted answers.

While all the ranting and raving was going on, Kenny hardly spoke. He just stood with his back against the wall staring at the floor. After about fifteen minutes, Kenny calmly declared that we would discuss our performance on Friday morning. We got changed and went for a beer in the bar with the Everton players where the inquest continued, but without the histrionics. Never in a million years did anyone think that Kenny was about to quit.

We had the Thursday off and knew we had to be in early the next day to travel to Luton. We wanted to train on their plastic pitch before the League game at Kenilworth Road. We knew there was something wrong when we arrived at Anfield on the Friday morning. The media were everywhere. This wasn't a normal press conference. None of the players knew what had happened but the feeling was that we'd probably signed someone. After all, our season had started to wobble a bit. Although we were top of the League and still in the Cup, we were grinding out results. Perhaps a new player would help steady things.

The girl on reception knew something was up but she wouldn't say anything. It was strange. We all went to sit in the players' lounge when suddenly Ronnie came in and told us to go to the dressing room. Then Kenny dropped his bombshell. At first we thought he'd resigned because the board had turned down a request for money for a new signing. We thought there was more to this than met the eye.

There was a lot of speculation on Merseyside, including a far-fetched story about a row between Kenny's and Peter Beardsley's wives. That was rubbish. I remember hearing Kenny on the radio explaining his reasons – people didn't seem prepared to accept the fact that he'd simply had enough, the pressure had become too much. He was fed up with all the rumours and wanted to put the record straight – as he later did in his autobiography. I think eventually Kenny thought that because he would be involved in football for a long time, the people he'd be working with needed to know why he'd left Liverpool – that's why he produced the book.

I've heard since that Kenny was covered in a rash as a result of the strain he was under. I don't remember seeing it during his last season, because we didn't get changed with him, but after the FA Cup semi-final against Portsmouth a year later, I recall discussing Kenny's resignation with Roy Evans. He told me that when he asked what was wrong, what the rash was, Kenny replied that he'd had enough, that he couldn't cope.

Looking back at his career and his involvement in the three tragedies at Ibrox, Heysel and Hillsborough, I'm not surprised that Kenny left Anfield. All three, especially Hillsborough, must have taken their toll. As well as those experiences, the stress of managing a successful club which had set itself such high standards had become too great. Kenny's desire to win was as great as anyone's I've ever come across, but this was obviously one battle he felt he had to lose. It seems he just had to leave Liverpool.

It was a difficult time for everyone at Anfield after Kenny resigned. I think Ronnie felt that the manager's job was a step too far for him. He had always been quite happy as first-team coach and, although he'd been offered the job once or twice before, he'd always declined. This time, though, we thought he'd accept it because of the Liverpool tradition of promoting from within.

Roy's name was mentioned but it was thought he wasn't quite ready to take over. John Toshack, Steve Heighway and Phil Thompson were also talked about, and then there was Jocky – Kenny's big mate, a fellow Scot and another man who knew his own mind. We thought he might be the one to take the job, and he did, briefly. One morning, we were sitting in the dressing room and Jocky walked in.

'Morning, chaps,' he said. 'I'm your new manager. I've accepted the job and I'm going to make a few changes.'

We just sat there and listened as he told us how life would be different at Liverpool under the Hansen regime.

'I know where all the boys on the Wirral drink,' he began, 'and that's out-of-bounds now. And I know where the Southport lads drink – that's out-of-bounds too.'

Some of us looked at each other in amazement. Were we hearing things or was this for real?

'I'll be changing training,' continued Jocky. 'There'll be a new club captain and certain club rules. We'll come in on a Sunday and watch Saturday's game on video -- we'll be together a lot more. OK?'

As he left the room, Jocky shook hands with Ronnie and Roy, who congratulated him on his appointment – and then it started. There was uproar, pandemonium even. Grown men almost reduced to tears as we tried to take in what Jocky had said.

'What's he playing at?' cried Steve Nicol. 'He's been here for God knows how many years and he's going to change all the rules? The one rule at this club is that you don't change anything!'

What really hit home with us was the ban on Sunday drinking. We remembered Jocky doing his fair share as a player. Wasn't it funny how people changed when they became managers? While all this was going on, Jocky was standing outside listening. After a couple of minutes, he popped his head round the door and spoke two words: 'Only joking!'

Jocky was delighted that his wind-up had worked. He then explained that he was retiring because of trouble with his knees. It really was the end of an era.

The next time we saw Kenny was a couple of months later when we went down to Highbury to play in Ray Kennedy's testimonial, after Graeme Souness had taken over. He came on the bus with us but nobody asked him about his resignation. He was that kind of man. Whatever decision he had made, we all respected it. But he was happy to talk about the long family holiday he'd just been on.

Ronnie made it clear when he succeeded Kenny that he would only do the job on a temporary basis. To be honest, even if he had wanted it to be permanent, our results did nothing to help his cause. In the first game as caretaker manager, the cameras were all over Kenilworth Road. None of the players wanted to speak about Kenny's resignation because nobody knew the full details. We lost 3–1 – I scored another penalty – and then our season started to fall apart in a big way.

Everton knocked us out of the FA Cup with a Dave Watson goal in the second replay, and then we lost at home to Arsenal, 1–0. We were still in with a chance of winning the League but we never really sustained our challenge. After Kenny left, we won only half of our fourteen League games. Ronnie's ten games in charge resulted in four wins, one draw and five defeats. He went out with a bang though. In his last game as caretaker we were 4–0 up at half-time, against Leeds at Elland Road, before hanging on to win 5–4. Under Graeme Souness, we won three and lost two in the League to finish the season in second place, 7 points behind Arsenal.

When Souness arrived at Anfield in April 1991, I wasn't worried. We all respected him both as a player with Liverpool and Sampdoria and as a manager with Rangers. The board wanted a big name to replace Kenny to satisfy the supporters. Souness fitted the bill. It might have gone against the principle of appointing from within, from the Boot Room, but Souness had been at the club before, so he wasn't a complete outsider.

I had played against him in the 1986 World Cup for Denmark and he'd also tried to sign me for Rangers. When Liverpool had clinched the League at Derby the previous year, we'd discussed one or two things afterwards, but nothing ever came of it. According to Souness, I could play sweeper until I was 40 in Scotland, so it was no surprise that he wanted to use the same system – me as sweeper with Gary Gillespie and Gary Ablett marking. It went well – we beat both Norwich and Crystal Palace 3–0 at Anfield – but towards the end of the season, he made it clear that he didn't want me in his squad at Anfield.

173

In Souness's third game in charge, we lost 4–2 at Chelsea and I was one of the players he blamed for the defeat. He said I wouldn't be part of his plans because I wasn't suited to the way he wanted to play. Two days later, we lost 2–1 at Nottingham Forest – I played in midfield and scored another penalty – and then the following day he took us down to Lilleshall on a fitness drive. Souness thought we weren't in good enough shape, but if you look in the Lilleshall records you'll find that we're one of the fittest groups of footballers ever to have gone there. Nevertheless, Souness said he would turn us into the fittest squad in Britain the following season. As well as me, he had a pop at one or two other players, like John Barnes and Peter Beardsley.

I must admit I was surprised by his U-turn. Two weeks earlier, I had seemed to be an important member of the squad, but then suddenly I was surplus to requirements – even though I'd just signed a four-year contract! I hadn't played any worse than anyone else against Chelsea, but that game had somehow changed his mind.

We'd heard he was a little rash in making decisions – I now knew from personal experience that the rumour was well founded. I might have been dubbed the 'new Graeme Souness' when I arrived at Anfield back in 1984 but, seven years on, the new Graeme Souness – the one in the manager's seat – had decided that my Liverpool career was at an end.

The 'New Graeme Souness'

I had a love–hate relationship with Graeme Souness. Sometimes I could do no wrong; at other times, it seemed he wanted me nowhere near his team. It was strange and, to be honest, I couldn't work it out. I didn't seem to have much of a future at Liverpool, and by the summer of 1991 there was talk of me moving to one or two clubs, including Everton. A trip across Stanley Park wouldn't have gone down too well with our supporters, but I was quite keen on the idea.

We wouldn't have had to move house and I could show Liverpool what they'd missed out on by letting me go.

I knew my prospects under Souness weren't looking good when he picked his pre-season-tour squad of eighteen players for a trip to Norway. I hadn't been included, but on the day they left, Liverpool sold Steve Staunton to Aston Villa and I had to take his place. I was really there just to make up the numbers because I hardly played. I came on as sub every now and then. When we returned to Anfield, Souness had made his mind up about me.

His nickname as a player at Anfield had been 'Champagne Charlie'. He'd always liked the good things in life – smart clothes, fine food and wine and, of course, lots of bubbly. The image of the man with the high-profile lifestyle will stay with him for ever, even though when he returned to Anfield he was more or less teetotal. He still liked his nice clothes and cars, but the champagne had long gone, replaced by a tendency to pay large amounts of money for mediocre players.

During his time as a manager with Rangers, Souness had made a name for himself as a big spender, and at the start of the new season the comings and goings at Anfield were well under way. He'd already sold Peter Beardsley to Everton, Gary Gillespie had gone to Celtic, Barry Venison was on his way out, and he was in two minds over Ray Houghton.

Souness thought it was time to change, to bring in new blood; but I think he was a little ahead of himself in that the replacements were either not there or not ready. He didn't want me because he thought Jamie Redknapp, Mike Marsh and Don Hutchison were all better. Fair enough – at least I knew where I stood. All I could do was get myself fit by playing for the reserves, so that if someone did come in for me I'd be all ready to go. Even the latest in a long line of injuries couldn't stop me. During our match against Newcastle reserves at Anfield, I nicked a cartilage in my knee. After an operation, I was back within three weeks and played for the A team against Everton. Apparently, someone from Goodison was at the match and it looked as if a move was on. Then came another example of the extraordinary way Souness could change his mind.

With the post-Heysel ban lifted on Liverpool competing in Europe, we had qualified for the UEFA Cup as runners-up to Arsenal. In late October, we lost 2–0 away at Auxerre in the first leg of the second round. The next day, all the players, apart from the kids, were off, and I was doing a bit of running on my own at Anfield to improve my fitness. I could hear somebody coming up behind me. It was Graeme Souness.

'How do you feel?' he asked.

'Not bad,' I replied.

'How do you feel about playing, Saturday?'

'What do you mean?'

'How do you feel about playing against Coventry on Saturday?'

The question caught me on the hop. It was so unexpected. I'd thought I wasn't part of his plans. He wanted to blood a few youngsters and an old hand like me was out of favour, out of the reckoning. As I was about to reply, Souness said we would discuss the situation over dinner.

During the meal, he asked me if I would start playing for him again. Apparently, he'd changed his mind and it was time to forget what had happened between us. Liverpool were struggling in 10th position in the table, we hadn't won for five League games, and I think he realized that Jamie, Mike and Don weren't quite ready. After all, they were still only young boys. As I'd recently signed the four-year contract, I agreed to come back, and the Everton move died a death. For the second time in about a year, I'd seen a transfer fall through at the last moment. Everton were no Barcelona, but I was disappointed not to be making a fresh start across Stanley Park.

In my first game we beat Coventry 1–0 at Anfield in front of more than 33,000. It was good to be back, and I played the majority of the League games through to the end of the season. The highest position we reached was 3rd in January and February before finishing a very disappointing 6th. The FA Cup was a different matter, and although I turned in a good performance when we beat Sunderland 2–0 in the FA Cup Final, I nearly didn't make it to Wembley. I'd had enough of Souness blowing hot and cold, so I blew my top when he decided to drop me for the semi-final against Portsmouth at Highbury.

I was annoyed because I'd been involved in most of our Cup games on the way to the last four. I remember we beat Crewe 4–0, thanks to a John Barnes hat-trick at their place in the third round, and then drew 1–1 at Bristol Rovers in the next round. I was injured in that game, so missed our 2–1 win in the replay and the 0–0 draw at Ipswich in the fifth round. I returned for the replay, which finished 1–1 at full time. They scored right at the start of extra time, before I equalized with what I now regard as one of my top-five goals. We had a free-kick outside the box and Istvan Kozma, a Hungarian we'd signed from Scotland, had just been put on as a sub by Souness to take it. As I lined up the ball, Kozma made it clear he thought the free-kick was his.

'No,' I said firmly. 'Go away. I'm taking it.'

And I did. Top corner. 2–2. And then a minute later Steve McManaman scored the winner. During the post-match celebrations, Souness didn't mention the free-kick.

The next round saw us beat Aston Villa 1–0 at home without me. Souness left me out, favouring John Barnes and Ronnie Whelan, who had hardly played all season. Michael Thomas scored the winner. I bit my tongue and found myself recalled for the next few League games.

Before the semi-final against Portsmouth, I did probably the only thing I've ever regretted in my whole career. The talk before the game was all about the choice Graeme Souness had to make: it was either me or Ronnie Whelan. I felt it was no contest, especially after my performance in the other big match of the season – against Auxerre in the second leg of our UEFA Cup tie in November.

In that game two foreigners – me and Ronnie – were vying for one place. I got the nod and scored our first after four minutes and made our third for Mark Walters as we won 3–0 to go through 3–2 on aggregate. After that game, Souness came into the dressing room and showed the other side of our relationship. He walked around and kissed all the players on the forehead and then went over and pulled a thousand pounds in notes out of his pocket.

'Go and take the boys out for a drink,' he said, throwing the money at me.

Souness was like that. He could be very generous when the mood took him. Unfortunately, he wasn't in the same frame of mind before the Cup semi-final against Portsmouth. I felt there was no way he would leave me out. I'd been a regular since being recalled and I was expecting to play. But an hour and a half before kick-off, he came up to me out on the pitch and hit me with it.

'Jan,' he said, 'it's going to be a frantic game, it's hot, I'm going to leave you on the bench.'

'No, you're not!' I replied.

'Yes I am,' insisted Souness. 'Once the game settles down and everybody gets tired, then I'm going to bring you on.'

'No you're not,' I repeated. 'I either play – or I don't get stripped.'

He looked at me. I stared back.

'I'm not budging on this,' I said. 'I either start or I'm not involved as a sub.'

'You can't do that,' said Souness.

'I can – and I will. I'm not going sub in this game. I've been your best player all season.'

'I know that, but it's tactical. I want Ronnie Whelan in there, biting!'

I repeated my ultimatum and that was that. We went back to the dressing room where Souness decided it was time for his team talk. He asked me what I was going to do. I repeated that I wouldn't be playing. I stood up and walked out.

Word must have travelled fast at Highbury because I was then approached by the former youth development officer Tom Saunders, now a Liverpool director. He tried and failed to make me change my mind, and then I went upstairs to the stand where I found my fiancée Mandy in tears.

'What's wrong?'

'I knew you were being left out last night,' she sobbed. She then explained how she'd been introduced to Souness's girlfriend, now his wife, during a meal for all the women. His girlfriend had told Mandy that I wouldn't be playing. Apparently, it was a very difficult decision for Souness to make. So difficult, in fact, that he'd told his girlfriend before the player involved!

Mandy was very upset and I think I was more annoyed about her being told the night before than about the decision itself. The game ended 1–1, we didn't play well, but Ronnie equalized four minutes from the end of extra time to earn us a replay. Of course, I wanted the team to win, so that we'd reach Wembley, but I hoped they would play badly so that I'd be recalled – and that's what happened.

After the game, I think Souness was expecting me to have a go at him, but I didn't. To be fair, he admitted dropping a clanger and said my name would be the first one on the team sheet for the replay. He brushed over everything very quickly and, in hindsight, it's easy to see why he was so brief.

We boarded the bus to go north, and halfway up the M1 Souness told the driver to stop at a hotel. He then announced that he would be having an operation on his heart the very next day. Now I could understand why he hadn't discussed the Portsmouth game in much detail.

We were absolutely amazed. Souness was such a fitness fanatic. How on earth could he have a heart problem? It didn't make sense. I felt a bit sorry for him because he was going to miss out on the rest of the season. Reliable Ronnie Moran took over again and we drew 0–0 with Portsmouth in the replay, before beating them 3–0 on penalties. They missed their first three and Dean Saunders, Rushie and John Barnes scored for us. I was due to take the fifth one if it had been needed.

In the build-up to the Final, the media obviously made a thing of us winning the cup for Souness. We said it was true, but we really wanted to win it for the club, the fans and ourselves as much as anyone. He was in hospital when we beat Portsmouth and he angered a lot of people on Merseyside by selling the story of his heart problems to the *Sun*, which, with great insensitivity, published it on April 15 1992 – three years to the day since the Hillsborough disaster. He made the mistake of miscalculating the depth of feeling against the *Sun* after the paper had accused some Liverpool fans of being drunk at Hillsborough.

It was a huge own goal – even though he said he would donate the fee to charity. He shouldn't have done it in the first place; later, he quite rightly made a public apology. Obviously the players felt very strongly about it too, but nobody had a go at Souness. It wasn't really the thing to do; he was the manager, after all. I think he's probably regretted selling his story to the *Sun* many times ever since.

Unlike some of the players, I didn't have a major problem with Souness. I just wish he'd been a bit more consistent when choosing his teams. Some of the lads didn't like his managerial style, and it's true he had a very short fuse. He'd come in after games and have a real pop at us. He was one of those managers who wanted to win so badly. Like Kenny, he was pretty calm before games, but afterwards he just couldn't control it.

In September 1993, we lost 3–2 to Wimbledon at Anfield in the Premiership. We really were pathetic. Souness was livid. After storming into the dressing room, he picked up a bottle of smelling salts and threw it at the mirror. It smashed into a thousand pieces. That was the worst I ever saw him after a game. He'd have a dig after most matches and then he'd go and sit down. But on a Monday morning, he was big enough to forget about what had happened if you were.

Personally speaking, I admired the way he admitted those two big mistakes he made with me. Having said I wasn't part of his plans at the start of his first full season in charge, he could have persevered without me. But he put the brakes on and went back to the tried and tested. And he was man enough to admit his error after Liverpool had scraped that 1–1 draw with Portsmouth without me.

For my part, I regret refusing to be a sub because it could have cost me dearly. If Liverpool had won, say, 4–0, I might not have played another game that season, let alone have gone to Wembley. And, of course, I was in breach of contract by going on strike. If I'd had more time to think about it, I probably wouldn't have refused to play, but at the time I did what I felt I had to do.

Despite his strange selection process, there was a side to Graeme Souness which I quite liked. We soon realized that he was fond of the occasional bet. On his first pre-season tour we were discussing

Scottish football on the flight to Norway. A few of the lads were pooh-poohing his achievements with Rangers by saying that anyone could succeed in such a Mickey Mouse league.

'Anyone?' said Souness. 'I'll bet you any money that Liam Brady is not the manager of Celtic by the start of next season. He won't be able to hack it up there.'

I scoffed – along with the other lads.

'OK then, Jan,' said Souness. 'Let's have a bet! I say he'll be out of a job before the start of the new season in a year's time.'

I thought he was thinking of having £50 on a friendly bet. 'OK,' I said, 'sixteen-to-one.'

'Right,' said Souness. 'One thousand.'

A grand! I thought he must be joking. When I realized he wasn't I couldn't back down, so we shook hands. I stood to lose £16,000, whereas all Souness would have to cough up would be his £1000 stake. I didn't really take much notice of the fortunes of one of my former heroes, but by the start of the following season Liam Brady was still at Celtic. Souness owed me the money. The only player to remember was John Barnes, and he kept reminding me of the unpaid debt in front of Souness.

During training, John would often shout very loudly to me in Souness's earshot: 'Jan! Have you had that one thousand yet?'

'No,' I'd say. 'But don't worry. He'll do an article for some paper soon, and when he's paid he will settle the debt.'

We would wind Souness up like that every now and then. One day, towards the end of the 1992–93 season, a group of us were lying around in the treatment room. I was with John Barnes, Phil Boersma and Sammy Lee. Souness came in.

'I owe you a thousand,' he said to me.

'I know you do,' I replied. 'Plus interest.'

'I tell you what,' said Souness. 'I'll give you a bet which will make you four thousand or nothing.'

'What do I have to do?'

'Guess my weight – plus or minus four pounds. I'll give you three-to-one. If you put that thousand on and you guess my weight correctly, I'll give you four thousand.'

181

I looked at him for a moment.

'Yeah. OK. I'll have a bit of that,' I said. Sammy Lee then put on £20 and John Barnes £50. Sammy guessed the manager's weight at 13st 10lbs; John went for 14 stone; and I said 14st 10lbs. So, with four pounds each way, my estimate ranged from 14st 6lbs to 15st. Quite a margin for error.

'No more bets?' asked Souness.

Phil Boersma was laughing, so I realized something was up. Remember this was over a year after his heart operation. Souness hopped on to the scales and weighed in at 15st 10lbs. Now I knew why he was so keen on having the bet! Nobody would have guessed that he was so heavy. So I didn't get my £1000 but I was more delighted that I didn't have to pay him £16,000 after the original bet. That would have broken my heart – not to mention Mandy's.

By the time the FA Cup Final came around, Souness had just come out of hospital. In fact, he'd been released only twenty-four hours earlier and came to stay with us at the Stockwell House Hotel in St Albans. It was all very low-key, he wasn't looking his best, and he hadn't regained all his strength. He gave us a team talk on the day of the match, but everything was mainly left to Ronnie and Roy. I think Souness just wanted to be there because it was the first time that a team he'd put together had reached Wembley.

Ronnie led us out and Souness came to sit on the bench. The club doctor was next to him to make sure he didn't get too excited, and I'm sure Souness had to restrain himself when our two goals went in. The game itself came and went. No disrespect to Sunderland, but we were never under any real pressure and we won quite easily through goals from Michael Thomas and Rushie.

It was nice to be back on the big stage, and I always looked forward to any occasion at Wembley, but although we were all excited before the game, I'm afraid it never took off as a spectacle. I don't think anyone got too carried away with our victory because Sunderland never managed to put us under any kind of pressure. We strolled through the game, Paul Bracewell – like me, making his third appearance in a Final – was trying to deal with us in midfield, but Sunderland just didn't manage to get anywhere near us. Michael

Thomas was a box-to-box midfielder who scored goals, and we worked well together. I came off feeling I had done OK – nothing out of the ordinary – and although it was nice to win the Cup again, it just felt like a training session. I was more aware of what was going on, but it wasn't the same sort of occasion as in 1986. That had been the first all-Merseyside Final and my first really big involvement in English football but, by 1992, I'd been there, seen it and done it all. I still had the tingle of playing at Wembley, but afterwards there just wasn't that special buzz of relief that we'd won. I was also pleased to be at Wembley again after my row with Souness before the semi-final against Portsmouth. It was a gamble I took at the time. I felt I had to say something – I wasn't going to let him push me around. After the Final, he didn't say anything to me in particular, but he was as pleased as anyone that we'd won – after the season we'd had, his heart trouble and the pressure he was under from selling his story to the *Sun*.

My one regret was that we weren't awarded a penalty in the first half when it was 0–0. Steve McManaman was brought down and it was a blatant spot-kick. A lot of my friends had had a double bet on me to score first and for us to win 2–0!

It had been a strange sort of season and it was nice for the club to pick up some silverware. Although I narrowly missed out on the man-of-the-match award to Steve McManaman, I was chuffed to become player-of-the-year in a competition organized by a local paper based on the most man-of-the-match awards during the season. Some of these polls are a bit Mickey Mouse, but it's nice to be recognized when you've done well.

Mind you, the Liverpool supporters' clubs' awards are something else. They all run their own competitions and I'm not sure how impartial they are. I know for a fact that the Cork one is always won by an Irishman, but as I was the president of the Scandinavian branch, I couldn't keep winning their award every season!

The summer of 1992 was another frustrating time for me because Denmark won the European Championships and I wasn't even in the squad. We hadn't originally qualified for the finals but the civil war in Yugoslavia meant they'd been thrown out a month before the tournament began. As group runners-up, we'd taken their place.

I knew as long as Richard Moller Nielsen was Denmark's manager, I wouldn't get a look-in. After being out of the team for a year, Brian Laudrup had made his apologies and come back, but his brother Michael and I were still not part of the set-up. I'd had a row with Richard after we lost 2–0 to Yugoslavia in what turned out to be my last game in 1990. He had a bit of a go at me by saying he didn't feel a Danish team could have Brian, Michael and myself in it (for Denmark, I played mostly in midfield). He wanted Denmark to be less attack-minded.

I maintained it wasn't a problem with the players, rather the manager and his tactics. I felt that as we'd been unbeaten at home in qualifiers since 1981, there was no reason to be defensive – we should get at teams, especially in front of a 45,000 sell-out crowd for every game. He didn't agree and that was that. End of argument and end of international career.

I had other things on my mind during the summer, anyway. Mandy and I were getting married. We went over to Denmark for a church wedding, and had the reception in a former summer residence of the Queen. It was a very special day. I was nervous – something I wasn't when I played at Wembley for the first time with Denmark in 1983! Your wedding day is often something you've never experienced before and you want it all to go well. My brother was my best man, and I had to make my speech in Danish and English.

It was a great day, especially after Denmark had just won Euro '92 the week before! We only invited a few footballers – among them John Barnes, who couldn't come because he was in plaster with his damaged Achilles, Ian Rush, who flew in from Portugal, and Michael Laudrup, who came from Spain. At the reception, Michael and I were just shaking our heads. We couldn't believe that Denmark were the European Champions – and that neither of us had been part of it. We thought there were some Danish players with winners' medals who shouldn't really have them.

Mandy and I didn't have a honeymoon because I had to go back to Liverpool for pre-season training. All in all, 1992 had been one of my better years.

A Weighting Game

With my track record, I should have known it was too good to last. After our Cup win and my wedding, I returned for the new season still on a bit of a high. We were all looking forward to the challenge of playing in the European Cup Winners Cup and Souness was back to full health after his heart problems.

I missed the first couple of League games but then established a regular place in the side – wearing my favourite number 10 shirt – until the end of October, as we made a pretty indifferent start. Then, the long-term injury jinx struck again.

Everything was going brilliantly at Old Trafford. We were 2–0 up against United when, out of the blue, Darren Ferguson, their manager's son, caught me accidentally on the Achilles. I thought at first that I'd broken my leg. Thankfully I hadn't but, as I hobbled off to the dressing room, I feared the worst. We decided to give it some rest and treatment for six or seven weeks. In the end, though, I had to have an operation in early December, which meant I missed the rest of the season – apart from making the bench for the 1–0 defeat of Everton in late March.

It was so depressing. Apart from this problem with my Achilles, the only other injury which kept me out for the best part of the season had been the broken foot in 1986. The rest were strains and pulls, which were short term. This one, I knew, meant the end of my latest attempt to re-establish myself in the team, and it hurt.

At least I'd had another taste of Europe. I played in our first two matches against Apollon Limassol from Cyprus, as we beat them 6–1 away and 2–1 at Anfield. In the second round, we came a cropper against Spartak Moscow, who hammered us 4–2 out there after Bruce Grobbelaar had been sent off. I was sick about having to miss the first game because of my Achilles problem and on the morning of the second leg, I was so desperate to play that I was trying to train!

Souness told me to go away: there was no way I would be fit, and he was right. On the night, they wiped the floor with us, winning 2–0 at Anfield (6–2 on aggregate). Europe was out for another season and so was I.

Every time I was injured at Anfield, I found myself putting on weight very easily. Nine times out of ten, I didn't do myself any favours by coming back from injury too early – either because the manager wanted me back or because I wanted to join in. I would start playing again before I was fully fit, and I was often carrying half a stone or ten pounds too much. I hadn't done enough work to come back properly.

I wasn't as careful with food and drink as somebody of my size should have been when not playing. I thought I could lose the weight as easily as I'd put it on, and I now regret not taking much more care of my body. The worst thing was that when I did come back to play, I couldn't really afford to diet. I needed something inside me so I could do the work. The best time to diet was when I was not playing but still training.

Over the years, I've got used to all the insults from the terraces – they're part of football and you have to grin and bear them. Even if I were only eight stone, I wouldn't look slim because of the way I'm built. I've got a big chest and big thighs, but I'm not that big an eater. I was pleased when Liverpool brought in a dietitian for the players, though. He tried to help everyone. I took particular notice of what he was saying and started to eat the right things.

In fact, during my last eighteen months at Liverpool, when I really worked hard at it, I didn't have a weight problem. I assumed dieting would mean one meal a day, but all of a sudden this dietitian was telling me I could eat six meals a day! He said that we could have as much fat-free food as we wanted. We could eat crumpets and jam with our cereal for breakfast, and he said we had to make sure we ate, say, bananas, just before training followed by a tuna salad straight afterwards. Scones with jam in the afternoon were fine, and then dinner in the evening should include potatoes and bread. He said we could eat our last meal at eight o'clock at night, and drink as much water as possible. This all knocked me sideways, but it worked. Without really realizing it, I lost ten or twelve pounds while eating more than ever before. I was just eating the right things.

The 1992–93 season proved a disappointment for Liverpool Football Club. We were knocked out of the Coca-Cola Cup by Crystal Palace in the fourth round and Bolton beat us 2–0 in a replay at Anfield in the third round of the FA Cup. The holders beaten by a First Division club at the first hurdle! On top of that, we finished 6th in the first season of the Premiership – our worst position in the highest League for thirty-odd years – and to make matters worse, our great rivals Manchester United finally broke their twenty-six-year jinx and won the title.

Towards the end of the season, Graeme Souness survived a vote of confidence from the Anfield board. As we lost at Norwich and Oldham, the press were predicting that he was about to be sacked. It certainly looked that way to us. In our final game of the season at Anfield, we beat Spurs 6–2, but Souness was elsewhere – watching Coventry City at Highfield Road.

His programme notes had gone missing too. Instead, the chairman David Moores took the opportunity to address supporters through the programme, and the next day he made an official announcement at a press conference. Souness would be staying as manager, and David hoped his contract would even be extended. We were surprised – the writing had looked to be on the wall – but we noticed that the board had made one change. Roy Evans officially became Souness's right-hand man – a move which some people saw as increasing the pressure on the manager.

Having received a stay of execution, Souness decided it was time to start brandishing his chequebook again. In the summer of 1993 Liverpool signed Neil Ruddock for £2.5 million from Spurs and paid Nottingham Forest £2.25 million for Nigel Clough. I thought Neil was a good buy, and Nigel was definitely my sort of player. If anyone was going to suit the Liverpool style of play, surely it would be him.

Under Souness, we had become a lot more of a physical side. With Nigel's signing, I thought we might see a return to the Liverpool passing game. I don't think the club persevered long enough with Nigel. He got a bit of a rough deal.

As we came bursting out of the blocks and scored 10 goals in our first 3 games, Nigel made a dream debut by netting both goals in a 2–0 win over Sheffield Wednesday at Anfield on the opening day. I remember that game pretty well because Carlton Palmer was sent off after trying to cut me in half after about a quarter of an hour. He was someone I'd always had a running battle with, and it was a shocking challenge. Nigel got another in an outstanding 3–1 win away at Queen's Park Rangers on the following Wednesday, but he didn't score in our 5–0 thrashing of Swindon live on TV the following weekend. Mind you, four other players did, because we had a special reason for winning that match.

On the previous Thursday, I was sitting at home reading the *Racing Post* and I noticed that the odds on us beating Swindon were 11 to 10. I think they must have printed the coupon before our Wednesday game against QPR. It seemed incredible, but these were odds we couldn't afford to ignore. The next day, I showed the paper to Rushie, who, like me, was fond of a little bet.

As I suspected he would, he suggested putting the players' pool money on the match. If we put on £2000, we'd pick up £2200 profit. I tried everywhere to get those odds of 11 to 10, but they'd changed to 10 to 11 on, and I don't like to bet odds-on, but eventually I found one bookmaker who accepted £2000 at 11 to 10. It was the first time we'd ever had a bet on ourselves – and footballers aren't allowed to bet against their team winning. When Souness walked into the dressing room to give us his pre-match team talk, one of the lads told him that he didn't need to get us going today.

'What do you mean?' asked Souness.

We pointed towards the notice board, where I'd pinned the betting slip. Souness took a quick look at it and confirmed there wasn't a problem. We went out and beat Swindon 5–0, and then had a few drinks with our winnings.

After such a great start, everyone thought it was going to be a good season for Liverpool. But we lost at home to Spurs in our fourth game, before beating Leeds 2–0 to go 2nd. Four successive defeats (to Coventry, Blackburn, Everton and Chelsea) meant we slumped to 13th, and never really recovered. I can't give one particular reason why we lost our form so badly. That was as good as we were, that was our level. We may have kidded a few people by our start; the excitement of the new season carried us along for a while and then we found our true level. We flattered to deceive. On our day, in a one-off, we could raise our game against anyone, but teams used to play out of their skins against us on a regular basis. It wasn't there for us.

My season, like Liverpool's interest in the Coca-Cola Cup, came to a premature end in December 1993 in a replay against Wimbledon. This time it was further up my leg, but an injury which produced the same devastating result. We had drawn 1-1 at Anfield and then, during the replay in London, I ripped my calf after 27 minutes and had to come off. At that stage, it was 0-0 and we managed to force extra time thanks to a last-minute own-goal by their keeper Hans Segers. But he made amends by saving a John Barnes penalty during extra time – a kick I would normally have taken – and then we lost in a penalty shoot-out after the scores were tied at 2-2.

Now there was no doubt about the writing on the wall, but Souness was having trouble reading it. We'd won only one of our six League games in December and a potential giant-killing was just around the corner.

In the New Year, our season, and the Souness reign at Anfield, was well and truly over when Second Division Bristol City knocked Liverpool out of the FA Cup by winning 1-0 in a third-round replay at Anfield. That was the last straw for the board – not to mention Souness, who resigned a couple of days later. I wasn't surprised to see him go – he was under a lot of pressure. The previous season it had been non-Premiership Bolton who had seen us off. Now it was Bristol City. Liverpool had become easy meat. The 1992 Cup win seemed an age away.

The Bristol game was one Souness just couldn't afford to lose, but he was too proud a man to tell the team that his job was on the line. I remember that he insisted John Barnes apologize in the match programme for a Sunday newspaper article in which he'd criticized his manager's 'abrasive manner'. I didn't want Souness to go but, after that defeat, there was really no alternative.

The story of his resignation broke two days after the Bristol City defeat. He didn't tell the players personally that he was going – I was just sitting at home at the time and heard it on the news.

Within a week, Liverpool went back to the Boot Room and gave Roy Evans a two and a half-year contract. Once the Souness era was over, people felt it was time to promote from within, to get back to the tried and tested ways which had brought so much success under Bill Shankly, Bob Paisley and Kenny Dalglish. Some stability was needed in the club.

Souness's main problem was that he wanted to change too many things too quickly – especially the playing staff and style. Under Souness, we had become a team known more for our aggressive approach than our footballing ability. He wanted hard men who could look after themselves because he felt Liverpool had become a soft touch. But it just wasn't true. We had our bogey teams – like Wimbledon – but it had nothing to do with losing the physical battle.

On the field, Souness was one of a rare breed, almost unique – hard as nails, but someone who could also play. As a manager, he felt that if he bought hard men he could *make* them play – but they weren't good enough, and he couldn't do it. I was a little bit disappointed to see that we'd become more of a snarling side. We seemed to be in trouble with referees a lot more, and in the 1992–93 season we had six players sent off – three in Europe and three in the League – which was completely unheard of.

Souness's judgement of players wasn't all it should have been either. I think he discarded too many too early without having good enough replacements. He made mistakes in releasing players like Gary Gillespie, Steve Staunton, Dean Saunders and Peter Beardsley, and he also made a few duff signings: Paul Stewart, Julian Dicks, Istvan Kozma and Torben Piechnik (even though he was a Dane!) to name just four. They all had their qualities, but they weren't out-and-out Liverpool players.

To be fair to Souness, Torben had had a sensational European Championship in 1992. He'd played well against strikers like Jürgen

Klinsmann and Marco Van Basten, not allowing them a kick. But Torben didn't try hard enough to fit into the Liverpool style of play. He wasn't happy with it and decided that, with his experience, he wasn't going to change.

Souness seemed determined to shake things up on the training ground too. He wanted Liverpool to be run along the lines of Sampdoria, whom he'd joined in 1984, but found it hard to get his ideas across. The famous five-a-sides were left intact but we first noticed the difference in his initial pre-season in charge.

We had been used to doing everything short and sharp at Liverpool, with runs taking a maximum of eight minutes. Under Souness, they suddenly lasted forty-five minutes! There was resentment among the players, but it was Ronnie and Roy who were most upset by the introduction of the Italian way. They'd been in charge of pre-season training for years and, on top of that, the new methods didn't work. We ended up with more injuries – most of them to the Achilles tendon – in the first three months of Souness's first full season than we'd ever had. We would take our grievances out on Roy – as we'd done when Kenny was in charge – and he would take it up with Souness, but nothing changed.

Souness also upset the very important relationship between the players and the Anfield staff. Before he came, we would drive to Anfield, get changed and then hop on a bus to the Melwood training ground. We'd had a laugh on the way there, and afterwards there would be a cooling-off period where we all wound down on the bus before returning for showers and food at Anfield.

Souness changed all that by having a dressing room and canteen built at Melwood, and we'd have to go straight there from home. The Anfield staff were unhappy because they felt the big Liverpool family was being broken up. The cleaning ladies and the office staff were part of the football club and they felt they were being distanced from the players. Before Souness, we'd see them every day and have a crack over a cup of tea, but they now felt we were being taken away from them. It meant we only came to Anfield for games, which upset a lot of people.

There weren't many problems with the players, but some people objected to the speed at which he was trying to change things. Ian Rush, for one, didn't like being told that he couldn't have a steak before a match. He argued that having scored more than 250 goals for Liverpool after eating a medium steak three hours before a game meant that he was entitled to keep things the way they were – and he did.

I sometimes wonder how Graeme Souness the manager will be judged by history. He was accused of squandering millions of pounds on, at best, average players, and if you look at our record under him, his critics may have a point. In 157 competitive games, we won 66, drew 46 and lost 45, and when Souness left we were 5th in the table before finishing the season in 8th position.

I think it's sad that despite a great playing career at Anfield, he will probably be looked upon as a failure as a manager. It's true that, under him, we did win the FA Cup, but we only met one Premiership team, Aston Villa, on our way to Wembley to beat Sunderland – a fact that rather took the gloss off Liverpool's fifth Cup victory in their centenary season.

When Roy took over in January 1994, I always felt that he would take stock until the end of the season. There was nothing left for us to play for. I think everyone agreed that he was really the only choice to replace Souness. I had no problem at all with Roy. He'd been part of the Liverpool Boot Room ever since I'd been at Anfield, he knew what I could do and I was looking forward to working with him.

For the first time in a long time, I spent a relaxing summer holiday in Denmark with Mandy and our two children, Kingsley and Karina, hoping that my calf operation – and a new manager – would see me back at the heart of the action . . .

The Boot from the Boot Room

The injury jinx which had dogged my Liverpool career showed no signs of letting up, even though the club did everything possible to get me fit for the start of the 1994–95 season. I was in the last year

Liverpool's figure-hugging away strip, April 1988
(Stewart Kendall/*Sportsphoto*).

Hansen looks on in another derby game against Everton
(above, Colorsport); another Championship celebration, with
Ian Rush and Glen Hysen (below, Popperfoto).

More comfortable in the baggy-style strip, April 1992
(Stewart Kendall/Sportsphoto).

Another highlight of the FA Cup-winning season, 1992
(above, Claus Bonnerup/Fokus); (below) at home with the family,
Kingsley, Mandy and new-born Karina.

Testimonial time, and a big night for Jan's two biggest supporters.

On loan from Liverpool, Jan couldn't make the Canaries sing but the seeds of management were sown at Carrow Road (Matthew Mayhew/Sportsphoto).

Early days as player-manager at the Vetch Field (Empics).

The pass-master at work (above, South Wales Evening Post);
(below) happier times in the dug-out (Colorsport).

of my contract and, despite the club making me feel really wanted by wrapping me in cotton wool from the off, it was the beginning of the end, and sadly my last two seasons at Anfield were a bit of a non-event.

Initially, I spent two weeks at Lilleshall before the other players reported back for pre-season training, and then I was handed over to our new physiotherapist Mark Leather. He was under orders to make sure that I didn't kick a ball until two days before the season started. Mark worked on strengthening my calf and, although it was a lot harder, I enjoyed being with him rather than training with the lads.

My pre-season training had been specifically designed for me. It meant I didn't have to plough through all those long runs which I used to hate. Mark had me doing all the short, sharp stuff, which suited me. In all, I spent an enjoyable six weeks working with Mark but I became frustrated when I missed the pre-season tour to Ireland. There was one game left before the season began and when I heard the team weren't playing too well, I talked Mark into letting me turn out for the reserves at Altrincham a week before the opening game. Luckily, it went OK and I managed to make the trip to Ireland for a game on the following Monday. Although I struggled for my general fitness, because I hadn't played for nine months, I came through OK, and was then thrown into the first League game at Crystal Palace.

It really couldn't have gone any better. I scored our first goal after twelve minutes, with a penalty, as we hammered Palace 6–1. I played quite well in the middle of midfield, bearing in mind my long lay-off, and I then stayed on for most of the 3–0 win over Arsenal, when Robbie Fowler scored a hat-trick. A heavy tackle meant I was doubtful for our next game against Southampton, at the Dell, but I came through and we won 2–0. Roy Evans then went and signed John Scales and Phil Babb when, at the time, we were playing four at the back with Neil Ruddock and Mark Wright as our two central defenders. John came in straightaway in the disappointing 0–0 draw against West Ham and then, after we'd lost 2–0 at Manchester United, Roy changed the formation. John and Phil joined Neil as our three central defenders in a five-man defence.

That defeat by Manchester United was a blow because we'd

dominated the game. Roy later admitted that one of the biggest mistakes he's ever made as a manager was taking me off at Old Trafford when it was 0–0. He thought we were getting overrun in midfield so he replaced me with Phil Babb after about 70 minutes. He felt we needed some fresh legs, but within five minutes we were 2–0 down. Although I admit I was feeling a bit tired, I was still dictating matters from the middle of the park. I wasn't happy about Roy's decision, and afterwards I told him so: I knew straightaway it was a bad move. We were never going to win the game but we were comfortable. All the substitution did was disrupt our momentum.

I played in the 1–1 draw at Newcastle, the 4–1 win over Sheffield Wednesday at Anfield and our first defeat of the season, 3–2 at Blackburn in the middle of October. With Alan Shearer and Chris Sutton up front, it was always going to be a difficult game. My memory is of John Barnes scoring with an overhead kick from 18 yards in a wonderful match. After missing a couple of games, I was then on the bench before returning for the 3–1 home win over Chelsea. We were going well in the Coca-Cola Cup, having knocked out Burnley, Stoke and Blackburn – gaining revenge for the League defeat with a 3–1 win at Ewood Park thanks to a Rushie hat-trick.

Then, right out of the blue, I was hit by my infamous injury jinx in the Merseyside League derby at Goodison towards the end of November. I was stretching to make a tackle and tore my hamstring. I stayed on for the last ten minutes or so but I knew I was in trouble. It was a bad day all round. We lost 2–0, Jamie Redknapp replaced me as sub and, alongside Michael Thomas and John Barnes, he became a regular in the Liverpool midfield. After recovering from my hamstring problem, I couldn't force my way back into the side until the middle of March, and then it was only for one game – a 3–2 home defeat by Coventry – which turned out to be my last appearance for Liverpool. I scored a penalty but I still think I got another one as well. A free-kick of mine looked to be on its way in when it took a slight deflection off David Burrows' head and was credited as an own-goal.

I hadn't been involved in the Coca-Cola Cup run as we knocked out Arsenal and Crystal Palace before beating Bolton 2–1 in the

Final. I made the squad but not the bench – the first time I'd been to Wembley with Liverpool and not played some part in the game. We'd reached the sixth round of the FA Cup – losing 2–1 to Spurs at Anfield – and finished 4th in the Premiership, four places better than the previous season, but still not good enough for a club like Liverpool.

To be honest, I had a more pressing personal problem. My contract was about to run out at the end of the season and it looked like the end of the road for me at Liverpool. I was really worried. I just hoped they would give me a free transfer. When Roy called me in and offered me another twelve months on improved terms, I almost bit his hand off! I was delighted to accept the contract and give it a last go.

After spending the summer of 1995 coaching in Canada, I returned to Anfield full of enthusiasm for the new season. This time I did go away on tour, where I picked up a tendon injury. As a result, I missed a couple of pre-season games and, with them, the boat. The chance to stake a claim for a regular place in the side had gone and, although I returned from injury to play in the reserves, it really was the beginning of the end of my career at Anfield.

I was back in Roy's office in September to hear him tell me that Barnsley were interested in signing me on a month's loan. Now a youngster would go to a club on loan three weeks into the season to gain some experience. But at my age, I realized that Liverpool just didn't want me any more.

My first thought was that Barnsley were a very unfashionable team, but then I remembered that I'd heard some good things about them. They were playing some neat football and they had a nice pitch at Oakwell so, much to Roy's surprise, I said I would go. I made my debut in a 2–0 win at home to Derby, who went on to win the First Division, but I didn't play particularly well. Afterwards, the Barnsley manager Danny Wilson said he was happy with the way I could influence his young team, and I started the next four League games.

The results weren't brilliant – we lost one and drew three – but I improved game by game, and I got the impression that Danny wanted to keep me for another month. The trouble was that he also wanted to buy the centre-back Arjan De Zeeuw from Telstar in Holland, and the chairman said he couldn't afford both of us. Danny had already asked me to stay, but I told him not to worry about the extra month falling through. Within weeks of me leaving, Arjan signed for £250,000 and ended up being voted player-of-the-year, so it was a very good buy. I had expected to stay a little longer at Oakwell, but I didn't go there with the intention of becoming a permanent fixture.

I really enjoyed my spell with Barnsley and I wasn't at all surprised when a year later they made it to the Premiership. I was telling anyone who wanted to listen that, after finishing 10th that season, Barnsley would go up, and I'm delighted they did. It's great that such an unfashionable club, with little money, made it to the Premiership. They had a good crop of youngsters coming through and Danny made some experienced signings, like Neil Redfearn from Oldham, to bring them along. He also picked up some bargains from abroad.

When I went back to Anfield, Roy said they'd been keeping an eye on me and were impressed with what they'd seen. Our Coca-Cola Cup win had meant European football was back on the agenda, and after beating Spartak Vladikavkaz in the first round of the UEFA Cup, Liverpool were due to meet Brondby from Denmark in October. I wasn't involved in the 0–0 draw we picked up in the away leg but I expected to play some part in the game at Anfield a fortnight later.

With my Danish connections, I was very keen to see some action and I thought my experience, at the very least, would be useful. So I couldn't believe it when Roy included virtually every pro in the club in his twenty-one-man squad apart from me! From that moment on, I knew my time at Anfield was up.

I decided to bite my tongue and, instead of playing, did some radio work on the game, which we lost 1–0 to a second-half goal. Afterwards, I asked Roy why he hadn't picked me in the squad when even the kids had been included. At the time, I thought he was talking a load of rubbish, but now I think Roy was telling the truth. His explanation was simple: 'I forgot about you, Jan,' he said. 'I've been so busy that I've had the blinkers on – I've been so single-minded. I completely forgot about you because you've been on loan to Barnsley.'

'I've been here eleven years, Roy,' I replied. 'Forget about one of the youngsters, but don't forget about me! If I can't get into a squad of twenty-one for a European game, can you ask the board if they'll give me a free?'

I knew I just had to get out of Anfield. Wherever I went, I realized it was going to cost me because I wouldn't be on the same salary, but money was never important to me. I heard nothing for the next three or four weeks, and carried on playing in the reserves. Then, in December, Roy told me the board had agreed to my request: I could go on a free transfer. I was fairly realistic about my future at Liverpool. It wasn't the end of the world, I could still carry on living, and I was prepared to move somewhere else to stay in the game.

When I became a free agent, Tranmere Rovers, the third side on the Mersey, were the first to express any interest. I went to see their manager Johnny King for a chat in his office. The move appealed to me because it was just down the road, but the talk came to nothing. There was vague interest from Ron Atkinson at Coventry – if anyone was going to fancy me in the Premiership it would be Big Ron – and there was a rumour that Ronnie Whelan might take me down to Southend. I was keeping my options open. I just wanted to go somewhere to enjoy my football.

I needed a club whose style suited mine, and when Gary Megson phoned Roy to ask about me going to Norwich on loan I thought I had found it. I didn't fancy trekking across to East Anglia much, but I liked the way Norwich played, and there was a big carrot being dangled in front of me. Gary had just taken over from Martin O'Neill and was under a lot of pressure. Nobody was really enjoying their football at Carrow Road because they had been expected to go straight back up to the Premiership and weren't even in the play-off places. It was just a case of putting a run together, but there was a lot of unrest at the club involving the chairman Robert Chase. The facilities were fantastic, both Norwich the city and the ground were lovely, but, football-wise, it just wasn't happening – at least in the

League. In the Coca-Cola Cup, though, Norwich were about to play Birmingham City in the quarter-finals.

I made my debut at home to Reading, near the end of the year, and we went 3–1 up. I'd been carrying a slight calf niggle after my operation so Gary took me off with fifteen minutes to go. We ended up drawing 3–3. On the Monday, against Derby, he left me out because of my injury – with the Birmingham game in mind – and the following Saturday I was Cup-tied, so I went down to watch them get beaten 2–1 by Brentford at Carrow Road in the third round of the FA Cup.

We drew 1–1 at home with Birmingham on the Wednesday and then won 1–0 in the League at Sunderland, who went on to get promoted. We should have won by a lot more and, with those results, we thought we might have turned the corner. But then, four days before the replay with Birmingham, we lost 1–0 at home to Luton. It was infuriating to be so inconsistent. The team weren't playing particularly well, they lacked confidence but, every now and then, they could pull themselves together and produce a result. All the unhappiness off the pitch, involving the chairman Robert Chase, filtered through to the players as well as to Gary Megson. I wasn't happy with the way I was playing, but I was just pleased to be getting more matches under my belt.

The Birmingham replay was probably the best game I had for Norwich. We went one down but then Birmingham had a man sent off. The equalizer, my one and only goal for Norwich, was a real cracker. I picked up the ball about thirty yards out, took a touch and lined up to shoot. As two defenders were trying to close me down, I dragged the ball inside and hit it with my left foot. It flew into the top corner via the inside of the post. I would include that goal in my all-time top ten. I knew it was going in as soon as I hit it. It was a lovely feeling because it was such a big game, but I'm afraid it didn't last. With 12 minutes to go, we couldn't make the extra man count, and only thirty seconds from time Birmingham won a corner and scored.

I was really disappointed with the result because Norwich were a great little club and Gary was the sort of manager you wanted to do well for. Later that week, he rang to say they wouldn't be extending my loan. Again, it was no surprise. I knew that it was coming, but I wasn't expecting Gary's next comment. He sowed the seed that eventually took me to Swansea. He said he'd been really impressed with the way I had imposed myself on the other players in training. He'd seen me explaining to the younger ones how I thought they should play and suggested I should offer myself to a club as a player-coach. He said it might be easier to find a position like that. I was chuffed because I'd only ever thought about playing.

Before I could do anything, the Birmingham manager Barry Fry was on the phone. I'm not sure if he could remember who I was before Norwich played them in the Coca-Cola Cup, but he told me he'd been impressed by my performance. I'd heard all about Barry being a bit of a character at Barnet and Southend and I knew Birmingham were a big club. What I wasn't too sure about was the set-up and the high turnover of players at St Andrews. Still, there could be no harm in talking to him, so off down the M6 I went.

It was the only time in my career that I was prepared to move to a club just for the money. I deliberately went in with a well-over-the-top opening gambit in a blatant attempt to make a killing. If I'd signed for Birmingham, they would be getting me on a free, but I knew I still had some value in the transfer market. I thought I was worth £300,000 so that's the figure I wanted as a signing-on fee, spread over three years on top of my wages. I wasn't entirely happy with the Birmingham set-up, but I thought that £100,000 a year for three years would make it OK.

When Barry Fry didn't go for that, I went back to Liverpool, and within a couple of days Ron Yeats, their chief scout, received a phone call from a fella called Paul Molesworth. Paul Molesworth? Who was he? The Swansea City saga was just about to begin.

PART FIVE

The Leaving of Liverpool

By exchanging Anfield for Vetch Field, Jan Molby became Swansea's latest folk-hero, the 'new John Toshack', following in the footsteps of another former Liverpool favourite who, by 1981, had taken Swansea from the old Fourth to the First Division in successive seasons.

Jan's arrival saw the ridiculous being swapped for the sublime. Cradley Town's youth-team manager was replaced by a former Danish international and Liverpool Double winner. With the failure of the Michael Thompson takeover bid and Kevin Cullis' return to obscurity in the West Midlands, Jan Molby's appointment as Swansea's player-manager in February 1996 ensured that sanity prevailed. It brought down the curtain on a Welsh Whitehall farce which had been playing to packed houses in its week-long run, as Jan became Swansea's fifth manager in as many months.

The club's chairman, Doug Sharpe, was instrumental in bringing Jan to the Vetch Field. After saving the club from bankruptcy in the High Court in 1986, Sharpe had decided enough was enough: it was time to sell. For nearly a month, he negotiated with Michael Thompson, a businessman from Shropshire. The appointment of the unknown Kevin Cullis preceded the dramatic collapse of the takeover.

'Those were the worst three weeks of my life in football,' recalls Sharpe. 'It was a disaster which I knew nothing about. Jan's name had been mentioned as a possible player under Thompson, so I got in touch with Liverpool's chief executive

Peter Robinson, whom I know very well. He did us proud by letting Jan come down here.

'Obviously, in the back of my mind, I was aware of what John Toshack had done. Like John, Jan had been a great player. I knew that I was going for a very experienced player and a very expensive manager. I was taking a risk, but after spending twenty minutes with Jan, I was confident he could do the job.'

He may have been appointed too late to avoid relegation, but Jan made an immediate impression on the beleaguered Swansea players – including then captain David Penney.

'It was a bit of a shock that Jan was prepared to drop down so far,' says Penney. 'To the depths of the Second Division. At first, we couldn't believe it when he walked into the dressing room – Jan had a little bit of an aura about him. He was someone most of the players had only seen on television – although I'd played against him a couple of times – and you could tell that he was a bit on edge. It was probably the first time he'd had to stand up and talk to everybody, but he came across OK.'

The former Swansea, Leeds, Southampton and Cardiff winger, Alan Curtis, was running the Football in the Community programme at the Vetch Field when Jan was appointed. He had played under Toshack and became one of Jan's backroom boys by replacing Jimmy Rimmer as youth-team coach.

'Jan had an immediate effect on the club,' recalls Curtis. 'He's a very big personality anyway, a larger-than-life character, and his arrival gave everyone a lift. The club was on a real downer, but I think everybody could see that, given a little bit of backing, Jan could be the man to steer the club to better things.'

Swansea eventually finished third from bottom of Division Two, five points and two places short of safety. Doug Sharpe decided his new recruit needed some help and enlisted the support of Billy Ayre as Jan's assistant. The Southport manager had extensive experience in the lower leagues as player, coach, assistant manager and manager, with clubs such as Halifax, Blackpool, Lincoln and Scarborough. He twice took Blackpool to the Third Division promotion play-offs at Wembley, losing to Torquay in 1991 but beating Scunthorpe on penalties the following season.

When approached by Sharpe six years earlier to work alongside manager Terry Yorath, who was also in charge of the Welsh team, Ayre had declined. In the summer of 1996, though, he decided to accept the challenge of taking Swansea back to Division Two at the first attempt.

'When I came down for a day in May to meet Jan, I said I would go home if he wasn't happy with the arrangement. But right from the start, Jan thought we'd get on well together – and that's how it's turned out.

'Our relationship worked very well,' says Ayre, now assistant manager with Cardiff City. 'Jan dealt with the press and media. He was brilliant with supporters and he had this high profile which lifted the club and the city. It suited me, because it meant I could organize all the training and coaching. It allowed Jan to come in and participate as just another player, which was what he wanted, because he had enough on his plate. He took on board my views but he then made his own decisions.'

Alan Curtis believes the managerial partnership worked well. 'They complemented each other. Jan leant very heavily on Billy, who impressed me with his organization and his know-how and was certainly as good if not better than a lot of managers and coaches that I worked with in the old First Division.'

'I think it was a bit of a culture shock for Jan when he arrived at Swansea,' says David Penney. 'It's hard to be a player-manager because you've got to get in with the players, and sometimes you have to distance yourself from them when you're a manager. I don't think he could do that for the first two months by himself, but when Billy became the go-between for the players and Jan, it worked well.'

In the 1996–97 season, Jan made 31 appearances for

Swansea, including the Wembley play-off final. On the park, he was the master of energy conservation. Patrolling the centre-circle as though directing traffic, he was a cajoling, rebuking, gesticulating barrel-chest of a man. With a frequent hitch of his shorts and an even more frequent word with the referee, he dominated the midfield, conjuring up inspired passes and visibly wincing at less-than-subtle clearances by his defence.

'Playing with Jan was an experience,' says David Penney, Swansea's top scorer in the '96–97 season before he moved to local rivals Cardiff in the summer. 'Obviously, when he had the ball, he was different class. He used to sit in front of the back four and we would mark two men in midfield and then just give him the ball. We'd then push on and he'd open all the doors for us with his passing and his quick feet. That's how I scored so often that season.

'He wasn't as mobile as he was at Liverpool, but his upper-body strength helped him hold people off in this division. He could hit a ball with hardly any backlift with either foot. And then there was his shooting. With teams who came to Swansea for a draw, Jan would open up their defences – he could see things which we couldn't quite see.'

'We were always a better team with Jan in the side,' says Alan Curtis. 'Our opponents were only too glad to see his name missing from the team sheet at two-thirty on a Saturday afternoon.'

Jan always appeared to be a figure of frustration in the Vetch Field dug-out. Billy Ayre, pen and paper at the ready, oversaw substitutions, leaving the manager free to berate the referee, his assistants and occasionally opposing managers.

During breaks in play, instructions were issued to his charges by hand and mouth. Under the watchful eye of his chairman, who leant forward on to the dug-out, Jan could both inspire and intimidate. First to the loose ball at a throw-in, he exhorted his team to play the game properly. First up to celebrate a goal with fist clenched, rank-poor defending also brought Jan to his feet, exasperation written all over his face. Nice'n'Nasty does not begin to describe the former Swansea managerial team.

'Jan could be a very hard taskmaster,' reveals Alan Curtis. 'Billy was the disciplinarian, but Jan had a ferocious temper and when he lost it everyone soon knew.'

While acknowledging his own hard-man reputation within the game, Billy Ayre agrees that his former partner is no pussycat. 'In the dressing room, Jan is generally quiet, but he has been known to raise one or two hairs on the back of people's necks! I am strict on discipline because I believe that footballers come to training to work, not to mess around. And if they do, then they get told in no uncertain terms where to go.'

Swansea's inability to repay a Football League ground-improvement loan meant they were barred from buying players throughout the '96–97 season. Alan Curtis is delighted that the youngest playing squad in the club's history was put together as a result.

'The average age was 23, and the great thing was that Jan was prepared to look at the youngsters and give them every opportunity to stake a claim for a first-team place. First thing on a Monday morning, after the weekend fixtures, we got together to discuss who was playing well and which ones could fit into the side.

'In '95–96 Jan gambled on Lee Jenkins, who was doing a marvellous job for us in the youth team. I thought it was possibly a little bit too early for him to come into a struggling side, but he ended up playing twenty-odd games and doing exceptionally well. Jan stuck his neck on the line and it paid off. Other former youth-team players who came through were Ryan Casey, Kristian O'Leary, Damien Lacey, Robert King, Jonathan Coates and Chris Edwards.

'It makes my job so much easier when I can show the youngsters that they can make it through to the first team – it's a great carrot for all of them.'

The 1–0 defeat by Northampton in the play-off final in May 1997 was a huge disappointment. John Toshack was always going to be a tough act to follow, but Jan very nearly succeeded in clearing the first hurdle. In the end, an injury-time free-kick at Wembley cruelly blew the whistle on Swansea's promotion hopes.

Protracted negotiations between Doug Sharpe and prospective new owners over the summer cost Swansea dear. Uncertainty over the club's future led to three members of the Wembley side being sold – including skipper David Penny.

'At the end of the day, it was all about money,' says Penny, now with Doncaster Rovers in the Nationwide Conference. 'I was quite happy at Swansea – the '96–'97 season was my best ever. I was club captain and top scorer; we had just been beaten at Wembley, and all I got offered was a 20 per cent pay cut!

'I've no regrets about leaving Swansea and joining Cardiff. I think me leaving brought things to a head, and the new owners acted to stop other experienced players from going.'

The new owners emerged as Silver Shield, a Coventry-based windscreen replacement firm, who paid nearly one and a half million pounds for the club – including £450,000 for Doug Sharpe's controlling interest. After a sixteen-year association with the Swans, the chairman, who runs a construction company at Gorseinon, eight miles away, finally decided a new face was needed. He felt he could take the club no further and the deal was eventually done less than forty-eight hours before the start of the new season.

Another local football fan, Steve Hamer, succeeded Sharpe as chairman. Born in Glyn-Neath, north-east of Swansea, but living in Hampshire, Hamer is a director of The National Sporting Club, a London-based company which specializes in sporting entertainment. He spent ten years working for London Weekend Television's *The Big Match* in the 1980s. His father Jack ran Dinefwr Engineering, which employed former

Welsh scrum-half Gareth Edwards as a marketing executive for fifteen years. A former player with Sutton United and Carshalton Athletic, Hamer also managed Corinthian Casuals in the Isthmian League. While in South Africa, he turned out for Berea Park, who number Labour MP Peter Hain and former Blackburn Rovers manager Roy Hodgson among their former players.

'We have made no secret of the fact that, as a commercial organization, we want the club to make some money,' Hamer said, soon after the takeover. 'Professional football clubs need to have the umbrella of a plc. The days of the Doug Sharpe-type private fiefdoms are long gone.'

Silver Shield's plan is to move the club to a new 25,000 all-seater stadium on the site of the current council-run Morfa Athletics Stadium in the city, as part of a leisure complex. 'I'm afraid the Vetch is now a decrepit and tired old ground,' says Hamer. 'I would love to stay here – I first came to the Vetch forty years ago and I have happy memories of the ground, but there's no room to develop it. There's no way that we can stay here if we are to fulfil the dreams of every Swansea City fan.

'The new ground will be a purpose-built football and rugby stadium without the athletics track. There's nothing worse than watching football in an athletics stadium with the track between the pitch and the crowd.'

On assuming control at the club Hamer had nothing but praise for the work carried out by his fledgling manager before the takeover. 'Jan has actually carried this club on his big broad shoulders for some time. They have been living under siege conditions and Jan has been the spokesperson. It has been especially difficult for him because Swansea had been treading water for a month before we finally came in. Jan has done a wonderful job, with little help, and we have endeavoured to introduce a better back-up team for him.

'I've told him that if, by the end of this season, we're a better organized and far-better equipped side on the field of play, then I'll be happy. I've told him we'll support him as best we can and give him every chance.'

As it turned out, Jan Molby was given about nine weeks – or ten League games – before being sacked. Silver Shield had embarked on a ninety-day appraisal of the club which led to chief executive Robin Sharpe being replaced by Peter Day, who had held similar positions with Spurs, Colchester, Swindon and Birmingham City. On Day 62, it was Jan's turn to part company with Swansea City.

When the new season began, though, a huge wave of optimism swept through the Vetch Field, with many people drawing parallels with the start of the Toshack era nearly twenty years before. After scoring the winner against Brighton on his debut in Swansea's opening game, the former Barry Town striker Tony Bird revealed why he had rejected Second Division Brentford for Swansea.

'I just respect Jan for giving me the chance of resurrecting my career after Cardiff let me go. I also respect the way he likes to play the game – everything to feet rather than being knocked sixty or seventy yards over the top.'

'I think the boys could relate to Jan,' says Alan Curtis, now assistant manager to John Hollins at the Vetch. 'They all knew him from his days at Liverpool and he was perhaps one of the players they had idolized since they started in the game.

'It's a tradition within the club that the YTS boys put on a bit of a Christmas show. In 1996, some of them took off Jan – the famous Harry Enfield scouser with the moustache and the curly wig – "Calm down, calm down – cool head!" and all that – and he thought it was a scream.'

Even the humour of his adopted Merseyside could not have prepared Jan Molby for the turn of events which led to his dismissal. His huge reputation as a player and his achievement – with Billy Ayre – in taking Swansea to the brink of the Second Division seemed to count for nothing when results turned against him.

Three successive home victories augured well but five

210

straight away defeats plunged the Swans to fifth from bottom of the Third Division. In an action replay of the '95–96 season, the club was in desperate trouble and the new board decided it was time to act. In a statement issued by Silver Shield to the Stock Exchange, Jan's contract as manager was 'reluctantly terminated with immediate effect'. Billy Ayre was sacked too.

'We were eighteenth in the League and spending more time squabbling internally than focusing on what matters,' said Neil McClure, Silver Shield's chairman and Swansea City's vice-chairman. 'We were not finding it possible to work happily as a team.'

Within two days, the former Fulham manager Micky Adams was appointed as Jan's successor. Having been sacrificed for the arrival of Kevin Keegan and Ray Wilkins at Craven Cottage the previous month, Adams was delighted to be back in football. When the dust had settled on the equally controversial sacking of Jan Molby, Steve Hamer elaborated on the reasons behind the change of manager.

'The decision was based on results,' said the chairman. 'I have no doubt in my mind that Jan had lost the respect of the dressing room. It was clear that the team were not playing for him. He set very high standards and I don't think he understood life in the Third Division or why the players were there.

'Early on I said to Jan: "Let's give it one more year. You're head-and-shoulders above everyone else in this division." He was on a high salary, he was the player-manager, but he wasn't training. He didn't seem to want to play and claimed injuries that might not possibly have been injuries. It was rather tragic, really.

'I wasn't unhappy to pay him his money as long as he justified it. We were suspicious about his injuries because we received no medical evidence from either him or the club physiotherapist. We didn't see the full medical breakdown of what was wrong.

'It's not true to say we didn't want Jan in the first place. In fact, I quite liked the guy and wanted to work with him. I wanted Jan to embrace us and not fight us.

'Jan's biggest problem was that for all his time at the club, he was its only spokesperson. He was allowed to do that and there were public newspaper battles with Doug Sharpe with "back-me-or-sack-me" type quotes appearing from Jan. He became bigger than the club. In that sense, he did a wonderful job by keeping Swansea City to the fore, but he wasn't prepared to understand that we would run the club as a professional outfit.

'He'd had too free a rein before we arrived and I don't think he liked being told anything by anybody. He had been allowed to run the club and, although he was manager, he was only in charge of the football team, not the whole club. At the end of the day, he was only 34 and I think he still thought like a player. I never thought he quite made the move up from being a player to a manager. He always wanted to be one of the boys.'

Steve Hamer has denied interfering with Jan's job as manager but admits having consulted half a dozen experienced contacts for their opinions on certain players. 'They were well-respected managers and former players who knew current players better than Jan and Billy. Jan's policy seemed a bit hit-and-miss to me. There was no consistency in his recommendations. It was a confetti bag full of different names – drawn up on the mood. Thank God I had my *Rothmans Football Yearbook* available – that's surely part of my job.'

When Swansea City sold Steve Torpey to Bristol City for £400,000 just before the start of the 1997–'98 season, most of the money was expected to be reinvested in buying replacements for the experienced players who had left during the summer. After £60,000 was used to recruit Tony Bird and Dave O'Gorman from Barry Town, Swansea then paid £108,000 to Wrexham for striker Steve Watkin.

'We agreed a down payment of £250,000 from Bristol City with the balance to be paid in a year's time,' explained Hamer. '£124,000 went on paying off a Football League loan, and £88,000 was due to Bradford City through a sell-on clause in Torpey's contract. So there wasn't a great deal left.

'It would be unkind to suggest that we didn't give Jan money to improve the team so that the results would get worse and we could get rid of him. We didn't want to sack a hero in the fan's eyes, but we needed a change.

'We wish Jan well for the future. I think his best role would be to become an agent bringing Scandinavian players into this country. I think he found it very difficult to adapt to the Third Division.'

Less than a fortnight later, Steve Hamer was being forced to explain the abrupt departure of Jan's successor. In the wake of three successive defeats, Micky Adams resigned after just thirteen days in the job. In a terse statement made outside the club's offices, Adams plunged Swansea into further disarray – recalling the even briefer reign of Kevin Cullis, when the club became the laughing stock of British football:

'I have decided with deep regret to hand in my resignation as manager of Swansea City,' he said. 'I'm bitterly disappointed that it's not worked out for me. I came down here with all the best intentions in the world.'

After thanking his former players and the club's supporters, Adams hopped into his car and drove away from the ground. No mention was made of the reason behind his resignation: the new board's refusal to honour a promise to make money available for new players. Adams had recently met with the club's directors in an attempt to resolve a problem which, in his view, threatened their Third Division status. With a six-figure pay-off from Mohammed Al Fayed in his back pocket, Adams had little need of a job managing a struggling Third Division side with little or no money to improve it.

According to the board, Adams resigned for 'personal reasons'. Peter Day and Neil McClure then revealed that Alan

Cork, an original member of the Wimbledon Crazy Gang, and assistant to Adams for thirteen days, would be his replacement; Ian Branfoot becoming the club's chief scout.

'I think Micky was still on the bounce from a bad experience at Fulham,' said Hamer. 'He was a young man in a hurry, a very capable manager and a very charming and decent man. He was fully aware of the position but he was eager not to be seen as a failure, and this wore him down in the end. I think he made a hasty decision.

'I think we were a little unlucky in that Micky was still probably emotionally involved with the problems he had at Fulham and was still deeply hurt by his experience. When you arrive and sadly lose a couple of games by the odd goal, it does have an effect. If we'd beaten Notts County and Mansfield, I have no doubt in my mind that Micky would still be with us.

'It's not strictly true that he left because we wouldn't give him any money to buy players. That's a slightly emotional outburst. I promise you I spent a long time with Micky. He was fully aware of what we're doing – our plans, our structure and the finance that was being made available to him to buy new players. We are not prepared to see Swansea City stagnate in the Third Division.'

Just over a fortnight after walking out of the Vetch Field, Micky Adams was back in football and back in London – replacing the sacked Eddie May at Second Division Brentford. Following his appointment, he reflected on his sacking by Fulham and his decision to resign as manager of Swansea.

'After Fulham, I was aiming to follow advice and take a break from the game to chill out and decide what I really wanted to do. Then Swansea came along with an attractive offer but, after just a day or two in the job, I sensed there were hidden agendas, not all to do with not having money to buy players. I just felt that promises made were not going to be fulfilled.

'I walked away from a better contract with Swansea than

I've got here, but I had to go. The players there were very keen and full of enthusiasm but basically that was all. They were youngsters doing men's jobs. I wanted to take them out of the firing line and bring in new players. I had the ones I wanted lined up and was just waiting for the green light – but it never came. Nothing materialized.

'I assessed the strength of the squad quicker than they thought I would and before I had signed a contract. I left because I felt I was bashing my head against a brick wall.'

When Jan Molby left Liverpool for Swansea, he wasn't the first former Liverpool player to take on the challenge of player-management. In recent years, Kenny Dalglish, Steve McMahon and Ronnie Whelan had, with varying degrees of success, made the transition. But none of them chose to begin at the bottom.

With an idiosyncratic chairman, little or no money but a wealth of goodwill, Jan's policy of make-do-and-mend almost paid off immediately. The decision to swap the prestigious Premiership for life in the lowest division met with almost universal approval from the people who mean most to him.

'It was strange for Jan to leave Liverpool after twelve years,' says his wife Mandy, 'but it was like a breath of fresh air. It really gave him the kick that he needed. I didn't think going to Swansea was a good idea because it split up the family for a while, but it was what he wanted to do.'

The coach at Kolding, where Jan began his career, Knud Engedahl, was not surprised to learn of his move into management. 'Jan has played football all his life – what else could he do but to stay with the game, become a manager?

'You can never tell whether a very good footballer will become a very good manager, but Jan has the personality to succeed. From what I have seen in TV interviews at Liverpool and Swansea, he's a great person, with real charisma.'

Jan's former Liverpool team-mate Alan Hansen and the man who coached him at Ajax, Aad de Mos, were both initially taken aback by his move down the divisions.

'I was a bit surprised,' recalls Hansen, 'but it's the same old story: what do you do when you retire from football? You become a TV pundit or a manager! I've no doubt that Jan will be a success. He was close to it already with Swansea and I'm sure he'll learn from that experience – that's what management is all about.'

'I was a little bit surprised to hear Jan had become a player-manager,' says Aad de Mos, 'because he didn't give me the impression at Ajax that football was the most important thing in his life. But in this game, everything is possible. People change, footballers change.'

'I wasn't surprised when Jan went to Swansea,' says Ian Rush, 'because I know what he was looking for. But I thought he might have gone to a Premiership or First Division club rather than joining one about to drop into Division Three.'

Five years playing under Kenny Dalglish undoubtedly left their mark on Jan Molby, as the principles of the passing game were transferred from Anfield to Vetch Field. The former Newcastle manager believes his former team-mate still has a successful career in the game.

'Jan's a very intelligent person – even though some of the things he's done in the past might not support that view! – and he's very knowledgeable about football. It seemed a natural progression for him [from playing into management], and I think he's got a right good chance to be a good manager. I used to ask him about certain people who played abroad and, although I can't think of anyone whom I dismissed or took on because of him, there was plenty of intelligent conversation with Jan about football.

'He must be disappointed that maybe he didn't achieve the success that his ability deserved, but he could put that to good use in his managerial career because he can cite himself as a prime example of what not to do. I think he has learnt from his mistakes and he'll take that lesson into the future.

'As a person, he's not a bad lad – despite the one or two things which have happened to him. He's a very pleasant lad, who never gave me any problems other than the well-known ones. He's somebody you can sit and talk to and enjoy his company, and somebody that I really enjoyed working with.'

Jan Molby was perhaps a victim of the revolution now sweeping through the British game. No longer a rich local businessman's hobby, football is big business – even in the Third Division. Shareholders have to be satisfied by performances both on the stock market and the pitch. Balance sheets have become as important as clean sheets; hitting financial targets as crucial as finding the back of the net.

Three wins out of ten League games may not have seemed the end of the world, but they signalled the end of Jan's reign at Swansea. It appears that Silver Shield's business plan did not take into account such a poor run of results. Unlike Doug Sharpe, whose faith in his charismatic manager was almost repaid with promotion, Steve Hamer preferred a hands-on approach to chairmanship. While Sharpe retreated to his villa in Spain and left Jan and Billy Ayre to turn the club around, Hamer set up camp in the boardroom before preparing to push the panic button and eject the pair.

Despite his sacking, Jan Molby is dedicated to football. He badly wanted success for the club which gave him the chance of a new career. Life at the sharp end at the Vetch Field could easily have deterred lesser men but Jan hung on in there. By giving the club back its pride, he reinvigorated a lame swan which had looked beyond recovery. Ultimately, an untimely relapse cost Jan his job but not his reputation.

For more than a year and a half after leaving the Vetch Field, Jan Molby trod water. As he waited for the opportunity to return to the game he loves, a new career opened up for him in football punditry. TV channels, radio stations and newspapers in Britain and abroad all made use of his expert knowledge yet still no chairman was prepared to offer him a second chance, until April 1999, when Lionel Newton, from Kidderminster Harriers, decided to grasp the nettle. Having made millions from selling his furniture-manufacturing company in 1995, the Welshman from Bridgend had already helped to redevelop large parts of the Aggborough Stadium in the quaintly named Hoo Road. The West Midlands side had won the Conference in 1994 but were prevented from taking their place in the Football League because their ground wasn't up to scratch. Now it was time for Newton to turn his attention to the team.

When long-serving manager Graham Allner left in December 1998, Phil Mullen was recruited from nearby Redditch as a caretaker before Newton made his move towards the end of that season.

'A third party told me that Jan might be interested in taking over,' recalls the chairman, 'and I immediately arranged to meet him. I was very impressed with everything he said, I knew the fans loved him at Swansea, and I felt he must have something. I didn't bother ringing the Vetch Field – I had taken a business from nothing to one with nearly a £30 million turnover employing 600 people, and I think I'm a good judge of people. After Jan met the board at a later meeting, we unanimously agreed to offer him the job.'

Jan took over as part-time manager at Kidderminster in June 1999 and two months later appointed the Barry Town player-manager Gary Barnett as his assistant. After a promising pre-season, the Harriers proceeded to lose four of their first five Conference games before their form picked up.

'We have both always remained positive,' says Lionel Newton, 'and I'm convinced we're moving in the right direction. Our goal is to reach the Football League at the end of Jan's two years here, and I will be very happy if we are in the top eight in May. I would be looking for him to fine-tune his squad next year and for us to be a serious contender, but as long as we are in there fighting, there will be no pressure on Jan.'

The big man with the big shot may be out of the big time, but he's not ready to shuffle off the stage just yet.

A Week is a Long Time in ... Football

It turned out that Paul Molesworth was someone Ron Yeats had used as a scout for Liverpool in the West Midlands. At the time, the story about Kevin Cullis taking over Swansea after managing Cradley Town's youth team was about to break. Paul was to become his assistant under the new chairman Michael Thompson, who in turn was about to buy out Doug Sharpe. Apparently, Thompson was very ambitious and when he heard that I might be willing to leave Liverpool, he told Paul to go and get me.

Money seemed no object. When he was contacted by Paul, Ron said I wouldn't be interested in taking a pay cut and, in fact, put a thousand a week on top of what I was actually earning. Paul said that sort of wage wouldn't be a problem.

I must admit I was quite attracted by the idea of joining Swansea on a two-year contract, so I drove down to Birmingham the following weekend to meet Paul, with my agent Dave Sheron. We then travelled to Swansea for talks with Kevin Cullis. Friday night and Saturday morning were spent trying to find Thompson, who finally turned up at the Swansea Hilton Hotel just before lunch. He confirmed that he would make everything permanent within the next three weeks, when he'd taken over the club.

On Saturday afternoon, I decided to go and watch Swansea play Swindon at the Vetch Field. They didn't sell themselves particularly well to begin with. They could have been three or four down after the first twenty minutes but picked up a little and were unlucky to get beaten 1–0. The result meant they were 22nd in the Second Division with 18 games to go. Paul had put me in the first row of the directors' box so that, if they needed to have a word about tactics, I would be on hand. Paul and Kevin, who'd been appointed only three days earlier, were in the dug-out for their first and, as it turned out, their only home match in charge.

I knew nothing about Kevin apart from what I'd read on Teletext about him becoming Swansea's fourth manager in as many months (after Frank Burrows, Bobby Smith and Jimmy Rimmer). When I met him on the Friday, he held his own as we talked about football. There didn't seem to be a problem.

After the game, Kevin and Paul asked me for my impressions of Swansea.

'Not too bad,' I said. 'Which one of you two is going to do the coaching?'

'I want to do my management in the office,' said Kevin.

Paul was just as adamant. 'I don't really want to be the assistant manager,' he admitted. 'I want to be more of a scout. I'd like to carry on living in Birmingham with my wife and four children.'

There was a pause while I digested their remarks.

'Why don't we make you the player-coach?' they said.

'If that's what you're looking at,' I replied, 'we can always think about it.'

And with that, I went back to Liverpool, not very confident that the whole thing was going to happen. I thought I'd never hear from them or Thompson again. Mind you, I wasn't complaining. It had been a pleasant enough weekend away, I'd watched a game of football and had a chat with an old Liverpool team-mate, Steve McMahon, who was managing Swindon. I'd also met Doug Sharpe, the Swansea chairman, for the first time.

We were having a cup of tea and a biscuit in the tea room after the game when Doug called us into the boardroom. He struck me as being very enthusiastic about football and well aware of the strong link between Swansea and Liverpool. Michael Thompson didn't even know who Jan Molby was. He was a businessman, whereas Doug was a football-mad businessman. I gave my agent Dave a couple of numbers for Thompson to see if we could get something down in writing. We could then sign the contract when Thompson took over.

Nothing much happened for the next ten days or so. Swansea lost 4–0 at Blackpool and drew 0–0 at home to Hull. Those results put them next to bottom. The situation was looking bleaker and bleaker. In between those two games, Kevin Cullis and Paul Molesworth left Swansea after only a week in charge. Doug Sharpe took over the reins again as the Thompson takeover deal collapsed, and Jimmy Rimmer returned as manager. When I heard the news, I felt that that was the end of my involvement with Swansea. And after the draw with Hull, I thought that was the end of Swansea's involvement with Division Two.

But, as we all know, football is a funny game. Two days later, I came home from picking the kids up from school to find a message on my answerphone from Doug Sharpe, asking me to ring him on his mobile. Since then I've learnt that the chairman had contacted Liverpool's assistant manager Doug Livermore for a reference before approaching me. The chairman was in Carlisle for Swansea's League game on the Tuesday and asked me to meet him at a hotel in the Midlands the next day for a chat. Swansea lost 3–0 at Carlisle, who were fourth from bottom. It was getting worse and worse, but I made the half-hour journey south all the same.

I met Doug, as agreed, at the Thistle Hotel in Haydock, not far from the racecourse. I told him I was interested in taking over at Swansea. We talked money, and then he got straight to the point.

'Do you think you can keep us up?' he asked.

'It's going to be difficult,' I said, 'but we'll give it a go. It's in the lap of the gods, but we might just make it.'

The meeting confirmed my first impression of Doug. He loved football and in particular he loved Swansea City. He was very keen and was desperate for the club to stay up. To be honest, the odds were stacked against us. We'd played 31 games and had just 25 points. We had relegation written all over us.

After shaking on the deal, we went up to Liverpool to see Peter Robinson to sort out my free transfer, before calling in at home to pick up my gear. We then watched West Bromwich Albion reserves play Tranmere and headed down to Swansea where I spent the night at the Hilton. There was no sign of Michael Thompson in the hotel!

On the Thursday, I turned up at the Vetch Field to put pen to paper and start work. At the press conference to announce my arrival, I could see Doug was excited to have signed me. For my part, I was pleased to be there. I just wanted to get on with the job of trying to keep the Swans afloat.

That Sinking Feeling

I must admit to being a little apprehensive when I first met the players in the dressing room, under the grandstand at the Vetch Field. I felt a bit like the poacher turned gamekeeper. From being on the receiving end of team talks as a player with Liverpool, Barnsley and Norwich, here I was about to deliver my first one as a manager! And that after I'd already been linked with them as a player through the aborted Thompson takeover.

I knew they'd been through a lot – I was their fifth manager that season – but I was just as nervous about the situation as I suspected they were. Like me, they probably felt the takeover had been pie-in-the-sky, and they seemed genuinely pleased that I'd become their manager. At least it would help stabilize the situation. My message to them was simple: let's just get on with it and collect as many points as we can. As far as I was concerned, survival was the only name of the game for the rest of the season.

When we went training for the first time, I could see the players were up for it. A new manager was the lift they needed. They were going through an horrendous run – just one win since November – and they hadn't scored in their last five games. At first, everything went like a dream. Three wins and two draws in our first five matches. It was important that we kept a clean sheet in our first game away at York. The point wasn't a bad start – especially as we then had two home games on the trot.

The players were also responding to the arrival of a Premier League player. I put myself straight into the team in the back four to steady

222

things down a little. We'd been leaking goals right, left and centre and we just took it from there.

Walsall were creeping towards the play-off places when we beat them 2–1 at the Vetch in midweek and then on the Saturday we surprised Bristol City with the same scoreline, and I got my first goal. We picked up a point with a 1–1 draw at Rotherham before bringing Brentford down to earth. They were having a tremendous run, we went 1–0 down but fought back and I scored the winner with a penalty in the 94th minute.

When I first arrived, I thought it was going to be easy – especially after the start we made. But it only lasted for a week or so, before I became aware of the shortcomings of players at this level. At Liverpool, we would always reach a certain standard in every game. Sometimes we'd be slightly better and other times absolutely wonderful, but we'd never slip below it. We all knew how to do the basics – like control the ball and pass – but there wasn't a consistency level at Swansea; the players could sink lower than we thought possible. I must admit that I found it difficult to come to terms with.

We were starting to move up the table until we met the leaders Blackpool at the Vetch. This time, it was our turn to be hit by the late, late show. They scored twice – in the 91st and 93rd minutes – to bring our revival to a shuddering halt. That defeat marked the end of skipper John Cornforth's time at the Vetch. There'd been talk of him going to Oxford, but that deal fell through because they couldn't agree personal terms, and he eventually went to Birmingham. At the time, I didn't really have a view on whether we should sell John or not. He was doing quite well, but £350,000 for a Second Division midfield player was a lot of money. In retrospect, I'm not too sure whether selling him did us any good.

We took a thousand supporters with us to Brentford and came back with a point which, for the first time, took us out of the bottom four. The trouble was we'd played four games more than all our relegation rivals. After the Brentford result, we then lost three of the next four – a run which sealed our season, despite three wins in our last four games.

I think the Jan Molby effect was beginning to wear off and the players realized that the air of invincibility they'd had for a couple of weeks had gone. We lost 2–0 at Blackpool but steadied the ship with a 0–0 draw at Brentford, but then lost 5–1 at Bradford (after being 4–0 down at half-time). There was nothing we could do about it, so we just carried on with what we thought was right. We drew at Peterborough but then lost to Wrexham and Bournemouth before coming back towards the end of the season. Our mini-revival had nothing at all to do with the Jan Molby factor – it was the fruits of the training we'd done. The players had actually improved and it showed in the results we managed to pick up.

I brought in Lee Chapman on a match-by-match basis for seven of our last eight games and he didn't let me down. I knew with his record at Leeds, Arsenal, Forest and latterly Ipswich that he would get us goals. He managed four, but while he was with us, everybody else stopped scoring! Lee enjoyed his time at the Vetch, and then spent the summer in Norway before deciding to retire.

I was sorry to have been proved right with the prediction I made when Doug and I met at that hotel in Haydock. We nearly stayed up, eventually finishing third from bottom. Doug was obviously disappointed, and he said it would be hard in the Third Division: 'It's a difficult league to get out of,' he told me. 'There are some tough teams down there.'

From what I'd seen at the bottom of Division Two, I wasn't about to argue. At the end of the season, Doug was still very keen and he was determined to get me some managerial help. Soon after I had arrived, we'd tried to bring someone in. My first choice was Kevin McDonald, whom I'd played with at Liverpool, but he didn't want to leave Aston Villa. We then spoke to Gary Gillespie, another old Anfield team-mate of mine, who was at Coventry, but we couldn't agree personal terms with him. So we decided to go with what we had until the end of the season.

I had found my time at the Vetch pretty tough. Jimmy Rimmer did his best to help me out, and towards the end of the season Ron Walton was brought in to give us a hand on the bench but, once we were relegated, the chairman insisted I had an assistant.

I was well aware of Billy Ayre, as a former manager of both

Blackpool and non-League Southport. Liverpool's reserve team played all their games at Southport, so I knew Billy well. What I didn't know was that he'd been approached by Doug Sharpe six years previously about becoming Terry Yorath's assistant at the Vetch. The chairman was unhappy with Terry doing the Welsh job at the same time and wanted to lighten his load by bringing in Billy. At the time, Billy decided to stay put at Halifax.

Billy was also very well thought of by Kenny Dalglish, whom I bumped into at John Aldridge's testimonial at Prenton Park, Tranmere. After we'd played in the game, Kenny asked me how things were going, and I explained I was on the look-out for an assistant. Kenny said it was important to have one. He felt I needed someone to organize things defensively and he recommended Billy. In the meantime Doug Sharpe had resurrected his link with Billy. This time he didn't turn Doug down, and turned up at the Vetch for a day in the middle of May.

Much to the chairman's delight, we got on well. We spent the day together discussing our approach to the game and watching Swansea play Wrexham in the Welsh Youth Cup Final at Cardiff Arms Park. I was happy that the responsibility was about to be shared but, at the time, I didn't know what sort of impact Billy was going to make. In fact, he was one of the shrewdest signings Doug made. It was vital for me to have someone who knew the lower leagues and who could make decisions when I was playing. Billy's a strong character; he was me off the pitch. And he'd been through it all.

As Billy went back north to Southport and Doug jetted off to his villa in Spain, I felt a lot happier about the prospects for my first full season in charge at the Vetch Field. All of a sudden, the chairman's warning about life in the Third Division didn't sound so daunting.

Life at the Sharpe End

Whatever his critics might say, Doug Sharpe certainly knew how to put his money where his mouth was. He did it in 1986 to save the club from folding in the High Court and, before leaving for his Spanish villa for the summer in 1996, he sanctioned the signing of full-back Joao Moreira from Benfica for £40,000.

It might be a drop in the ocean for a Premiership club but it was a lot of money for what was now a Third Division team in the Nationwide League. Unfortunately, Joao injured his knee and missed our pre-season tour to Denmark. It was a tough trip and we weren't very good, but I've always felt that pre-season games should be for getting players fit rather than for winning or playing well.

I was a little surprised to see that we'd been made joint favourites for promotion with Wigan by the bookmakers. I suppose they must have based their optimism on our performances during my fifteen games in charge the previous season and, it was true, there was a feeling at the Vetch that we might well go straight back up.

Our first League game, at home to Rochdale, was a mixed bag for me. We won 2–1 but I missed my first penalty for ten years and was then sent off. I didn't hit the ball too well from the spot and the keeper made a reasonable save. I received my marching orders for two bookable offences: shirt-pulling, which was fair enough, and trying to elbow an opponent. I didn't mean to be malicious but I must admit it looked bad on the television the next day! Anyway, a 2–1 win in front of a 4000 crowd was a wonderful way to kick off the new season.

The dream start then turned to a nightmare over the next six matches. We lost them all – two in the Coca-Cola Cup to Gillingham and the rest in the League. A lot of players were struggling to find their form, we were a little too adventurous, and some of our defending left a lot to be desired. Our second match was at home to Gillingham. We hit the post four times in the first 20 minutes but ended up losing 1–0 to an own goal. If we'd won that game, everything could have been so much different. The defeat took a little bit out of us and we just couldn't recover. We lost away at Darlington, Chester, Gillingham and Carlisle and were beaten 2–1 at home by Lincoln after being 1–0 up at half-time.

In all those games, apart from the last one at Carlisle, I felt we had a chance of winning – I was very upbeat about our prospects. At Carlisle, though, I just knew we were going to lose. It had nothing to do with me being suspended. Carlisle were a strong team and were well fancied to go straight back up. We'd just been beaten 2–0 at Gillingham in the Coca-Cola Cup and, as I looked at my players, I realized there was no way we could lift them before Saturday. Sure enough, we took the lead, but ended up on the end of a 4–1 hammering. We'd lost six on the trot and the chairman had lost patience.

The following morning, a Sunday, a press conference was called at the Vetch Field. Doug didn't attend, but his son Robin, the club's chief executive, and Ian Cole, Swansea's accountant, announced that the chairman was putting the club up for sale. Apparently he didn't feel he was the man to take Swansea forward. I think it was partly because of the dreadful start we'd made to the season and partly because he thought he'd made a mistake in appointing me. I came to the ground in the afternoon to be told by Robin to carry on as normal.

Our next game was a midweek match against Hereford at the Vetch. We didn't need to motivate the players much – we simply told them it was now or never. We had never needed a win as badly as we did that night.

Having been left out at Carlisle, club captain Shaun Garnett returned to central defence for the Hereford game. I also brought Keith Walker in for his first game of the season to partner Shaun. And 17-year-old Lee Jenkins made his debut in midfield. After the Carlisle game, Billy and I were pulling our hair out, wondering how we were going to get it right. We decided to try something different by picking the best eleven players in the club. That meant playing Lee, who was a trainee. He was from Pontypool in the Gwent Valleys,

227

and we'd heard good reports from Ron Walton and Alan Curtis, two of our backroom staff, as well as seeing him ourselves. Ron, in particular, was forever going on about Lee.

Lee was slightly different from everyone else at the club in that his main strength was the work he did off the ball. When either making forward runs or closing people down, he got through so much work, without people noticing. He hardly ever gave the ball away and just got on with it in his own little way. Sadly, he later smashed his cheekbone in an Auto Windscreens Shield tie against Bristol City, which knocked the stuffing out of him. But he'll come good again because he's got the right attitude and the right appetite.

Keith Walker is a rugged central defender from Scotland who, at the time, was on a week-to-week contract with Swansea. He'd played more than 200 times for the club but had been up to Preston and Burnley on trial before returning to the Vetch Field. I told him he'd be in the shop window if he played for us, and that was fine by him. He'd always done his own job well, but I had my doubts about his ability to become the organizer and leader at the back to help the youngsters to his right and left. I felt it was right for him to return against Hereford.

It was also a blessing that, straight after the Carlisle hammering, we were playing a fairly weak team in Hereford. For all these reasons, I had a feeling about this game – I was sure we would win, so I told a couple of my friends who liked a bet to put on as much as they could. We were 3–0 up at half-time and won 4–0. The defence kept a clean sheet, Lee scored and it was a very important win, which I hoped we could build on.

The next Saturday, we played the leaders Fulham – again at the Vetch Field. The revival could have started on the back of the Hereford result. Fulham were the runaway leaders and we were in the lower half of the Division, but we'd had a good win and there was a reasonable crowd willing us on at the Vetch Field. After being 1–0 up at the break, when it could have been two or three, a couple of silly mistakes cost us the game, as Fulham won 2–1. It was back to square one. I remember thinking that this was the way it was going to be. It would carry on happening. We would win a game and then lose one which we should have won. We weren't over the hump yet – we hadn't got the consistency level right.

After beating Doncaster away and then drawing at home with Hull, we were preparing for a game at Leyton Orient when Doug dropped his second bombshell. Again, it was Robin who gave me the news, as Doug was in Spain. I was sitting in my office on the Monday when the phone rang.

'Jan . . .' said Robin. 'Just to let you know that I'm faxing the Football League to let them know that all the players are up for sale – including you.'

As you can imagine, I was more than a little annoyed. The chairman had made this decision without consulting me at all. I felt that we were a couple of players short of getting it right and I wasn't looking to offload anyone, even if the price was right. A lot of people made more of the chairman's move than I did, but I'll admit I wasn't impressed. It would have been nice for Doug to have had a word with me beforehand. After all, I was the manager.

For a while, the decision really shook the players. They were looking over their shoulders all the time, but gradually we used it to our own advantage to gee them up. Billy and I played on it and the whole thing brought us closer together. We told the players it was us against the world, and team spirit improved. We turned in our best performance of the season in losing to a late goal at Orient and then we drew our next four matches. I felt we were playing some reasonable football and we were on our way back. The trouble was that we were still sliding down the table.

During this terrible spell, my confidence took a bit of a knock. My biggest worries were: Have I got it right? Is it my fault? Not everyone does it, but certainly my first reaction was to look in the mirror and ask myself those rather awkward questions. At times, I didn't think I was getting it right. Even so, I was still pretty confident in what I was trying to do. I wanted to make us a passing team, even though people kept warning me that I couldn't. I was told we had to be big, tough and strong. My view was that we could be all of those things but still play as well. And I must be honest, I didn't take much notice of all the advice I was given. I think that I was eventually proved right because we came through with the same players, in the end, to reach Wembley. I drew on the people around me – Billy, Alan Curtis and Ron Walton – and we decided that we were on the right track and we would stick at it. We thought about changing things but never did.

We hit rock bottom in our very next game – away at Torquay. I had a spot of groin trouble so Lee Jenkins returned for one of those games that I knew we were going to lose. I could just see that we weren't up for it: we weren't organized and, even when Torquay had a man sent off after half an hour, I couldn't see us winning. We ended up losing 2–0 on a day when Torquay didn't play particularly well. But we were appalling. It was so galling because Billy and I both felt that in recent games we had been making progress. The players had seemed to be grasping what we were trying to do and then came the Torquay game. But maybe things had to get worse before they really got better.

After the game, Billy and I had a right go at the players in the dressing room. The majority of them were putting in as much effort as they could but it wasn't coming right. You have to be careful how hard you go in on players. You've got to remember to encourage them and not always jump down their throats. But the Torquay result meant the gloves came off. They weren't good enough – and we told them so.

We made it clear that if they didn't buck up in the next couple of games, then we would go with the kids. We'd already shown we weren't afraid to. Apart from throwing in Lee Jenkins, Ryan Casey, another trainee, made his full debut against Colchester at 17 and Damien Lacey, who was only 18, had played in the first five League games. Ryan, who was born in Coventry, had the ability to go past people and deliver crosses and, in doing so, provided us with a very useful outlet. Damien comes from Bridgend, just down the road from Swansea, and has been very unlucky with injury. After figuring in the team early on, he developed a kidney disorder, which ruled him out for the rest of the season. I think all the young players at Swansea are ahead of their time, but they still need a couple of seasons before they're ready to take on the responsibilities themselves.

I think the players were pretty upset because, as we were travelling back on the coach, we heard that all the other results had gone against us and we'd dropped to second from bottom. Ninety-first in the Football League! The second-worst team in the country, with just 14 points from 15 games. We were second only to Brighton. The table made pretty grim reading in the Sunday tabloids and there was no hiding on the Monday because the Swansea paper, the *South Wales Evening Post*, was out and it was all over the back page.

The Torquay defeat was a turning point. It was the first time that I'd come out in public and had a go at my players. Up until then, I'd stood by them, come rain or shine, but I now compared their performances and approach to the standard found in the Conference. We were as bad as that. The league table doesn't lie.

The Cygnets Start to Swim

Almost immediately, the players had a chance to put right the wrongs of Torquay. We played Wigan at the Vetch on the following Tuesday night and we couldn't have asked for a better game. They were up near the top of the table, one of the favourites for promotion, and we didn't need to motivate the players at all. We played really well and, after being 2–0 up at half-time, eventually won 2–1.

Before that, we'd had three wins in the League but none of them gave us the confidence to think that we could compete with the best. This one did. It made the players believe in their ability and we then beat Northampton 1–0 at home in a very scrappy game. Two weeks earlier, we would have drawn that game, but now we were getting the breaks. We started to see some quality in training as well. Six points in a week – we'd nearly doubled our number of wins for the season in two games!

After losing 2–1 at Cambridge to a fluke goal from the former Swansea player Paul Raynor, the press suggested we were once more back to square one. I disagreed – I thought the result was just a blip and, to prove it, we then hit a real purple patch: six League wins on the trot, which propelled us up into the promotion play-off places. The players had the confidence of their wins over Wigan and Northampton, they believed what we were trying to do was right, and we brought back Pat Ampadu into midfield after having left him out for a couple of weeks. Pat was one of our most experienced players (Arsenal and West Bromwich Albion were among his former clubs) and the kick up the backside produced the right response. This showed that we weren't issuing hollow threats. If players weren't doing the business, we'd act. It worked with Pat, who knew that he'd play when I wasn't available. Very rarely would we appear together. He was disappointed because, although he was playing well, he could sometimes find himself on the bench.

Our second turning point in the revival was the 3–1 Welsh derby win at Cardiff in early December. They were 5 points ahead of us with a game in hand so we had to beat them. I think we came of age against Cardiff. We won quite comprehensively with a very impressive performance which made me think we really were getting somewhere.

By a quirk of the fixture computer, we had an eighteen-day break without a game, and the rest did us good. We then won away at Exeter and Hereford over Christmas and started to set our sights on the top three. Our supporters seemed to share our optimism too: nearly seven-and-a-half thousand turned up for the Boxing Day match against Carlisle. We lost 1–0 to a late goal and the team now faced a new test. How would we react to a defeat after six straight wins?

In the event, we responded well, drawing at Hull and beating Barnet and Leyton Orient at the Vetch. It was important to get back into the swing of things. We suffered another hiccup at Wigan, where we lost 3–2, but again the players reacted well, bouncing back with three wins on the trot – the last, 2–1 away at Northampton.

This spell showed that the players were becoming better at recovering from setbacks. We realized that our problems were over – we could handle getting beaten without falling apart over the next few games. We could deal with the situation; the players began to grow up. It was important that everything didn't come in twos or threes – draws or defeats – and we felt we were making real progress.

The third turning point came at Fulham in the second week of February. Along with Wigan and Carlisle, they'd been the Third Division pace-setters and we were 5 points behind them having played a game more. This was the big one – a win and we'd be just 2 points adrift. We started well and went a goal up. They equalized. We hit the post straightaway, then a defensive mistake gave them the winner 6 minutes from time. That defeat put paid to our chances of going up automatically. We then went on to lose the next three games, against Scarborough, Brighton, and Cardiff, in a nasty, bad-tempered derby at the Vetch.

It was weird. Normally, a string of defeats means a drop down the table. We'd been in 4th position since the end of January but despite losing those four on the trot, we stayed there. None of our rivals did enough to catch us, everybody was beating everybody else, which just showed how tight it all was. I always felt that once we beat Cambridge at the end of January to go 4th for the first time, and then lost at Fulham, the players were waiting for the play-offs. They picked the games we had to win, and they were dying to know who we would meet in the semi-finals.

After those four successive defeats, we went on another little run – four wins and a draw – to consolidate our 4th position. We then slipped up at Lincoln, Colchester and Scunthorpe, but made sure of a play-off place by beating Mansfield 3–2 at the Vetch. A 2-2 draw at home to Hartlepool on the last Saturday meant we finished 5th – one point behind Northampton, who would meet Cardiff in the semi-finals. Only Chester stood between Swansea and a place at Wembley. I could sense that the team were up for it now that they knew our play-off opponents.

It was time to pamper the players a little so we took them away to a secret hideout in North Wales for a couple of days before the first leg. We sensed they were starting to regroup and look after each other. Although a hamstring injury made me a non-starter for the game at the Deva Stadium, we didn't make that public. Instead, we indulged in a little bit of psychology, because we knew that Chester's manager, Kevin Ratcliffe, an old Merseyside rival of mine, would be worried if he thought I was playing.

We had decided to change our formation anyway. With 4–3–3, our defence had been a bit dodgy, so we switched to 4–4–2 to give us a more solid look. We wanted to get our wide men back to stop their full-backs getting out. We always felt that keeping a clean sheet at Chester was going to be the key to the semi-final game, and so it proved. We were delighted with the goalless draw at the Deva Stadium.

I could have played in the second leg at the Vetch but I felt that everybody had done enough to keep their places. Richard Appleby was suspended but Carl Heggs was more than due a start after recovering from tonsillitis, so we threw him in. He was raring to go. We reverted back to 4–3–3 and went after Chester.

I'd signed Richard Appleby on a free transfer from Ipswich after he'd spent six years at Newcastle as a schoolboy. I'd heard about him at St James' Park, so when I knew he was available we got him down to the Vetch. Thanks to his background, he picked up drills in training quickly and passed the ball well, but, at that time, he didn't quite have the experience to deal with the rough and tumble of the Third Division.

Carl Heggs was one of the most frustrating players I found at the Vetch. For the majority of the time, we tried to play 4–3–3, but that means your front men have got to work, and he didn't. His goals-per-game ratio in the reserves was sensational, but we felt maybe that was his level. Every time we gave him a chance in the first team, he couldn't do it.

Anyway, we gave him another opportunity against Chester and, for the first 25 minutes, we put them under tremendous pressure. We knew it would be intimidating with the crowd behind us so we kicked everything into the box. We didn't score during that spell but we laid the foundations for the rest of the game. The one setback was the horrific injury to Steve Jones after about a quarter of an hour. He broke his leg after colliding with Pat Ampadu as they tracked back at a corner and the game was held up for a good

234

10 minutes. Steve's injury disrupted our momentum for a while, because one or two of the players started to feel sorry for him. We hit the post and had two attempts cleared off the line before scoring twice just before half-time. From then on, I never felt we were going to lose the game.

Steve had been with the club for about six months before I came, after signing from Cheltenham Town. I first thought he was a centre-back, so that's where I played him, but when he was moved to right-back, he really made his mark. When we were playing 4–3–3, he had all the right-hand side to himself. It may have been too much for some people, but it wasn't enough for Steve. He loved ploughing up and down when he was attacking and, as a defender, he was tremendous in the air. He hardly lost a ball in the air all season. Through his injury, we not only lost Steve against North-ampton at Wembley, but also the drive of David Penny from midfield. He moved back to replace Steve in defence and with him went our bite and our appetite to go forward.

We used Steve's injury to our advantage in the half-time team talk, though. He would want us to go on and win the game so that at least he could go to Wembley, if not play there. It was ironic, because we'd been kidding Steve about the way he never seemed to get injured. He'd been our best player through the season, but the joke was that he wasn't brave enough to get injured, though of course his commitment caused the tragedy.

In the second half we scored our third, but we had so many chances it could have been five or six.

It was fantastic to be back at Wembley for the first time for five years, but the build-up was completely different to the last time I visited the Twin Towers.

As a player, everything is done for you. You train all week before arriving at the team hotel on the Thursday. You don't know what goes on behind the scenes. As a manager, I suddenly learnt what a football club goes through in the time between reaching and playing at the famous stadium.

There were so many things to do! I was involved in virtually everything: from kitting out the players with new blazers and

235

leisurewear to sorting out the venue for the post-match party in Swansea. I had to fix tickets for friends and make travel arrangements, not to mention sorting out everything for eleven people coming over from Denmark for the game.

We struggled to find a hotel in London which could put us up on both the Thursday and Friday. I tried ringing some of the ones Liverpool had stayed at but eventually we booked in at Burnham Beeches, north of Slough. As well as being England's HQ, it had been used by Swansea when they won the Autoglass Trophy at Wembley three years earlier. The chairman was keen to stay there again because he saw the hotel as a lucky omen after Swansea had beaten Huddersfield on penalties.

We also had a problem finding training pitches because by May many were being prepared for the next season. And then, to cap it all, we had to find a new kit. Northampton had won the toss and chosen to wear their home strip – claret shirts and white shorts – which clashed with our white shorts, but because I didn't like our away colours (black shirts and shorts with red stripes and trim) we had to get some new shorts and socks made up. We'd had some horrific results in that away strip and I didn't want to wear it at Wembley. Instead, we had our normal white shirts with black pin-stripes and black shorts and socks. We were sweating a little at the hotel, because the new kit didn't arrive until late on the Friday afternoon.

Then there was all the media attention. As well as all the regular reporters from Wales, it was the first time all season that we'd been live on Sky, and they wanted to do a piece on us. Danish TV and papers were also interested. The world and his wife seemed to want a slice of the action. I must admit to enjoying it all, because you only get that sort of coverage when you're successful, but it was a relief to leave Swansea after training on the Thursday to seek some sort of sanctuary at Burnham Beeches.

One-off at Wembley

Saturday 24 May 1997. I'll remember it until I die. Swansea City's date with destiny at the home of football. Wembley Stadium, the scene of my greatest triumph, was about to become the graveyard of our promotion ambitions.

We kept to our normal routine for away matches by having a walk around the hotel grounds on Saturday morning. The pre-match meal came next, but by that stage the players just wanted to be on the coach and on their way to Wembley. We finally left the hotel at about a quarter to one and headed towards north London.

Every time I'd been to Wembley with Liverpool, I'd sat at the back of the bus playing cards and occasionally looking out of the window. As Swansea's player-manager, I had to be down the front. The lads wanted the music on loud so they wouldn't have to talk to anyone. They were happy to sit there with their own thoughts and enjoy every minute of the day.

The nearer we got to Wembley, the more we saw of the Swansea and Northampton fans as we drove along Wembley Way and up to the tunnel. It's always a special moment arriving at the big door and the lads were in good spirits. The only things worrying us were the Northampton supporters. They were all over the place, easily outnumbering our fans by about two to one. We were inside Wembley an hour and a half before kick-off.

Once inside the dressing room, I braced myself for the worst moment of my managerial career so far – having to tell those unlucky players who were in the squad but wouldn't be on the bench. We'd already named the team the night before but decided to leave announcing the subs until just before the match. It's always best to keep everyone involved for as long as possible. The result was awful – the last thing I wanted to happen. Lee Jenkins, who was only 18, burst into tears in front of everybody when I told him the bad news.

He wasn't going to be taking part in the biggest game of his life. There was no nice way of telling him and he just couldn't stop crying.

Billy and I had simply picked the fourteen we thought were the best to do the job on the day. We moved Dave Penney out of position to right-back in place of Steve Jones, which meant naming Damien Lacey on the bench. If Dave had to move into midfield, Damien could fill in at full-back. Lee was the unfortunate one to miss out. A couple of the senior players put their arms around him and took him out on to the pitch. I had a word with Lee when he came back in. He said he was just so disappointed – the sort of reaction I expected, and was pleased to hear. All he wanted was for us to win. I felt so sorry for him, but there was nothing I could do to ease the pain.

As usual, I didn't warm up with the rest of the lads out on the pitch. I never have done before any game I've played at Wembley. I just prefer to prepare on my own in the dressing room. Billy asked if I wanted to take a look at the pitch but I said no. I felt drained and tired and, to be honest, I wasn't really up for the game. I thought I would spend a bit of time by myself while the other lads were trying out the sacred turf. I splashed some water on my face to try to liven myself up a bit, but I felt drained by the whole week – I think it had finally got the better of me.

I didn't tell the players or Billy until the next day. Looking back, I suspect that's how Kenny Dalglish must have felt as player-manager in the 1986 Cup Final. I'm not trying to make excuses for my performance – it's just the way I felt. When we announced the team on the Friday, I was bubbling and buzzing, all ready to go. Even on the Saturday morning, I felt OK, but as the game drew nearer it got to me, especially leading out the team. Perhaps I shouldn't have played, but we had made the decision and that was the way it was.

To be honest, it wasn't much of a game and I didn't make a great contribution. I was on the fringe of the action. Although we had the majority of the play, I think we saw too much of the ball in our own half. It took the urgency out of our game on a hot afternoon. Northampton gave us the opportunity to take it easy and we did. If we had been under a bit more pressure, perhaps we would have gone on to win the final – who knows?

I thought we'd gone in front after about 5 minutes. The ball was cleared to me on the edge of the box and I spotted Carl Heggs moving across the eighteen-yard line. I cushioned a header into his path, he took the ball on his thigh and then swivelled and shot in one movement. It was a lovely strike (I know because I was right behind it). It looked a goal all the way until Andy Woodman tipped it over at the very last moment – a fantastic save.

I was quite happy with our start. When we'd begun brightly in the past, we'd normally done well. My next significant involvement nearly cost us dear. After about 20 minutes, I was caught in possession in the centre-circle and Chris Edwards ended up having to clear a shot which seemed to be heading towards the goal. He wasn't to know it was going wide and his clearance back across the goal hit my leg as I was tracking back. I managed to cushion it, the ball was picked up by our keeper Roger Freestone and he cleared upfield. Luckily, the referee didn't consider it to be a back-pass. A goal, or a free-kick leading to a goal, would have been a hell of a story – they both would have been traced back to my original mistake.

The rest of the game was pretty forgettable. We dominated large parts of it without really creating any clear-cut chances, and then got caught by that sucker punch in injury time. It stemmed from a throw-in out on our right which ended up just outside the area. We might have disagreed with the original decision to award a free-kick, and it shouldn't have been taken twice, but there was nothing we could do but defend. The fact is we didn't defend well enough. The rest is history.

Gosh, it's Tosh . . . Again

I suppose it was always going to happen. There was no way when I took over as player-manager at Swansea that I wasn't going to be compared with John Toshack. I could see it coming from the moment I met Doug Sharpe at Haydock.

The link was so obvious. Two former Liverpool internationals with FA Cup and League-title medals coming down to Swansea to try to perform a minor miracle. It had to happen, and I understand why it did, but people should realize that the circumstances were totally different. Times have changed, and unless the Premiership bubble bursts, football won't ever be the same again.

When John first came to the Vetch Field, he could bring First Division players down to Wales because the wage gap wasn't that big. Tommy Smith and Ian Callaghan jumped at the chance to prolong their careers by a couple of years as Swansea made their way up the divisions. Nowadays, lower-division clubs wouldn't have a chance of buying players from Liverpool – even on loan – because they couldn't pay their kind of wages.

I remember it taking me eighteen months to get rid of the 'new Graeme Souness' tag at Liverpool. I was never the same sort of player as Graeme and I'll never be the same sort of manager as John. I think in some ways the success achieved in the Toshack era is still weighing Swansea down. The fans reminded me of the good times, although they didn't call them the John Toshack days – his name wasn't mentioned all that often. I'll admit we're similar looking, but let's just say that my first touch was better than his and he was much more dangerous than me in the air!

Our accents are similar too. As former ports, Cardiff and Liverpool have quite a lot in common, and the Cardiff accent has a touch of the Scouser in it. I'm not really sure why I speak such strong Liverpudlian. When I first arrived in Merseyside, I spent the first nine months living in a hotel in the city centre mixing with people with very strong accents, so I must have picked it up from day one. Then in the Liverpool dressing room, I always got changed next to Sammy Lee, one of the greatest living Scousers, so people shouldn't be too surprised by the way I talk.

Merseyside will always hold a special place in my heart because the people there took me to theirs. Their humour, generosity and support were a great help during the difficult years and my family – Mandy and the children Kingsley and Karina – still live there in Wallasey. I had a flat in Caswell Bay, about two miles from the Vetch, out on the coast, and the family came down to stay during school holidays. It was not ideal, seeing so little of them, but with football being such an insecure business, we didn't think it was right to take the children out of school and move down permanently.

Looking back over my two years at the Vetch, I don't see myself as a failure. In fact, I really enjoyed my time at the Vetch Field. We had three eventful seasons, which all ended in disappointment. If I'd had a lot of money to bring in new players and hadn't taken us up, then I think you could say I had failed. I tried to set myself as high a standard as possible and, although we didn't win promotion, I don't think anyone can point the finger.

The transfer market was almost a no-go area in the 1996–97 season. The club had borrowed £120,000 from the Football League for ground improvements, and when it wasn't repaid we were banned from buying new players. All we could do was beg, steal or borrow. We let three players go during the season (John Hodge, Andy Cook and Shaun Garnett), and we signed three on loan – John Hills, Paul Brayson and Thomas Willar. Apart from that, we stuck with the players we had and I think they benefited because were able to spend more time with them rather than driving up and down motorways looking for new ones.

We kick-started one or two careers as well. David Penney probably had his best-ever season, and re-paid us by signing for Cardiff in the summer!, while Jonathan Coates, Chris Edwards and Dai Thomas were regulars in the side. Steve Jones was sensational before breaking his leg against Chester, and youngsters like Lee Jenkins and Ryan Casey came through well.

Towards the end of my first season at the Vetch, I gave Jonathan Coates a free transfer . . . on the insistence of chairman Doug Sharpe. Jonathan was a Swansea boy and a former trainee who played in midfield. But before he had the chance to find himself a new club, I saw him in the reserves and decided to hang on to him. I pleaded with the chairman and, to his credit, Doug gave him a one-year contract. Jonathan turned out to be one of our best players in our play-off season.

Chris Edwards, from Caerphilly, north of Cardiff, was described to me as a central defender who would go a long way in the game. My first impression, though, was that Chrissie lacked confidence. Without confidence, you can't play. For the first couple of games, I think he was helped by having me alongside him, and he went on to have a good season for us, and, like Jonathan, he was in the Welsh Under-21 squad. He later moved to Nottingham Forest.

Another Caerphilly boy was Dai Thomas who, again, it was suggested to me, we should let go. The chairman said a number of managers had been banging their heads against the wall with Dai, who had ability but didn't want to use it. The thing that worried me was his fitness, so we sent him up to Lilleshall where he was given a programme to work on during the summer. When he came back at the end of the close season, I knew he'd kept to it. He was extremely fit and, although he didn't play in every game during his first full season, we later sold him for £100,000 to Watford. And this was a player we were going to throw out! Stories like that give me a lot of pleasure.

On a personal note, I was more frustrated with the way I played than the injuries which restricted me to fewer than thirty matches. Before Christmas I was poor but, in the New Year, when our form in general picked up, so did mine. I'd probably put it down to the pressure of player-management, because it was tough. We definitely wouldn't have achieved what we did without Billy. I needed someone to take charge of the training sessions, as when I was fit I became one of the lads. His knowledge of lower-league football meant he knew how much the players could take on board tactically.

A lot of the training was obviously geared towards the games, but Billy did it without the players realizing it. We didn't try to confuse them with too many ideas; they knew they had one or two specific jobs to do and we kept it as simple as we could. Billy and I had a very good relationship. We disagreed on a lot of things, which I think is good, but I had the final say.

There is no distinct Jan Molby style but I have been brought up on a passing game at Ajax and Liverpool, and that's the sort of game we liked to play at the Vetch. After our defeat by Northampton at Wembley, where we were the better footballing side, some people suggested that we should concentrate more on route one at the expense of our short-ball approach. In 1996–97, two passing teams, Carlisle and Wigan, and two more direct teams, Fulham and Northampton, were promoted. We beat Northampton twice in the regular season.

When we began in August 1996, we didn't have the right people to play the passing game. We were asking certain players to pass the ball from the back, but gradually we more or less abandoned that because too many mistakes were being made. We were getting caught out playing from the back four into the midfield. Eventually we sorted it out: our centre-backs would put the ball in the corners for the forwards to chase, and we'd started playing from there. If we got caught out, it was through the centre-forward playing it back to the midfield, which meant there were still seven or eight men behind the ball. So we looked a lot more solid.

The future of the club looked anything but solid in the summer of 1997, what with Doug wanting to sell it and talks taking place with various interested parties almost all the time. At times, the uncertainty helped us – like when Doug put the club and the players on the market – but I think we have to accept that players outside the Premiership are all up for sale all the time. If the offer's right, the chairmen will accept it because they need the money. But it's one thing putting players up for sale, it's another thing selling them.

By and large, Doug and I had a good relationship. We had our disagreements, but then show me a manager and chairman who don't fall out every now and then. There were one or two flashpoints, like the time we had to declare an uneasy truce after David Seal's transfer from Bristol City fell through at the last moment and Doug had a go at me on the Swansea ClubCall line. (Billy, Robin Sharpe and I had agreed a deal with David and his agent on a Thursday night but the contract wasn't signed as expected on the Friday morning because of a misunderstanding over figures. As a result, my frustration led to me criticizing Doug in public. He then used the ClubCall line to answer back. He said he was paying me enough money to do the job, and he expected a little more loyalty from me. According to Doug, I should have stopped moaning and just got on with it.)

The chairman exploded again a few days later when a planned takeover by a London consortium collapsed. He vowed he was never going to set foot inside the Vetch Field again and, for a few matches, he was true to his word. But those comments were made in the heat of the moment, and because Doug's a Swansea fan through and through, back he came for the play-offs. His heart's in the right place but, by the end of the season, he felt he had taken the club as far as he could – a position I could understand.

My relationship with the Swansea supporters meant a lot to me. I wasn't sure why it was so good. I suppose it might have had something to do with the fact that I'm a younger manager, someone perhaps they could relate to. We tried to tell them as much as we could about what was going on at the Vetch via ClubCall, the local press and media.

The two or three thousand who make up the hard-core of the supporters are tremendous. They're fanatical, they want the club to do well, but in all the time I was there they never once turned on me. Even when we were ninety-first in the League, they were on my side. Three hundred and fifty of them came all the way down to Torquay to see us lose to ten men, but they gave the players a standing ovation at the end.

During our spell of six straight defeats in 1996, Mandy and the children came to the home game against Lincoln. I said they should go home if the crowd started to bad-mouth me. I didn't want them to hear people having a go, but nothing happened. There were always one or two regulars who wrote letters about team selection, but I never received any hate-mail.

One side-effect of joining Swansea was my involvement with horse racing. I used to be a regular at the Cheltenham Festival but I missed two years because of the Swansea job. In my time, I've part-owned six horses with, among other people, Ian Rush and my agent Dave Sheron. The three of us bought one horse, Great Marquis. It won half its fourten races and was then retired injured – a bit like one of its owners.

My interest in racing began in 1988 when I had a couple of hundred pounds in my pocket. I was going home for a sleep and I asked a mate of mine to put the money on a horse whose name I just picked out of the paper. Willie Carson was on board and as he was the only jockey I'd ever heard of, I decided to back it. When I woke up, I looked up the result on Teletext and found the horse had won at odds of 7 to 1 and I was £1400 richer. When my mate turned up with only £700, he claimed he just couldn't put the whole £200 on such a novice so had only backed it with £100. He returned the other hundred, and I was hooked.

For a while, betting became quite easy. On my first visit to Haydock, I backed four winners out of six and went one better the next time. I was coming away with £700 every time I went to a meeting. I had met the champion jockey Peter Scudamore during one of my visits to Lilleshall, and he supplied me with some information about form.

Then for about a year, I couldn't pick any winners. I was getting idle, I was becoming too clever and I thought I knew everything about it. But I didn't, and had a bad year. I then decided that if a job's worth doing, it's worth doing well. If I was going to bet, I ought to do it properly by reading racing papers and books and watching the horses every day. So that's what I did for three or four years, and I won quite a bit of money.

But my biggest win came not on the horses but a double tennis and football bet. If you win the first part, then all your money goes on to the second bet, but if you lose the first one, then you lose everything. In 1990, I decided to back Stefan Edberg to win Wimbledon and

Germany to lift the World Cup in Italy. The only reason I laid the bet was that the finals were being played on the same day on a Sunday in July. I had just won £1000 on a horse and I was just about to go back to Denmark for the summer when I thought I'd have a flutter. It would be a bit of a risk, but what the hell.

I split the double bet right down the middle – £500 on Edberg to win at 7 to 1 and £500 on Germany to win at 8 to 1. I went home to Denmark and watched the two events on the television. First Edberg did the business by beating Boris Becker. And then when the final whistle blew in Rome, and Argentina had been beaten 1–0, any animosity I felt towards our near-neighbours over the border suddenly disappeared! The Germans were the greatest as far as I was concerned. I'd won nearly £36,000! I seem to remember that was a very good summer.

PART SIX

Back to the Drawing Board

It took me a while to recover from Wembley. Everything was very flat during the next four or five weeks, whereas when we had been relegated, I couldn't wait to get on with it. At that time, I felt I wanted to make my mark, but in the summer of 1997 I almost called it a day as a player. I couldn't seem to get going. I knew I needed something to excite me, but I came back for the pre-season feeling very depressed.

Normally, we would have been quite busy preparing for the new season, but because the takeover was expected to go through straight after Wembley, everything was put on hold. The club virtually stopped trading. We were in a state of limbo, waiting for the new owners to come in. It was very frustrating.

It was nice to be involved with the talks and, as I was kept informed by both sides, I realized how difficult it is to buy a business. Both sides were jockeying for position, there were meetings when everything seemed to be settled, and then it would all be off – sometimes the very next day. Some sort of takeover deal looked to be on three or four times, but it kept falling through and the players were rightly concerned about their future.

All the uncertainty over the future of the club took its toll. We had the heart ripped out of the team which took us to Wembley when we were hoping to build on it. We had identified three or four areas which needed strengthening, but when three players went, suddenly our shopping list contained six or seven replacements.

Our captain Dave Penney was the first to go. He was looking for a two-year deal to take him to his pensionable age of 35, but because of the possible takeover we couldn't make that sort of commitment. He couldn't hang on for ever and the offer from Cardiff was too good to turn down. I don't blame him, but I just wish he'd given us another week. Dai Thomas, our second-top scorer, had only played one full season with us and I felt he should be in the middle bracket of our wage structure, not up with the big boys. I wasn't prepared to pay him the money he wanted, so he went to Watford for £100,000.

I was sad to lose Dai, but very annoyed when Carl Heggs went off to Northampton. I found him very frustrating when I arrived, but eventually the message got through. He had a great run-in to the end of the 1996–97 season and so I offered him a two-year contract as a reward. We talked and talked, we thought we had an agreement on an improved contract, but in the end, after playing us off against Northampton, he went there. I didn't mind him signing for the team who beat us at Wembley – he can play for whom he wants – I just didn't like the way he conducted himself.

On the other side of the coin, some of the players showed real commitment to the club. Straight after Wembley, we called the squad in to announce the retained list. We offered contracts to most of the players, and two of them, our keeper Roger Freestone and Jonathan Coates, both said they would sign as long as I was staying at the Vetch. I was really pleased with their attitude and it cheered me up no end but, by the time all the transfers had been sorted out, I was pretty down. I knew that my presence on the field was needed even more than ever, but I just didn't feel up to it. That was, until Billy delivered a few home truths. When we returned to the Vetch Field for pre-season, I told him I'd retired.

'Not officially?' he said.

'No, not officially,' I replied. 'I'm going to do all the pre-season work, but I don't really want to go on playing. I'll let the boys get on with it.'

'But you know how important you are,' said Billy. 'You know what you mean to them – that's just the way it is. You must carry on.'

As it turned out, the first two pre-season games were crucial. I didn't play in a 1–1 draw at Morecambe or a 4–2 defeat by South-port. Billy had another word.

'We need you out there,' he said. 'If anything, just to get them back playing and winning. To show them what it's all about, because they've forgotten during the summer.'

So I played in the next two games as we trounced Burscough 4–0 and Llanelli 8–0, in front of a crowd of about 800. I realized the buzz was back. I had missed playing. Billy was right. The boys would be looking to me for a lead. I had a duty not to let them down.

Unfortunately, the takeover and then a foot injury I picked up in training meant my return to the first team was delayed for seven weeks. I was finding the role of player-manager pretty demanding. Towards the end of our build-up to the new season, the takeover by Silver Shield was coming to a head and I was spending every moment of every day in meetings. Training took a back seat as last-minute details and transfers were ironed out, so I decided to delay my return as a player until a couple of weeks into the new season. The chairman Steve Hamer wanted me to play in every game, but if I could make 46 appearances a season I would still be at Liverpool. They let me go because I was picking up too many injuries, and it was no different at Swansea.

When I picked up injuries in the nineties – say, to my calf or Achilles tendon – I probably wasn't doing myself any favours by coming back before I was fit. Sometimes I felt the team was looking for something which I could supply – if I had been 100 per cent fit. Half the time, I played before I was ready, which is the worst thing you can do because you then pick up other injuries. It wasn't helped by the fact that Liverpool didn't have a physio to guide you and tell you when you were ready – it was left to you. When Ronnie Moran asked me if I was fit, I'd always say, 'Yes!' There was no way in a million years that I would have said I wasn't fit, because I badly wanted to play.

In the 1996–97 season, I could have played more games for Swansea but I didn't feel there was any need. I missed some through injury, but I also sat out others when I could have been involved. I wasn't just at Swansea to play. I was employed to manage as well, which meant not playing unless I was needed. Doug Sharpe actually suggested I should pack in playing and concentrate on being a manager – the complete opposite of the advice I received from the club's new owners who bought him out!

I wanted to play as much as I could, because it was so frustrating being in the dug-out and only being able to influence events from a distance. And I didn't want to be one of those players who are always complaining that they retired too early.

I suppose I took a bit of a risk dropping down to the Third Division, but it was a challenge I couldn't refuse. I knew my time at Anfield was up, yet I wanted to stay in football, and Swansea gave me the chance to do just that. I love the day-to-day involvement, the camaraderie of the dressing room – just being part of a club. I know Kenny Dalglish feels the same – I'm sure he's taking part in the five-a-sides at Celtic with our old Liverpool team-mate John Barnes.

Life in Swansea was a world away from Liverpool, not just three divisions. The difference between the Premiership and the lower leagues isn't just about players' wages. It's more to do with the shortage of money and the way it affects the running of a club. When I was at Liverpool, I didn't have to worry about anything. It was all done for me and money was no object. At Swansea, every penny had to be accounted for.

Before every away game, we discussed whether we needed an overnight stay. We looked at the map, saw how far the journey was and how long it was likely to take. It's been proved that you win more games if players get a good night's sleep and don't spend the morning of a match on a coach, and I just think that staying overnight removes the excuse. If they're not performing well, players can always blame bad preparation beforehand. The trouble was that we couldn't always afford to go away. When we had to go to Mansfield and Scunthorpe in the 1996–97 season, Swansea's chief executive Robin Sharpe said we couldn't stay overnight because there was no money. We decided to ask a few local firms to help us out, but when they offered to, Robin declined. He claimed that wasn't the way to do business, so we didn't go the night before.

At the other end of the scale, we went through a spell when money was so tight that we couldn't afford strappings for the players to put around their legs and ankles! After a while, I became used to expecting nothing, then you're grateful for what you eventually get. It was no good looking back to the way I'd become used to doing things for twelve years at Liverpool and wishing it could continue. I had to adapt.

It helped being at Swansea, which is a great football club with great traditions. What I really liked were the players and the fact that so many of them were really promising youngsters. That's a tribute to people like Alan Curtis, Ron Walton and Billy, who spent a lot of time with them. Senior players, like Keith Walker and Roger Freestone, who pledged their futures to the club, also needed to feel that Swansea were going places.

It may seem funny, only a little thing, but the players needed to be wearing new training kit at the start of the 1997–98 season, to replace the gear that was on its last legs. It was used every day of the season in all kinds of weather and a new strip gave the squad a lift. Keith could have gone to Wycombe and Roger was wanted by Gillingham – teams playing in a higher league – but they decided to stay at the Vetch, and Swansea need to repay their faith.

Loyalty doesn't seem to count for much in football these days. With the amount of money sloshing around in the game, players are quite prepared to up sticks and move if it means a pay rise or a huge signing-on fee. I must admit that I was disappointed by the way in which my loyalty to Liverpool was rewarded in August 1996 in my testimonial at Anfield.

I was very proud to be the first Liverpool foreigner to be given one but I didn't have much to do with the organization of the game, against PSV Eindhoven – I left that to the committee. I remember, weeks before the game, reminding them of the saying 'out of sight, out of mind'. As I hadn't played for Liverpool for eighteen months, I suggested we ask them down to the Vetch Field where we'd be guaranteed a good crowd, perhaps 15,000, which was almost the ground's capacity then.

The committee felt we would get more at Anfield, but I had my doubts. I'm afraid I was proved right. Only 8360 people turned up, the lowest-ever attendance for a testimonial at Anfield. It was partly because I'd been gone too long and partly because of the time of year, early August, when everyone was away on holiday.

The choice of opponents wasn't brilliant either. Some people thought PSV were a good choice, but they wouldn't have been mine. We had an opportunity to bring down Newcastle and we tried for Ajax, but dates were the problem, so we ended up bringing PSV over on a Friday night for a £40,000 appearance fee. The game couldn't be staged on the Saturday because Liverpool were hosting a wedding.

I think I was unfortunate because there wasn't much interest in testimonials at the time. In the past, players had made hundreds of thousands of pounds out of them, but with the Premiership bringing in Sky money testimonials aren't seen as a way of rewarding players any more – they're generally doing pretty well through their normal wages.

It was disappointing to end my connection with Liverpool on such a low note, but that's the way it goes. I didn't lose any money, but it certainly wasn't a night to remember – Liverpool lost 3–2 and I was taken off midway through the second half!

A year to the day, 9 August 1997, our new season kicked off with a home game against Brighton at the Vetch Field. If results had been slightly different in May, then Swansea and Brighton might have been two divisions apart. In the week building up to the match, I began to get a glimpse of the sort of pressure Brighton must have been under.

When our takeover deal was finally signed, sealed and delivered at half-past five on the Thursday before the season kicked off, I had mixed emotions. I was relieved it was all over, and yet sad because Doug Sharpe was leaving. Since he'd put the club up for sale, and especially since Wembley, we'd got closer. We spoke more than ever, and we spent a great day together going to Sheffield for the Carl Heggs tribunal ruling on his £25,000 transfer fee to Northampton. We had a good laugh, Doug's got a great sense of humour, and I felt a little sad to see him go. But he'd made the decision to get out because he felt he couldn't take the club forward to the next stage.

The new owners have a five-year plan and I hope things will gradually improve during their time at Swansea. It wasn't the ideal time to take over a club – barely forty-eight hours before the new season began – but at least it finally happened.

The new owners are very ambitious and they know that Division Three is not the place to be. Even the First Division now is big business, and the next one to be hit will be Division Two. I look around and see all sorts of clubs having a go, spending some money to get themselves higher up the pyramid. They're all prepared to spend to attract players; they all want to get out of Division Three. Swansea have got to be with them, and if that means leaving the Vetch Field, then so be it.

The Vetch has a wonderful atmosphere but it badly needs improving. I loved playing there, and if you get more than 4500 inside the ground it's tremendous. The new owners want to move to a new sports complex at Morfa in Swansea and play football alongside rugby union. It might prove to be the right decision, but it's always sad to leave a football ground with tradition.

The new owners were shrewd enough to know and say that improvements weren't going to happen overnight. People always want success yesterday, but it never happens immediately. I think everybody realizes that a football club has got to be run like a business; you can only keep putting money into something without getting a return for so long. But the new owners also realize that, for a period of time, it's going to cost them before they turn the corner. It's the only way to do it.

I was really pleased with how everybody at the club worked together to sell Steve Torpey to Bristol City for £400,000 on the Thursday before the season started.

We had turned down an earlier offer from Bristol because Steve was our only recognized striker, but then he came in for a chat with me. I could tell by his attitude in training that something was up. Torpey made it quite clear that he wanted to leave, even though he had two years left of his contract. He said he wanted to return to the Second Division to better himself – he had made his mind up.

Now I know that unhappy players can have a bad effect on the rest of the squad, so I contacted John Ward, the manager at Ashton Gate, to see if we could resurrect the deal.

The main problem was time. Bristol wanted Torpey for the opening day of the season but, before we sold him, I wanted a replacement. We'd had Tony Bird and Dave O'Gorman on loan for a week from Barry Town, the League of Wales Champions, and we were close to agreeing a price for them when Brentford declared their interest in Bird. He'd scored 47 goals for Barry the previous season and our decision to take him on loan had obviously alerted Dave Webb, Brentford's then managing director. I spoke to Tony before he went to London and asked him not to sign for them without coming back to me.

When Barry told us the Brentford deal looked likely, I was worried. It was all getting rather complicated. We needed to sell Torpey to pay off the £120,000 loan from the Football League for ground improvements so that they would lift our embargo on buying players, and we could then get Tony Bird. We managed to match Brentford's wage offer, there was a flurry of late-night phone calls, and eventually we got our man – but not without me having to talk to his mother.

She was adamant that she didn't want Tony going to London – she would prefer it if he stayed at home in Cardiff, so that she could look after him. She wanted her son by her side, which was very sweet, and great news for us. It helped a little because I knew if he signed for Swansea, he'd carry on living at home. I knew we had that in our favour and, in the end, it all worked out well.

We finally agreed a £60,000 fee with Barry at about half-past nine on the Friday morning, and then came the mad rush to get all the paperwork done in time for the midday deadline. We met the players, they had their medicals and then signed their contracts, and we faxed the registration forms to the Football League. On top of that, we also signed David Puttnam on loan from Gillingham – and all that between half-past nine and twelve o'clock, thanks to some very hard work by Robin Sharpe, our chief executive.

It was very satisfying but very stressful. After we'd done the deals, it suddenly dawned on me: I was sitting in my office and I realized that we'd lost four of last season's five strikers – and the fifth, Linton Brown, was in the process of being released! The next day, three players would make their debuts and two of them – Bird and O'Gorman – hadn't played in the Football League for at least a couple of years (they started out with Cardiff and Wrexham respectively, before joining Barry). It was going to be a hell of a gamble, and I began wondering if we'd sold Torpey too early. But on the other hand, the £400,000 deal had been very good business.

Most important of all, our transfer embargo had been lifted by the Football League. Then, as well as off-loading an unsettled player, we'd bought a replacement and two other forwards and had some money left in the kitty for other strikers. Under the circumstances, it was the best thing we could have done.

On the morning of the match against Brighton, I was exhausted. I'd spent the last ten days in takeover and transfer talks. I hadn't trained, so there was no way I was going to play. I was really looking forward to the game after such a useful pre-season but I really felt under pressure as I made my way to the dug-out. As I walked from the tunnel, not one single supporter had a go at me about selling Torpey, but I knew we just had to win. We had to justify the decision but, in all honesty, it was unfair to expect us to pick up three points after all the upheaval over the summer and with three debutants in the side.

During the first half, I thought it wasn't going to be our day. We dominated large parts of the game but Tony Bird missed three reasonable chances. The longer it stayed goalless the more anxious I became, and Brighton began to think they might be able to sneak something. Sure enough, Roger Freestone had to pull off three excellent saves and then, 10 minutes from time, we scored. A short corner from the left, the ball swung to the far post and a Birdy header into the net. It couldn't have been more perfect. He was the high-profile signing and it was nice for him to score on his debut.

I wasn't too happy about him pulling off his shirt and running towards the crowd with it, but I can forgive him for that. He had come up with the winner, the North Bank had a new hero and, despite being a Cardiff boy, Tony was now 100 per cent for Swansea.

He didn't just come down to play professional football, he was totally committed to the Swansea cause. He's not an out-and-out goalscorer – I think he's got a lot more to offer than that.

We found that out when he came to the Vetch on trial for a week. We realized that Tony was very good in the air for somebody his size. What really struck us, though, was his desire. He had missed the boat once with Cardiff, and he was making sure it never happened again. He works so hard – like Ian Rush, he's the first line of defence. He's so honest and he wanted to do so well that, some times, we had to stop him chasing back. It's a long time since I've come across a footballer as fit as Tony, or one who spends as much time improving his game.

On the bench, Billy and I hugged each other. It was such a relief; our judgement was on the line. The expectations were so high but the fans got what they wanted and so did we. That first game was very much like the play-off at Wembley. After the build-up all week, with everyone talking about the match, we just had to win. We knew we could play better, but it was now out of the way. The players could relax. The pressure was off.

On top of that, some friends on Merseyside and I backed Swansea to win as part of a double bet. We put £50 on us to beat Brighton at 4 to 5, and then put the £90 winnings on Mansfield to beat Hull at 6 to 5. We made £140 and got our original stake back, which went into the kitty. Not a bad way to start the new season!

From Play-off to Pay-off

I'll never forget one of the first things the new chairman Steve Hamer said to me when the takeover had been completed: 'We're now going to give you an opportunity to manage,' he explained, 'which I don't think you'll ever be given again.

'You'll have the chance to bring in players and do what you want to do,' he said.

258

It was music to my ears, but over the next eight weeks it became pretty clear that we weren't singing from the same hymn sheet. And, sadly, it turned out that I was the one who was out of tune and, eventually, out of a job.

I must admit it sounded too good to be true, but I think the new board felt that my hands were tied under the Doug Sharpe regime because there wasn't a lot of money available. The implication was that things were going to be different – the trouble was I didn't realize just how different!

I first met Steve Hamer when he took me out for dinner after our 2–1 defeat by Fulham back in February 1997. He wanted to know what I was looking for. I got the feeling that it was never going to work between us. I was never sure of him and I never felt comfortable with him. I felt he was taking advice from people outside the club and that he respected their opinions more than mine.

But on the opening day of the season, such thoughts were the last thing on my mind. The club had new owners, and it was wonderful to begin the new era by beating Brighton. With Tony Bird scoring the winner, it couldn't really have been better, and I wanted to use the momentum generated by that result and the takeover. Six and a half thousand people had turned up at the Vetch Field for the Brighton game and I felt we should move pretty quickly to bring in some experienced players to replace Steve Torpey, David Penney, Carl Heggs, Dai Thomas and the injured Steve Jones. In fact, even before the takeover, I'd given the chairman the shopping list that Billy and I had drawn up.

'No problems,' replied Steve Hamer. 'We are well aware of the need for new faces. But you must bear with us. Money won't be a problem.'

I don't think it's fair to reveal all the names of the players we were after, but they were all experienced and they would all have done a good job for Swansea City. We were interested in Barry Horne, the former Welsh captain (who later moved from Birmingham to Huddersfield when Terry Yorath became coach), and Vince Oversen, a big, strong centre-half at Burnley, who then went to Shrewsbury. We were looking short term. The long-term future of the club was

OK with so many talented youngsters coming through, but we needed to stop the rot there and then. Even if it meant getting someone in on a month's loan, at least we could have built from there. We needed some experience to help the youngsters through what turned into a very difficult patch, but whenever I went to see the chairman about my list of players, nothing happened. He suggested I was throwing names at him like confetti, but there were a thousand players in the country who would have improved our team. He would scuttle off to consult his copy of *Rothmans Football Yearbook* to check their age, weight, height and previous clubs, before making a decision based on that rather than on my judgement. Invariably, the answer was no, and so I assumed it was because the chairman didn't rate the players I was after. I now suspect that the real reason was the club's financial situation – maybe there wasn't any more money at the time to buy players. I had a feeling the new owners were still in the process of raising money to fund the proposed move to the Morfa Stadium. We weren't talking about huge transfer fees but a signing-on lump sum and then wages. The board criticized me for trying to sign what they called 'geriatrics', but I now wonder if that was because they didn't have the ready money to sign anyone else.

When I spoke to the chairman at that time, he led me to believe there would be money available, but the question for me was 'when'?

On the pitch, we attempted to maintain our good start. After the Brighton win, we lost 2–0 at First Division Reading in the Coca-Cola Cup but then beat Scunthorpe 2–0 in front of nearly five thousand at the Vetch in the League. We turned in a good performance to hold Reading to a 1–1 draw in the second leg of the Coca-Cola Cup tie at home. We were doing pretty well without the new blood Billy and I felt we needed. Our results masked the problem, but we were papering over the cracks, which soon started to show in our results – especially away from home. After losing 7–4 at Hull in a freakish game, 2–0 at Barnet, 3–2 at Darlington and 3–0 at Macclesfield, where we were pathetic, I started to feel that the rot was setting in in earnest. I then reminded myself that we'd been in a worse position twelve months ago and had managed to turn it around. I felt that we had a more talented squad but we just needed two or three new, experienced bodies and away we would go.

We knew we would have problems at the start of the season because the heart had been ripped out of the team. We didn't even have the players to go away and fight for a 0–0 draw. We needed characters in the team. We missed Steve Torpey's sheer physical presence – in attack and defence – and David Penney's bite in midfield. He could gee people up, but he was gone. On top of that, I was missing. I told the chairman all this, and he listened at the beginning, but he just couldn't believe how bad we became after those first two impressive wins. We knew it was a natural progression because there was no one there to lift the rest of the team and they were sinking virtually without trace. None of the senior players left covered themselves in glory, but only one of them, Pat Ampadu, would admit it.

In terms of the results turning against us, I would say the 3–2 defeat at Darlington was the key. We were 2–0 up but let in two late goals in two minutes of madness. Our experienced players didn't respond when we needed them to. The characters weren't there, and the character had gone from the side. The chairman didn't seem too worried by that result. He said he thought we'd played well, and these things happened in football. The Darlington manager, Dave Hodgson, told me that, in the first half, Swansea were the best team he'd seen all season. Some people say things started to go wrong with the 7–4 defeat at Hull, but I don't agree. How we lost, I'll never know. They had eight efforts on target and seven ended up in the back of the net, but we played really well.

We were constantly in touch with the chairman about bringing in new players. We even set up deals only to have to pull out of them later. One Monday, I spent nine hours talking to three different clubs. When I told the chairman, he was happy with the progress I'd made but the next day he rang up to say it wouldn't be possible to complete them. I had to phone the clubs in question and say we weren't in a position to do the deals. It was then that I started to think the board were stringing me along. Two of the deals are too delicate for me to talk about – they involved established players leaving the Vetch Field in part exchange – but the other concerned Steve Watkin, the Wrexham striker, who eventually signed for £108,000 just before our home game against Leyton Orient in late October.

Steve had been on our wanted list from the start. He'd scored more than 50 goals in 200 games for Wrexham, his home-town club, but we didn't see him as an out-and-out striker. Billy and I had been talking about bringing in a central defender but we decided to go for someone up front who could hold the ball up and relieve the pressure on the back line instead.

After our 1–0 defeat at home by Colchester, the chairman said we would go after Watkin. Nothing happened until the middle of the week when Steve Hamer asked me to try to change the payments he'd agreed with Wrexham. When their manager Brian Flynn wasn't happy, I handed the negotiations back to Steve Hamer – that was fine by me because it was the chairman's job. He then told me the deal was done so I rang Steve Watkin and asked him to come down the next day.

When we arrived back from training, Swansea's chief executive Robin Sharpe told me Steve had arrived, but it looked as if the deal was off.

'We've tried to change the down payment again,' Robin explained, 'but I don't think Wrexham will go for it.'

As we were discussing the problem, I jokingly suggested to the chairman that maybe I should lend the club some money to make up the difference. I was trying to shame them into doing something.

Steve Hamer's response was staggering. Thinking I was deadly serious, he said: 'That's not a bad idea – maybe we should suggest that to Neil McClure!'

The matter wasn't discussed again but I said it was important for us to not only sort out the fee but to make sure we agreed personal terms with Steve.

'If we agree with Wrexham but then fail to sort out personal terms with the player,' said Hamer, 'then I'll resign.'

Later that day, we reached an agreement with Steve Watkin and the following morning, the chairman was on the phone: 'Looks like you'll have to put up with me for a while longer!' he said. 'Steve Watkin is a Swansea player – are you happy now?'

'Yes,' I replied, 'but we still need more players.'

'Let's just see how we do with this one,' was his reply.

Steve Watkin made his debut the following day in our 1–1 draw with Leyton Orient in what turned out to be my last League match in charge at the Vetch Field.

I remember the time Billy and I went to Southampton with the chairman to watch their reserves. Steve Hamer wanted us to bring in young and inexperienced players from the Dell but, no disrespect to anyone, that wasn't what I was looking for. I needed proven bodies in the lower level not a talented 20-year-old who hadn't played in the Football League. OK, the wages for experienced players would be higher, but, nine times out of ten, you only get what you pay for. They need to be paid more than the average Third Division player.

I looked down the M4 to Cardiff, who were busy buying all through the summer, as players left the Vetch Field. Every signing they made, I would have bought. David Penney, Mark Harris, the former Swansea defender who came from Gillingham, and Scott Partridge from Bristol City, to name just three. The Swansea board were reluctant to pay out what they considered to be high wages for experienced short-term players. It's no good trying to sort things out long term off the pitch when all that matters on the pitch is short term. The important thing is the next game. I thought they were being very naive by not being prepared to put their hands in their pockets. I admit that the initial outlay to buy the club was close to £1.4 million, but you can't go on buying £20,000 cars and not have a tenner for petrol.

From what I could gather, it was all to do with the ninety-day appraisal of the club. At first, we all thought the ninety-day appraisal was genuine enough. It made sense to come in and take stock of everything, but that wasn't the real story. I think the appraisal was to give them the chance to raise money for the planned move to the Morfa Athletics Stadium. They were hoping that the team would be OK during that period and that's why they were so delighted with our first two wins. It meant not having to spend anything on strengthening the team. I think they were trying to buy themselves time to try to raise some money.

The other problem I had with the chairman, apart from our disagreements about buying players, was personal, to do with my role in the club as player-manager. The board may have been unhappy about the amount of money I was earning – about £3000 a week – but they knew that when they were negotiating to buy the club. I came as part of the package. If they didn't want me, they should have got rid of me then and there.

I suspect that I might have been at the club under sufferance – in that I'd signed a contract with Doug Sharpe and not them – but they didn't give me that impression at first. Steve Hamer said they wanted me to be part of the football club – mainly as a player. I wouldn't have to go scouting, Billy would relieve me of all those duties, including office work, and I was to give the club a year playing. If I did that, he said, then they'd reward me. I'm afraid I just never felt comfortable with anything he said.

As I've already mentioned, I wasn't in any sort of shape to play when the season started and then, after two League games, I picked up an injury to my right foot in training. I thought it would clear up in a week or two and, as we weren't under any pressure at the time, I wasn't too worried.

As the weeks went by and the injury didn't clear up, the chairman said I had to play. He was right – I could see my experience was needed. But I hadn't told him about my foot. Our physiotherapist suggested I might have broken a bone, so I had an X-ray at a local hospital. It proved negative, but while all this was going on, I believe the chairman thought my injury was a smokescreen. He felt I didn't want to play, which was rubbish because I love playing. I saw the doctor twice for some cortisone injections and the second lot did the trick. On the Monday after our 1–1 draw with Orient, I began training and played my first game of the season (and my last game for the club) in our 3–1 defeat at Peterborough on the Saturday.

Between those two games, we had lost 2–1 at home to the League of Wales Champions Barry Town in the new FAW Invitation Cup competition. We were awful, and I said so publicly. We had been beaten by a better team and, although they were the only full-time League of Wales side, we shouldn't have lost. It was a bad night for Swansea City Football Club.

I told the chairman I would play against Peterborough, and fifteen minutes before kick-off on the Saturday, after our warm-up, we shook hands in the tunnel.

'It's your kind of playing surface,' he said, pointing at the pitch. And that was it. That was the last time I spoke to him before he fired me. My relationship with the chairman hadn't changed much during our bad run away from home – there was simply a lack of mutual respect. I didn't take to his comments about our performances. He said some of them were disgraceful – including the one at Macclesfield, which he didn't see as he was playing golf in Scotland! One of his advisers had obviously given him a match report.

Although we were beaten by Peterborough, I was a little upbeat, because it was the best we'd played for a while. I was pleased with my own performance – especially after the break, when I'd set up our goal – and I realized we were a better team with me in the line-up. I'd also seen a new side of Tony Bird. In the second half, he seemed to step up a gear in what was his best 45 minutes for the club. I was quite excited, because Steve Watkin and Keith Walker were due back from injury and Pat Ampadu was due back from suspension.

I wasn't particularly worried about not seeing the chairman afterwards and spent Saturday night, Sunday and Monday at home with the family in Merseyside, before returning to Swansea on Monday evening. I had no inkling of what was about to happen.

On Tuesday morning, I went to the local leisure centre to work out by myself, while Billy took the players for a run on the beach just down the road at Mumbles. When I came back around lunchtime, Billy said that Chris Evans, Silver Shield's financial director, had rung up: the club's chairman wanted to meet us both at half-past three that afternoon.

We looked at each other.

'Nah,' said Billy, 'it'll be about players!'

'We're going,' I said. 'This is the end.'

I'd known something was wrong since about twenty-to-nine, when I arrived at the Vetch Field to find the chairman already in. If everything had been fine, he would have either phoned me or come to my office some time during the day. Even after I'd returned from the leisure centre, he did neither. I thought something fishy was going on – especially as Chris Evans and not the chairman had rung about the meeting. Billy wasn't so sure.

'When you make an omelette,' said Billy, 'it's all about the ingredients you put in. Once we put the players over that white line, it's up to them. We've told them they're not good enough at the moment, but they will be.'

At half-past two, I received a phone call telling me I was about to be sacked. I can't reveal the person's identity, but it was someone who is still actively involved in football.

'Anything scheduled down there?' he asked.

'Yes,' I said, 'we've got a meeting with the chairman in about an hour.'

'Hold the line a minute,' he replied. When he returned, my worst fears were confirmed.

'Micky Adams has got your job,' he said, 'and Ian Branfoot will be involved as well.'

'Thanks,' I said, 'I appreciate it. You didn't have to ring me.'

'No,' he replied, 'I just felt I ought to.'

I put the phone down and looked at Billy.

'Nah!' he insisted. 'I still don't believe it.'

'I tell you what,' I suggested. 'When we walk into the chief executive's office to meet the chairman, I'll know straight away if we're getting the sack.'

'If we are,' said Billy, 'scratch your nose!'

As it turned out, I didn't get the chance to scratch anything – not even my nose! When I walked in, the chairman stopped Billy and said he wanted a word with me by myself. He came straight to the point.

'Things haven't been going too well,' he said, 'and the directors have decided to terminate your contract.'

'Fine,' I replied.

'We'll honour your contract until the end of July,' said Steve Hamer. The club's new chief executive, Peter Day, who'd replaced Robin Sharpe a couple of weeks earlier, then spoke to me.

'Were you expecting this?'

'Yes,' I said. 'I had a phone call an hour ago warning me.'

They both looked very surprised and asked me to call Billy in. As we passed in the corridor outside, I gave Billy the thumbs-down and went downstairs to make a few phone calls and clear my desk.

Billy still couldn't believe it when he came down. I had no feelings at all about being sacked. The board were in charge, and if that was what they wanted to do, then fine. We arranged to take the coaching staff out for a meal that night and then went home to Caswell Bay.

The really awful gut feeling you get after being sacked didn't arrive until the next morning when we went to see the players. We went up to the Morfa Stadium to say thanks and goodbye before they began training. They'd all gathered in the dressing room and by the time we arrived they already knew.

I can't remember any of their reactions because I was really choked – it was just a blur. The captain Keith Walker made a short speech thanking us on behalf of the players, and we arranged to take them for a farewell drink that night.

On Thursday morning I packed my car and drove back home to Liverpool. Twenty months after being brought in to save the sinking Swans, I was out on my ear.

Looking back on my sacking, I can't point the finger at the players in terms of lack of enthusiasm and work-rate. At times, there was a lack of experience and thought. As for the board, I feel there's no way the club would have been struggling had the Steve Torpey money been used straightaway to buy replacements. Even without any money being spent between my sacking and the end of the season, I still think Billy and I could have turned it around – as we did the previous season.

I don't know if the board deliberately withheld money for players from me so that the results would get worse and they could sack me. The impression I got was that there would be money because they told me – and the world – that there would be no shortage of funds. One hundred thousand pounds for Steve Watkin was a big transfer fee for a club struggling near the foot of the Third Division, but then I only got ninety minutes use of him because he was injured in his first game.

I must admit to being very unhappy about being sacked by someone like Steve Hamer. If it had been Doug Sharpe, I think I would have respected him because he'd put his money into the club. He knew quite a bit about football, we used to have our disagreements, but he never interfered in the football side. Steve Hamer was always suggesting players we should buy and, half the time, I was wondering where he was getting the names from. I didn't take much notice of his suggestions because, in my view, it wasn't his job. While Silver Shield had been successful in business, nobody connected with the company ever gave me a straight answer about the club's financial position.

My time at Swansea was nothing if not eventful. We had relegation, an unsuccessful play-off final at Wembley, the takeover and then the trouble. There was always something going on and I certainly enjoyed it. I made a lot of mistakes – in team selection and handling players – which hopefully I can learn from. It might seem incredible that one minute you can be losing to an injury-time goal at Wembley and the next, not five months and only ten League games later, you can be out of work – but these things happen in football. It's the nature of the game and you know the risk you run when you take on the job. The only thing that's missing from the contract you sign is the date of your dismissal! The more you can put back that date, the more successful you'll be. But I don't regret taking the Swansea job for a moment. It was a great experience and I'd like to think I made one or two friends along the way, especially among the supporters – they were terrific.

It wasn't nice being out of work for the first time since I arrived in England in 1984 but, to be honest, I was half-expecting to be sacked in my first season before we managed to turn things around. I think it's sad that football has become a victim to the money men. Instead of clubs being the expensive hobby of a local businessman like Doug Sharpe, they've now become just subsidiaries of plcs like Silver Shield. The fact is you can't be a Third Division manager and expect to have bucketfuls of money to strengthen your squad, but when you sell players, like Swansea did in the summer of 1997, you'd like to think that a fair share of the proceeds would be made available for replacements.

My abiding memory of Swansea City will be the players. When Billy and I took them for a drink the day after I was sacked, they all seemed sorry to see me go, and one or two of them apologized for giving me problems. In his broken English, Joao Moreira came up and said he was sorry if he hadn't done enough.

'Out of respect,' he said, 'I'd like to thank you for everything you've done for me.'

Richard Appleby said he'd never enjoyed himself so much, and there were kind words of appreciation from both the youngsters and their parents. We had always tried to involve the boys as much as possible, and we wanted to give everyone their own identity within the club. The worst thing about being sacked was leaving the players that Billy and I had brought through. What would happen to them? Would they be given the chance to show what they could do, or would they be gone? So far so good. As long as there are players I worked with at the club, I'll keep an eye on the Swansea results.

There can't be too many worse things than losing at Wembley to a late goal in a promotion play-off, but I discovered one of them on Tuesday 7 October 1997. After the Northampton defeat, I was still in charge of a football club and had the chance to put it right by winning promotion in the next season. We could have either gone straight up, or made it via the play-offs. After what's happened, I still have the opportunity to prove myself as a manager but it won't be with Swansea. I certainly don't see myself as a failure. I know our results weren't very impressive because we weren't good enough, but there were extenuating circumstances.

As I drove back to Merseyside with a car full of belongings and memories, it saddened me to think that my only contact with the club I'd grown to love would now be through agents and lawyers. I may have been relieved of my duties as a manager but I was still registered with Swansea as a player – and they owed me more than a hundred thousand pounds under the terms of my contract until the following July. What I wanted was a quick agreement so I could get myself fit and start playing again.

Negotiations hadn't even begun when Swansea City were again making headlines, but for all the wrong reasons. Barely a fortnight after I was sacked, Micky Adams resigned. I couldn't say I was surprised when I heard the news. It seemed that he had found the same problems at boardroom level which I'd had to deal with since the takeover. Micky only hung around for thirteen days – that was enough for him, after he didn't get the assurances he was looking for.

I would have thought that when he was appointed, Micky had been promised some money for team strengthening. By the sound of it all, the board didn't come up with any, so Micky packed his bags. I also wasn't surprised to hear that Alan Cork had become the new manager. Micky got a healthy pay-off after being sacked by Fulham, whereas Corky had just left Craven Cottage and needed to work. I expect he was just happy to be in a job.

As it happened, I was able to see Corky's first game in charge – a Friday night match at Doncaster. Billy and I had decided to spend a couple of days at the races, so we crossed the road from the course to Belle Vue for the match. It was strange sitting in the main stand just a few yards away from the man who had sacked us just over a fortnight earlier. I didn't have anything to say to Steve Hamer and, at half-time, he was invited into the boardroom while we went into the supporters' bar for a cup of tea.

After three defeats on the trot, Swansea badly needed to win and were fortunate to be facing the team propping up the whole Nationwide League. It was great to see two of the young players who we'd brought to the Vetch, Tony Bird and Dave O'Gorman, giving Swansea a 2–0 lead after 12 minutes and another who we'd brought on, Damien Lacey, wrap things up ten minutes from time. In between, there was an awful lot of poor football played by two not very good sides. Experienced new blood was needed more than ever.

But a win is a win and it was Swansea's first away from home all season. They weren't the only ones to enjoy their trip to Doncaster either. I'd put £25 on a horse in the last race and it came in at 25–1!

EPILOGUE

Hooray for Hoo Road

In May 1997, I was one game away from fulfilling my dream of taking Swansea City back into the Second Division at the first attempt. Two years and three managers down the line, the Swans had again narrowly failed to win promotion. After Micky Adams and Alan Cork, John Hollins is now the man in the Vetch Field hot seat. I felt a little sympathy for him as Swansea missed out on another Wembley appearance by losing to Scunthorpe in the play-off semi-finals but, to be honest, I had other things on my mind. I was about to re-enter the rough and tumble of English football.

After a twenty-month enforced sabbatical, when I'd gone from player to pundit, I was preparing myself to start out on the long journey back. Once bitten but certainly not twice shy. From Anfield to Vetch Field to Hoo Road. Kidderminster Harriers, one of the most respected teams in the Nationwide Conference, had thrown me a lifeline. My exile was over. No longer would I just be talking a good game, I'd be helping to shape one too.

When I was sacked by Swansea in October 1997, the phone just didn't stop ringing. Hardly a week went by without somebody calling up to offer me work. I went to games all over the place – Liverpool, Manchester, Copenhagen, London and Paris. It was wonderful to be so much in demand! The only trouble was that I was on the outside looking in. I'd crossed the white line and become a professional pundit. I was involved with football but not in the way I really wanted to be. My bank manager was happy, my family were happy and I was happy. But in my heart of hearts I knew I'd be happier if I were handling players instead of a microphone. I really enjoyed my new life as a football expert but I was dying to swap the studio for the training ground. Kidderminster Harriers, and in particular their benefactor, Lionel Newton, finally gave me the chance.

For the first time in a long time, I took the family home to Denmark for Christmas after leaving the Vetch Field. Mandy, Kingsley, Karina and I spent three lovely weeks back in Kolding, and it was wonderful to have Christmas off. But it wasn't long before I got the itch.

On the way home to Merseyside in the middle of January I received a phone call telling me that Chris Kamara had been sacked as manager of Bradford City. Would I like to apply? Would I? Of course I would, and I did. I spent an enjoyable day with the chairman Geoffrey Richmond and was offered to job of assistant manager to Paul Jewel. I told Geoffrey that I would probably accept his offer but I'd like to think about it before signing anything. When I got home and gave the situation some serious thought, I changed my mind.

I knew Paul from our Liverpool days. He was at Anfield for about a year and we played a few games together in the reserves. We were initially going to work together at Bradford until the end of the season, when the situation would be reviewed, but I just didn't think it would be right. It was short-term and I didn't feel there was enough time for us to make an impact. But, to be fair, Paul proved me wrong. Good luck to him, he's done very, very well at Bradford. It was a fantastic achievement to reach the Premiership for the first time in the club's history, and I just hope Paul can keep them there! In hindsight, I maybe have to say that I regret my decision a little, but it's not something I dwell on. I made the choice there and then and, at the time, it felt right for me to turn the job down. Life is all about making decisions.

I must admit that I felt more clubs would be interested in me because I'd done quite well at Swansea with limited resources. The truth was that, during my time out of the game, it was very quiet. I was offered a job by one club, which I won't name, while they still had a manager. I told them to come back to me when he'd gone, but they didn't. I formally applied for vacancies at Bury, Norwich, Stoke and Port Vale, with no success. You take a chance when you apply, you don't really expect anything, and if something does materialize, then it's a bit of a surprise.

It was true that I now had one less string to my bow because I'd stopped playing. I thought about starting again at the beginning of the '98–'99 season but I had lots of other commitments and I didn't think it would work out. At the end of the day, I turned out for Swansea in Division Three only because I was the manager. If I hadn't been manager, I wouldn't have played in Division Three. Having been out of football for almost a year, I knew I wasn't going to go back in at the top level so I just decided, in the summer of 1998, that it wasn't for me. I've now taken my pensions after playing in Denmark, Holland and England and there's no way back. I've signed a declaration that I'm never going to play professional football again, and that's that.

I could probably have kept going for three or four more years in the lower divisions but I didn't want to. I had enjoyed my time and I always knew it was going to be over one day. I still get Liverpool fans saying to me now that I finished too early at Anfield, but life's too short to regret anything. I now play five-a-sides a couple of times a week and in veterans' tournaments both at home and abroad.

During my sabbatical, the one thing I really did miss was that three o'clock Saturday afternoon feeling – there's nothing to beat it. It's a special feeling as either a player or a manager. It was all very well sitting in the stand with a microphone in my hand, but it wasn't quite the same. Don't get me wrong. I really enjoyed being a pundit – whether for radio, TV or newspapers and magazines – and I made a very good living out of it. While I was at Swansea, I did some work for Danish TV at Euro '96, and after leaving the Vetch Field everything just snowballed. I worked for BBC Radio 5 Live, Eurosport and Sky, as well as Danish Television – mainly as a pundit or co-commentator.

But then a full-time job materialized with Century FM, a commercial radio station serving the North West, based in Manchester. Every weekday night, between 6 and 7, I hosted *The Jan Molby Football Phone-in*. Century is one of the fastest-growing stations in the area and it's going really well. They had heard me on Radio City in Liverpool when I was sitting in for Ian St John on his Saturday phone-in, and they offered me the job for the '98–'99 season. It was great but you could never call it work – I talked about football for an hour!

The station had exclusive rights to all the Manchester United home games, but there are nineteen professional clubs in the North West and we talked to supporters of all of them. It wasn't just Liverpool and Manchester United fans who rang in. We heard from Bury, Burnley, Stockport and Crewe supporters – you name them, we put them on the air! I felt I had to prepare, so I began to find out more about the clubs in our region. I went to see them play and I think some callers were surprised by the amount I knew about their teams and their players. I couldn't just go on and be knowledgeable about our four Premiership clubs – that would have been rude to the rest of them. I remember receiving a lot of stick from the Manchester United fans but it was all good-humoured. We had plenty of slanging matches and sometimes I was deliberately provocative just to get a response.

We received loads of calls about the current Liverpool side because people were frustrated, and I could only agree with them. I put the boot in on the evidence of my own eyes. The team weren't very good, and they needed some new players to be able to challenge for the Championship. The Liverpool fans rang in to say it was nice to hear someone telling the truth. They heard other ex-players maintaining that the team weren't too far away from being as good as they were, when everyone else could see that it was going to take another four or five years and possibly £50 million to put right. I regularly had a go at Liverpool and the board, but nothing was ever personal. When Liverpool brought Gerard Houllier over from France, I said he was a super signing. I think he's been very surprised at the big job he has on his hands, but he's one of the few people who's capable of turning things around.

As well as my Century work, I also covered the occasional Liverpool game for Today FM, a commercial radio station in Dublin, and then, at the beginning of 1998, I started my other career, as columnist with the *Liverpool Echo*, the evening paper in the city. The former Liverpool hard man, Tommy Smith, had been badly injured in a car crash and I was asked to take over his job of replying to readers' letters on a Wednesday and a Saturday. I stood in for him for a while and then they offered me a weekly column. I agreed on condition I could write it myself but, because of all my other commitments, it's now ghosted. I'm rung up once a week by a reporter and he writes it up for me. I've also got a column in the official Liverpool monthly magazine, *The Kop*, which I write myself.

All in all, life as a pundit post-Swansea was pretty busy, but I never gave up hope that someone would give me the chance to return to football management. And when the opportunity finally arrived towards the end of the '98–'99 season, I was delighted. To be honest, I didn't know much about Kidderminster Harriers when I went to see their chairman, Lionel Newton, at his home in April 1999 – apart from the fact that they'd won the Conference by three points five years earlier but weren't allowed into the Football League because of the state of their Aggborough Stadium in Hoo Road. The whole place has been transformed since then, and you can't help but be impressed by the set-up for that level of football. The ground's in terrific nick, there's a thriving social club and the board came across as united and ambitious. The chairman felt the club had been living off their success in 1994 and, although he didn't want to start all over again, because some good foundations had been laid, he thought that someone with a fresh view would be able to make sure that certain things were done.

My first appointment was my assistant Gary Barnett. He'd been very successful as player-manager with the League of Wales Champions Barry Town, and I felt it was important to have someone who would be good on the training ground and thorough in his preparation for matches. At first glance, the squad looked OK but one or two players had grown old together and there certainly wasn't a lot of future in the squad, so I started looking around for fresh blood – making regular use of my Football League contacts like Billy Ayre.

My first signing was defender Andy Brownrigg from Rotherham on a free transfer. In fact, all but one of the new players – Rene Petersen from St Truiden in Belgium – cost me nothing. Rene joined for an undisclosed five-figure fee in July and was followed by another Danish midfielder, Thomas Skovbjerg, who came on a free transfer from Esbjerg a month later. Phil King arrived from Brighton, having made more than 350 League appearances for clubs like Sheffield Wednesday, Swindon and Aston Villa, and I went back to the North West to pick up Ian Foster, who was released by Liverpool before joining Hereford and then Barrow. He's just turned 23 and is a very good striker who's been playing slightly out of position – wide on the left – but he'll do anything to please his manager! Later, I bought a new keeper – Tim Clarke, a local lad from nearby Stourbridge, who's played for Huddersfield, Shrewsbury and York as well as his most recent club, Scunthorpe.

I immediately noticed the difference between the standard of football in the Third Division and the Conference. The full-time League players were a lot fitter and stronger, but a lot of my squad have come from professional backgrounds – like Aston Villa, Norwich and Liverpool. They've had good upbringings so you can actually influence them in terms of how you want to play. My way of working isn't that strange to them because they've been used to doing similar things at their previous clubs.

After a pretty good pre-season – which included a 1–0 win over a strong Villa side – we made a disastrous start to our Conference campaign: four defeats in our first five games! It could hardly have been worse, but I wasn't worried because I felt that, from what I'd seen of the players in training and during the games, there was nothing to suggest that we were going to carry on losing. I thought they had done well and basically we just needed to fine-tune the team a little. It was annoying that I didn't have the players every day (we only train on Mondays and Thursdays) but I must admit I had no doubts at all. I always felt we were capable of turning it around and I think we can improve even more.

We stopped the rot with a great 2–0 win at Stevenage at the beginning of September. They were Conference leaders and one of the favourites to win the title but, despite being hit by injury and suspensions, we won well. The players needed that result just to confirm that we were on the right lines. We had to change things around a little but I felt we couldn't afford to go to Stevenage and be defensive, so we had a go at them and surprised them. The only hiccup was me being ordered to the stand for the second half after making a few choice comments to the fourth official following Tim Clarke's sending off for bringing someone down outside the penalty area! The win really helped lift the players' confidence and they started to believe me when I told them we should be higher in the table. I stressed that we needed to beat both the good *and* the bad terms.

We operate a 4–2–3–1 system – the same one which won France the World Cup in 1998 – with a back four, two defensive players sitting in midfield, a right winger, a left-winger and then a midfield player in behind the lone striker. The lads seem to enjoy it and they've adapted well. They know we're never going to be out-numbered anywhere on the pitch. In an ideal world, I'd like to play 4–4–2. A system of three central defenders doesn't appeal to me – you put them there just to defend, but I think you should defend from the front.

After the win at Stevenage, we then beat Scarborough 2–0 at the Aggborough Stadium before making history in a local derby against Nuneaton. For the first time anywhere in the world, a first-class match was controlled by three women – referee Wendy Toms and her two assistants. When I first heard about the line-up of officials, I didn't give it much thought, but then the media bandwagon started to roll and I felt that, for a minute, we forgot what we were there to do – play a game of football. My team did well but I think the whole occasion fired up Nuneaton. They won 2–1. It was a big night for them and their manager Brendan Phillips said afterwards that he'd never seen his team play better!

I think Wendy did OK but I'm not sure about her assistants – perhaps they'd been promoted a little bit too fast. The fourth official was a man but I didn't reserve my worst comments for him. I certainly didn't temper my language because a woman was running the game and two others were running the line! There's been talk of Wendy refereeing in the Premiership but I don't think she'd be able to keep up with the pace of the game. The Nuneaton match was very fast and she visibly tired. I don't have a problem with women officials – as long as they're good enough. If they're there on merit, then fine.

We're still only two thirds of the way through the season but, in my view, there will be three main contenders for the Conference title – Rushden and Diamonds, Kingstonian and Nuneaton – although I suspect Stevenage will be there or thereabouts. It's amazing (and so unfair) that only one team can be promoted! It's a real problem and there's a growing tide of opinion within the Conference to have the situation changed. It's crazy – we have one going up and three being relegated, so the Conference is more or less the only league where, come January or February, eight to ten clubs have got absolutely nothing to play for! It'll be very difficult to get any change, though. You don't see turkeys voting this Christmas, do you?

I think we've given ourselves a little too much to do in terms of winning the Conference. Those silly defeats – like the opening day one against Dover – will probably come back to haunt us, but we're building a team to gain promotion by the end of my two-year contract. Most of the players are now the right age and when we put out our strongest team, there's only one over 30. I'm hoping to finish in the top six this season.

We can't change the past but we can do something about the future. It's very difficult to say what's going to happen next in the world of football, but I'm very excited by the potential for success at Kidderminster. It's a new challenge and one which I'm really enjoying.

I have never wanted to be a manager because of the financial rewards it might bring – I will always get more pleasure out of being successful on the field. Being part-time suits me down to the ground because I travel to Kidderminster three times a week and I haven't had to move the family. Kingsley has just started secondary school and we all like it here on Merseyside. It's particularly good at the moment because of the way Liverpool are doing – the former players are bigger heroes than we ever were! I'm seen as Jan Molby, a

279

member of the Liverpool team who used to win everything. There's not been anyone to take over from us. We were the last great Liverpool side so I always get a fantastic reception on Merseyside.

I can't tell you how pleased I am to be back in football management. I know now – if I didn't already – that I'm an addict. As I said, it's not the money I'm attracted to but the game, the everyday involvement of working with players and the special feeling you get just before three o'clock on a Sunday afternoon. There's nothing quite like it. Football's been my life, it's like a drug and it's a habit I find very hard to kick. I'll be forever grateful to Lionel Newton and his board for giving me another shot.

I'm getting such a fantastic buzz with the training, the Craic in the dressing room and, of course, the games. I join in the training but there's no need for me to lace up my boots any more – we've got plenty of good players here. The Conference has been an eye-opener and I've been surprised by the standard of football. Those people who know the Conference appreciate what a difficult league it is. We have to do it properly: we have to work hard and make sure that when we sign players they're the right ones and we have to improve the ones we've got.

Obviously, I'm doing less and less media work now but I'm back with Radio 5 Live as a summariser and, with Kidderminster being in the West Midlands, I've now got a column with the *Sports Argus* in Birmingham, as well as my work in Liverpool. I don't miss the Century FM commitment and I've still got my involvement with Danish TV, so there's a nice mix of media and football work. In many ways, it's the perfect life – expect that we're not winning enough games!

It's sometimes said that I've taken a big risk in coming down to the Conference but I'm not worried – I think I can make it as a manager. Some ex-players looking to get into the game tell me they want to make sure the job is right. I think they're talking absolute rubbish. There's no such thing as a job that's right. You have to get in there and prove yourself – wherever it is. Kidderminster have shown faith in me and I aim to repay them.

Index

de Mos, Aad 16–18, 19, 32–4, 43–7, 216
Denmark 13, 16, 36, 46–7, 67, 81–2, 88–95, 102, 161, 163–4, 173, 183–4, 273–4
Derby 160, 173, 195, 198
De Zeeuw, Arjan 196
Dicks, Julian 190
Doncaster 229
Dooley, Kevin 123, 124, 131–3, 134

Ebbrell, John 101, 169
Edberg, Stefan 246
Edwards, Chris 207, 239, 241–2
Edwards, Gareth 209
Elkjaer, Preben 36, 82, 91, 93
Engedahl, Knud 14–15, 29–30, 215
Eriksen, Johnny 91
European Championships (1984) 46–7, 63, 65
European Championships (1992) 25, 183–4, 190–1
European Cup 42–3, 63
European Cup Final (1984) 48, 53, 120
European Cup Final (1985) 56, 70–1, 109, 114, 117–20
European Cup Winners Cup 185
Evans, Chris 265
Evans, Roy 61, 62, 69, 76, 80, 86, 118–19, 150–1, 156, 165, 170, 171, 172, 182, 187, 190, 191, 182, 193–5, 196–7
Everton 55, 61, 69–70, 73, 75, 76, 80–3, 95, 101, 105, 141, 143, 153, 154, 156, 158, 160, 169–70, 173, 174, 175, 176, 189
Exeter 232

FA Cup Final (1971) 47
FA Cup Final (1979) 47
FA Cup Final (1985) 69
FA Cup Final (1986) 7, 58, 79–83, 149, 238
FA Cup Final (1988) 9, 83, 103–5, 176, 192
FA Cup Final (1989) 83
FA Cup Final (1992) 58, 83, 189
Fagan, Joe 53, 54–5, 56, 61, 62, 65–7, 71, 74, 86, 102, 118–19
Fairclough, David 160
Fayed, Mohammed Al 213
Ferguson, Alex 141
Ferguson, Darren 185
Feyenoord 35, 37, 40, 43
Fortuna Sittard 37
Fowler, Robbie 193
Frain, John 7–8
Freestone, Roger 7, 239, 250, 253, 259
Fry, Barry 199
Fulham 228, 233, 243, 259, 270

Galje, Hans 41, 44
Garnett, Shaun 227, 241
Gascoigne, Paul 167
Gillespie, Gary 58, 68, 70–1, 76, 79, 102, 173, 175,190, 224
Gillingham 226–7, 254, 258
GM Vauxhall Conference 25, 231
Gould, Bobby 102
Gray, Andy 69, 159
Great Marquis 245
Grobbelaar, Bruce 61, 69, 79, 80, 82, 84–5, 156, 170, 185
Groningen 34
Groves, Perry 96
Gullit, Ruud 35, 38, 167

Hadjuk Split 30
Hafnia 69
Hain, Peter 209
Hamburg 133, 164